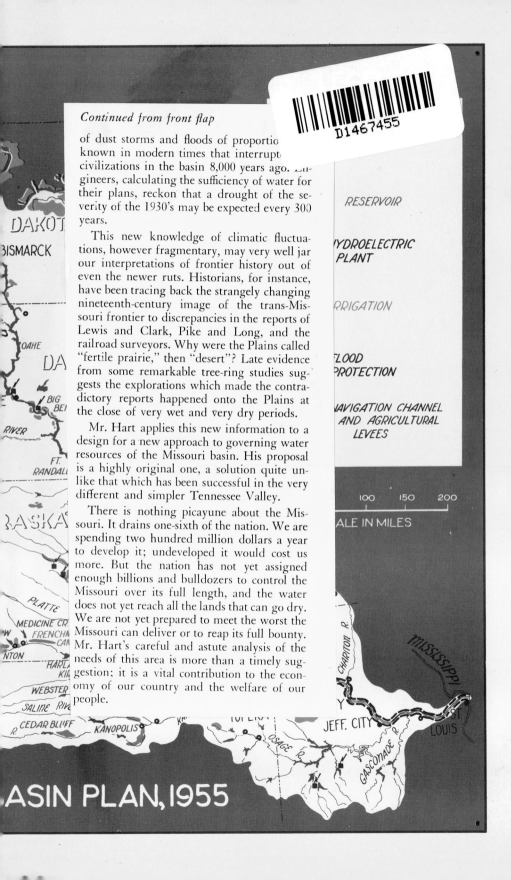

Continued from front flap

of dust storms and floods of proportio[...]
known in modern times that interrupt[...]
civilizations in the basin 8,000 years ago. [...]
gineers, calculating the sufficiency of water for
their plans, reckon that a drought of the se-
verity of the 1930's may be expected every 300
years.

This new knowledge of climatic fluctua-
tions, however fragmentary, may very well jar
our interpretations of frontier history out of
even the newer ruts. Historians, for instance,
have been tracing back the strangely changing
nineteenth-century image of the trans-Missouri frontier to discrepancies in the reports of
Lewis and Clark, Pike and Long, and the
railroad surveyors. Why were the Plains called
"fertile prairie," then "desert"? Late evidence
from some remarkable tree-ring studies suggests the explorations which made the contra-
dictory reports happened onto the Plains at
the close of very wet and very dry periods.

Mr. Hart applies this new information to a
design for a new approach to governing water
resources of the Missouri basin. His proposal
is a highly original one, a solution quite unlike that which has been successful in the very
different and simpler Tennessee Valley.

There is nothing picayune about the Missouri. It drains one-sixth of the nation. We are
spending two hundred million dollars a year
to develop it; undeveloped it would cost us
more. But the nation has not yet assigned
enough billions and bulldozers to control the
Missouri over its full length, and the water
does not yet reach all the lands that can go dry.
We are not yet prepared to meet the worst the
Missouri can deliver or to reap its full bounty.
Mr. Hart's careful and astute analysis of the
needs of this area is more than a timely suggestion; it is a vital contribution to the economy of our country and the welfare of our
people.

RESERVOIR

HYDROELECTRIC
PLANT

IRRIGATION

FLOOD
PROTECTION

NAVIGATION CHANNEL
AND AGRICULTURAL
LEVEES

100   150   200

SCALE IN MILES

BASIN PLAN, 1955

THE DARK MISSOURI

THE DARK
MISSOURI

HENRY C. HART

THE UNIVERSITY OF WISCONSIN PRESS

MADISON, 1957

Published by The University of Wisconsin Press,
430 Sterling Court, Madison 6, Wisconsin

Copyright © 1957, by the Regents
of the University of Wisconsin.
Copyright, Canada, 1957.
Distributed in Canada by Burns and MacEachern, Toronto

Printed in the United States of America
by Vail-Ballou Press, Inc., Binghamton, N.Y.

Library of Congress Catalog Card No. 57-7704

TO VIRGINIA

AUTHOR'S NOTE

CARTER GOODRICH has kindly permitted me to use in Figure 3 some of the maps by C. W. Thornthwaite from *Migration and Economic Opportunity* (Philadelphia: University of Pennsylvania Press, 1936).

This book owes a very special debt to
John M. Gaus
Harry A. Steele
The people of Lake Andes, S.D.
H. L. Walster
Kenneth P. Middleton
Randall Sale, who drew the maps

I have not named the others who gave their time to help me write it, especially the men in state and federal agencies who explained their work on the Missouri basin development. But I thank them all.

Henry C. Hart
Madison, February, 1957

FOREWORD

IN THE HEART of America civilized man has yet to make his peace with nature, even after a century of effort. For him the ways of the Missouri are dark still. Below the big dams in the Dakotas the water this year is olive drab, not coffee colored. Farther up, the Yellowstone still muddies the Missouri, and farther down the Missouri still muddies the Mississippi with the soil off farms and grass and sage lands. The dark haze in certain middle western skies has been, and may be again, the airborne upper inches of America's wheatfields. Nature is still making the Missouri basin. When the rains come they carry the earth that is the refuse of the Rockies a few miles nearer the Mississippi and the Gulf. When the rains fail the winds pick up the burden. No generation knows how long the rains will come or fail.

The buffalo once fattened where the Missouri flows. But the buffalo drifted with the rains, and when the Sioux got on the Spaniards' horses they drifted with the buffalo. By that time Europeans had conquered the forests and the prairie openings. They had become Americans. At the bend of the Missouri they came to a halt. The arid region which stopped their relentless progress from the coast of the Atlantic they called a "desert." But they missed the rains less than the timber, and presently they crossed the desert to the forests of Oregon and California. And the nation that would not be divided by slavery refused to be divided by a desert. The nation put rails upon the desert, converting it into plains, and prairie homesteads spread along the tracks. As for trees, the pioneers would plant them and make the Plains like all America.

Then the rains failed, as they have at least once in every generation. They failed too long in the sixties, the nineties, the twenties, and the thirties. American pioneers had never retreated before, but they fled the drought of the Missouri basin. Whether they moved east or west, by Conestoga or jalopy, they turned their backs upon the last frontier.

On the margins of the Plains, the cities hesitated but grew. Chafing at the dominion of the railroads, they demanded a waterway so that they could grow without hesitation. They edged out onto the alluvium which the river was slowly moving from the flanks of the Rockies. When floods came—and they came with record force in 1943, 1944, 1947, 1951, and 1952—the river laid its silt on hardwood floors and sluiced it gently into sewers and cylinders. Almost as quickly as the city refugees moved back, the nation decided to stop the floods in the Missouri basin.

Engineering against drought came more slowly than engineering against flood. To the bitter survivors of the Dust Bowl it had to come. Embattled westerners blocked the engineering of the Missouri for barges and riverbank cities until irrigation had been planned. That was in 1944, and that was the occasion and the subject for the meeting of East and West, of surplus-water and scarce-water laws, bureaus, programs, and pressure groups. Few people had realized before that America had two water policies, and the time and place of their collision did not favor reconciliation. To the nation, the sixth of its area drained by the Missouri River was a montage of conflicting images.

In 1944, a war year, the plans were made. By 1957, two billion dollars had been spent on Missouri basin projects, including 700 million spent on earlier irrigation and navigation works. Each year, Congress adds about 150 million dollars to the nation's investment in the Missouri River and its tributaries. There is much to show for the money. Through Montana and the Dakotas, engineers at Fort Peck, Garrison, and Fort Randall dams can turn the main river on and off—on during drought and off during flood—by working the gates of the biggest earth-fill dams ever built. In the last fifty years, three-quarters of a million acres of marginal land have been reclaimed by federal irrigation. But floods and droughts still come. The men whose business it is to plan the basin's agriculture warn that another 100 million dollars must be spent each year to hold the soil where the rains fall and to make irrigation safe for agriculture.

Cleverly and elaborately man fits his harness on the river. Even more elaborately and expensively he builds his cities and plants his crops beyond the security of his controls. Through little cities whose names look strange in headlines, through Topeka, Kansas City, and St. Louis, and out upon a cresting Mississippi, the Missouri basin has still the power to disgorge its floods. Over the Middle West and out over the Atlantic, soil off the basin's wheatfields can still darken the sky of an unpredictable summer. The nation has not yet assigned enough billions and bulldozers to control the river all the way. The river does not yet reach all the lands that can go dry. For most years the present plans will be enough. Perhaps only once in a lifetime will we fail, as the pioneers failed, to meet the worst the Missouri can deliver.

There is nothing picayune about the Missouri basin, either in the plans it invites or the disasters it visits. Its problems no more stay put than its climate or the channel of its main river. It is a wonderful next-year country. There have always been men and women living in the basin who have sensed its peculiar way with water, and some of them have studied and measured it. But civilization's plans are made in cities, and these are not upon the Plains; they are where it is always wet or always dry. So the great plans to stop the floods, stabilize the farms, and keep the young people at home in the basin are next-year plans. But next-year nature, which by wind and water is still making the Missouri basin, may show a revised plan, too. That is why to the engineer, as to the pioneer, the ways of the Missouri are still a little dark. On the other hand, that is why it is a frontier.

CONTENTS

LIST OF PHOTOGRAPHS

LIST OF MAPS

LIST OF TABLES

THE DARK MISSOURI

Hast ever been in Omaha
Where rolls the dark Missouri down,
Where four strong horses scarce can draw
An empty wagon through the town?

Where sand is blown from every mound
To fill your eyes and ears and throat;
Where all the steamboats are aground,
And all the houses are afloat?

—A traveler on the Pacific Railroad,
Harper's Magazine, 1869

Chapter 1

WET LAND, DRY LAND

SHAPE

No MAN can see the valley of the Missouri River. From Three Forks, Montana, seventy miles outside the northwest gate of Yellowstone Park, where its tributaries, the Madison, the Jefferson, and the Gallatin, converge, to the Mississippi twelve miles above St. Louis, the Missouri River cuts through a continental plain that stretches north from the Rio Grande to Hudson Bay. In much of its 2,473 miles the Missouri meanders in a trench which may measure one mile or ten miles from bluff to bluff. You will be understood if you call this immediate floodplain the Missouri *valley*. For the great drainage area of one-half million square miles, Missouri *basin* is the term. The Tennessean who climbs one of the bare knobs of the Smokies on a clear day can see the level wall of the Cumberlands closing the Tennessee Valley on its far side. But the resident of Robsart, Saskatchewan, Luverne, Minnesota, Cheyenne Wells, Kansas, or Rawlins, Wyoming, must check the marks of the surveyors on the map to discover he is in the Missouri drainage.

One sector only of the basin's edge is sharply defined on the ground: the Continental Divide in Montana, Wyoming, and Colorado. The knife-edge here has made it feasible to tunnel ducts for Colorado River water east through the Rockies into the Missouri basin. State legislators at Denver carefully balance the votes and the benefits of water used in or out of the Missouri basin. They know where the divide is; and they treasure every solitary slope of the Rockies, two miles high, as a watershed. A basin rimless on three sides is the shape of the Missouri drainage. It is a sixth of the United States. But it is only an oversized lobe of the true basin, the Mississippi.[1]

The geological history of the basin explains clearly enough why it is no valley in Webster's sense of "an elongate depression, usually with an outlet, between bluffs, or between ranges of hills or mountains." The folding of the earth's crust which raised the Rocky Mountains also tilted the ancient ocean bed which forms the center of North America.[2] Hence the steady rise of prairie and plain, eight feet per mile, westward from the Mississippi to the foot of the Rockies. "That slanting slab of prairie sod," as William Allen White called Kansas,[3] is the center of a larger terrace. A parallel series of

3

rivers originating in the high Rockies flowed eastward, slowly carrying onto the plain the softer strata overlying the granite core of the peaks. Evenly deposited over the basic grade of the continental plain, this alluvial blanket was attacked from the east by gullies working their way upstream from the rivers' mouths, where more rain fell.[4] A resulting low escarpment drops off to the east from the original level of the alluvial plain. It is called the Break of the Plains in Kansas, the Pine Ridge Escarpment in Nebraska, and the Missouri Coteau in the Dakotas.

The rivers draining what is now the Missouri basin diverged below the escarpment. Progenitors of the upper Missouri and the Little Missouri turned north in central North Dakota to Hudson Bay. Most of the Dakota streams —the Heart, Cannonball, Grand, Moreau, Bad, and Cheyenne—flowed farther eastward to what is now the Red River of the North, thence also finding their way towards Hudson Bay.[5] The White, the Niobrara, and all the lower tributaries of the modern Missouri appear to have followed much their present course to the ancient channel of a shorter Missouri River rising somewhere near Yankton, South Dakota.

During the last (Pleistocene) ice age, the polar ice cap invading the northeastern part of the basin cast up against the Missouri Coteau its Altamont Moraine. The glacier blocked off the outlets to Hudson Bay. Dammed by the glacier and fed torrentially by its melting edge, the upper Missouri and all its Dakota tributaries were forced to cut a new channel southeastward in the edge of the plateau against which the glacier halted. This is the deep, narrow course of the new Missouri River through the Dakotas which joins the wider original channel at Yankton.[6] It was thus in an arbitrary manner, geologically speaking, that the glacier threw together an enormous watershed, one-sixth of the United States. To a drainage which had not had time to carve its valley, it gave, not a natural divide on the north, but a great amorphous annex. Moreover, the glacier left its stamp on only part of the basin it assembled. It worked and reworked the low eastern plains of the Dakotas; it never touched the high plains to the west. The Missouri River runs between. "East-river" and "west-river" are the popular divisions of South Dakota; they form its two Congressional districts. The Missouri basin is a natural unit to the hydrologist but a contrived region to anyone else.

From Sioux City south to Kansas City the wide floodway of the river and the current of the Missouri itself create a significant physical obstacle. Both above and below this stretch, the Missouri and its western tributaries run east and west. The lower river, with its extension westward from Kansas City via the Kansas (called by initiates the Kaw), forms a straight westward route for upstream travel. The Platte, though notoriously unnavigable, affords water and forage for a second great upstream route due west from Omaha. The upper Missouri itself may be ascended from central North Dakota to western Montana. It was, of course, the pressure of advancing population on the east and the attraction of fur, minerals, and transcontinental passes in the western mountains that gave significance to the east-west routes and the north-south barriers. The middle river, constituting the only general hindrance to east-west travel, became a political as well as a geographic boundary, separating Iowa and Missouri from Kansas and Nebraska. From the Mississippi to the Rockies there is no other evident border. Nature draws a line north and south each season across the basin. Unfortunately it corresponds with no feature of topography which might arrest the eye. It is the subtle but fateful border between climates.

CLIMATE

A rainfall of 20 inches per year is the classic boundary between humid and arid climates. The 20-inch rainfall line runs south and a little west from the northeastern corner of North Dakota to the northeastern corner of Colorado. Thence it retreats east a bit and runs south to Laredo. In the land drained by the Missouri, precipitation ranges from 6 inches in the Big Horn basin of Wyoming to 44 inches in central Missouri. Climatologists, however, have long since improved upon rainfall as an index of humidity. Learning from plant ecology, they discovered that it is *available* moisture that counts: rainfall in proportion to the need for water as measured by potential evaporation and transpiration. The ratio, moreover, must be examined through the procession of the seasons: the surplus of winter and the need of summer.[7] Climatologist C. W. Thornthwaite, who has most rigorously developed the concept of water balance, mapped it as shown in Figure 1.

On this basis, almost the whole state of Missouri is definitely humid, as are the islands of mountains at the basin's western edge. The summit of the Front Range west of Denver is, in fact, superhumid. The Big Horn basin at the Wyoming-Montana line is definitely arid, for encircling mountains drain moisture from clouds approaching it from all directions. To the remaining nine-tenths of the Missouri drainage, weasel words apply: subhumid to the eastern half, semiarid to the western. When Major John Wesley Powell coined the term subhumid in 1878, his ambiguity was deliberate. Neither wetness nor dryness but marginality is the essential character of most of the basin's climate.

But the climatic transition, subtle in itself, produces sharp contrasts in the end product of the end product of the hydrologic cycle—streamflow. For rain and snow reach the rivers, except in unusual storms, only when the more even demands have been satisfied: evaporation from the ground, transpiration from the plants, and storage in the vast reservoir of the soil. Beyond these demands, small increments of precipitation reach the river channel virtually *in toto*. Contrast two Missouri tributaries. The Moreau in western South Dakota is a typical semiarid climate stream. Its watershed gets 15 inches of rain, but less than one-half inch reaches the river. The Little Sioux in Iowa, draining a moist subhumid zone, delivers eight times as much water per acre of watershed (3.14 inches) though it receives only twice as much rain.

That is why the relatively tiny mountain areas in the western basin are such important water providers. Their extra rainfall is greatly exaggerated in the relative flow of the streams they feed. The forested and timberline surfaces of the Rockies and Black Hills, 7 per cent of the basin's area, yield half of the water that flows past Sioux City—more than the runoff of all the short grass Plains.[8]

For that part of the basin in which water is the critical resource, these relatively small high watersheds are the sole dependable providers. Their yield is circulated underground as well as in surface streams. A geological cross section of the basin would look like a laminated saucer tipped up at the west. Into the upturned edge along the Rockies, the Bighorns, and the Black Hills soak portions of the mountain rainfall and snowmelt. Percolating slowly downward and eastward in the porous Dakota sandstone strata, this ground water sinks deep below the surface, sometimes (as in North and South Dakota) sandwiched between impervious layers of shale. At the lower edge of the saucer, along the mainstem of the Missouri, boring into this layer produces an artesian well, sometimes of great pressure. But the artesian ground water supply, dependent upon the small area of intake hundreds of miles to the west, has long since been overworked. Its level has sunk steadily until pumping is now general. Local controls have had slight effect upon a resource of broad extent and remote origin.[9]

"The Platte River has a wide circulation but a narrow influence," wrote Bill Nye, editor of the Laramie *Boomerang* in the eighties. Since then its flow has been both stabilized by upstream storage and robbed for irrigation. Typifying the rivers traversing the semiarid zone, it loses water as it flows. Such is the case perennially with the upper Missouri itself. In the whole of 1931, a dry year, the Missouri carried 2 per cent *less* water past Mobridge, South Dakota, than it brought out of Montana, four hundred miles upstream. Five tributaries which entered in between could not make up for seepage and evaporation in the semiarid zone.

The Missouri is the longest river in the United States. At 2,473 miles, it is

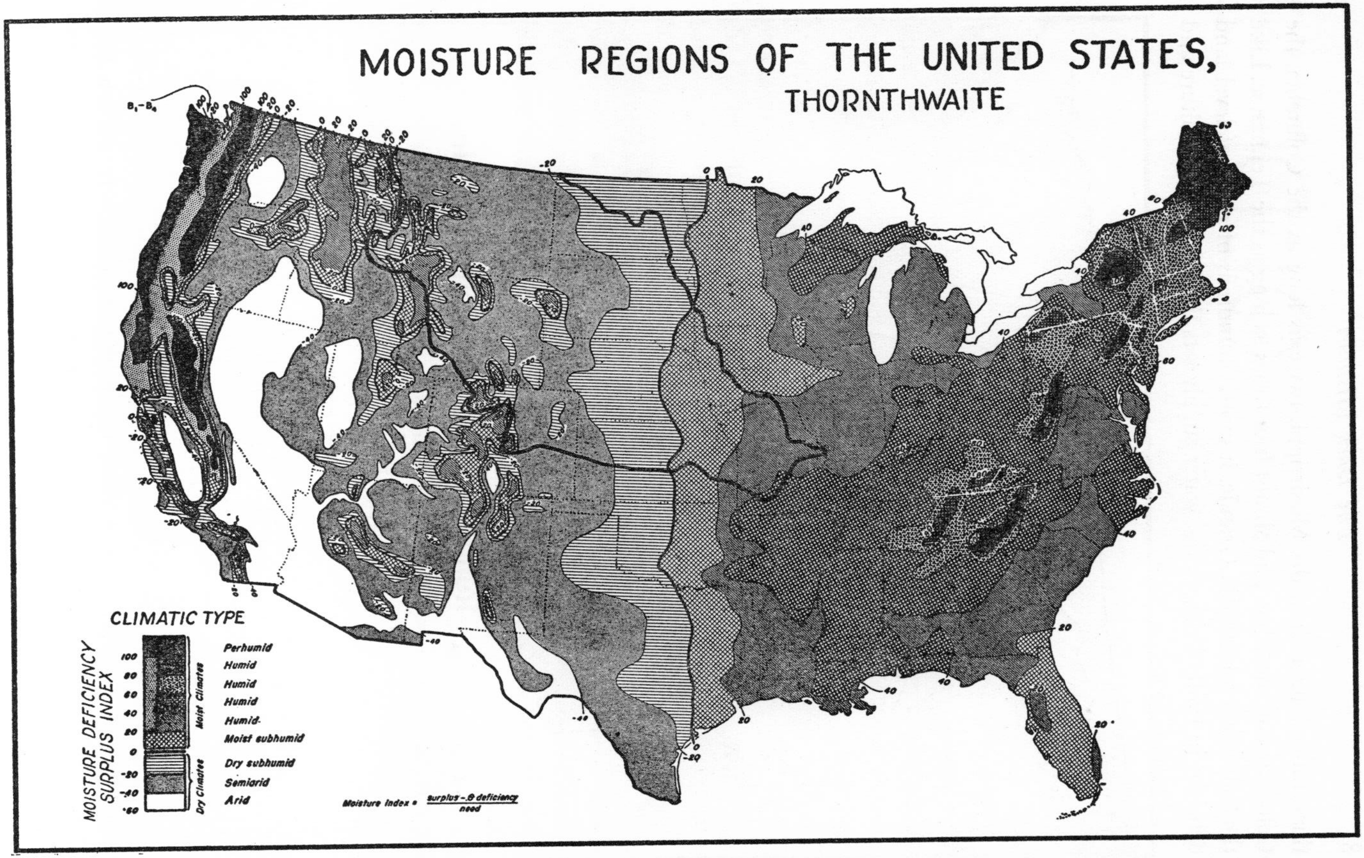

MOISTURE REGIONS OF THE UNITED STATES,
THORNTHWAITE

CLIMATIC TYPE

Moist climates
- Perhumid
- Humid
- Humid
- Humid-
- Moist subhumid

Dry climates
- Dry subhumid
- Semiarid
- Arid

Moisture Index = surplus–.6 deficiency / need

MOISTURE DEFICIENCY SURPLUS INDEX

100
80
60
40
20
0
-20
-40
-60

Fig. 1

7

three miles longer than the Mississippi, twice as long as the Columbia, the Colorado, and the Ohio, and almost four times as long as the Tennessee. Like the Colorado and the Rio Grande, it crosses hundreds of miles of level land deficient in rainfall, where the water supply sets the limit to agriculture and

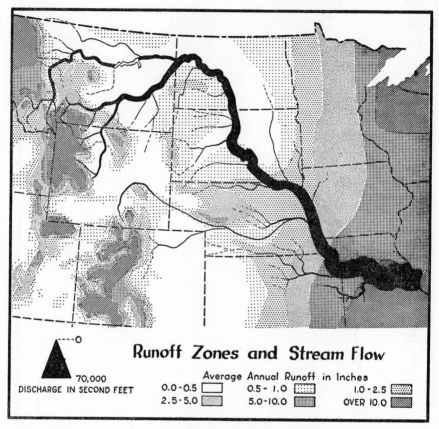

Fig. 2. The average amount of water flowing in the Missouri and its main tributaries is indicated by the width of the black line. The Missouri conveys the runoff of the western mountains into the humid zone at the east, crossing a wide expanse of water-deficient Plains. The Platte actually dwindles in the transit —its water is taken out for irrigation.

population. Any continuous increase in the flow of the river through this great area depends entirely upon the treatment of relatively small mountain watersheds, most of them remote from the area where the water can be used. In the case of the Missouri, comprehensive development is further complicated by the fact that at Yankton, sixteen hundred miles below its source, it re-enters a relatively moist climate, which becomes definitely humid for its last four hundred miles, Kansas City to St. Louis. Moreover, it then enters a river system draining the humid heart of the United States. Here water is in nature a surplus, subject to uses which in semiarid America would be insanely prodigal. Yet until the Missouri receives its tributaries from humid lands of Iowa and Missouri, water for surplus uses can only come across a thousand miles of semiarid country from the Rockies. Figure 2 illustrates the point.

This no man's land of uncertain moisture between the Rockies and the subhumid eastern basin is the Great Plains. It overreaches the Missouri basin in Canada, Oklahoma, and Texas, just as the basin extends east and west beyond the Plains.[10] You cannot understand the basin without knowing the Great Plains, which make up two-thirds of it. Moreover, the links between the Plains and the remainder of the basin are obvious: the Rockies provide the strategically important watershed of the Plains; the humid eastern basin was their base of settlement. Basic climatic factors give rise to an accepted distinction between Southern and Northern Plains. The basin takes in almost all the Northern Great Plains.[11] And the continental forces which make Plains climates work throughout the basin, and even east of it.

Yet the conformity of the two regions remains precarious. The Missouri basin is defined by the behavior of water in a poorly marked topographic area; the availability of water is a function of climate in an overlapping but not identical area. Precisely because the tilt and shape of the earth are not decisive from the Rockies to the line of the Mississippi, where the continent narrows between the Great Lakes and the Gulf, the Missouri basin is a creature of climate, but a climate which, in a real sense, is not its own.

Much of the moisture which falls as rain or snow in the basin originates in the Gulf of Mexico. Much of it is precipitated and re-evaporated on the way; more than anywhere else in the United States it is second-hand rain.[12] But it reaches the upper basin as a function of remote forces—of the difference between continental and ocean temperatures and, even more fundamentally, of solar energy. Pacific air must climb the mountains to enter the continent; if temperature variations force it over in the north, Gulf moisture is precipitated on the Plains by cold Arctic air masses. If the basic circulation is from the southwest, the hot, dry current off the Mexican plateau scorches the Plains and replaces moist currents from the Gulf. In the entire zone between the Rocky Mountains and the Mississippi, writes a meteorologist exploring the underlying causes of drought,

the influence of the Pacific Ocean is a vital factor. The rainfall of the region varies between extremes which are flood-producing at one time and dust-blowing at another. The north-south orientation of the mountain ranges permits the rainfall center to sweep back and forth over the entire region, bringing rain to the north when the south is dry, and vice versa.[13]

Equally subject to extreme variations are the factors which affect demand for water—temperature and wind. Montana and North Dakota are the states of extremes in temperature; their average annual low temperature is 130 degrees colder than their average summer maximum. The Missouri basin holds the present United States cold record of 66 degrees below zero. It was recorded at the Riverside Ranger Station in Yellowstone Park in 1933. Close by at Glendive, Montana, the minimum temperature was 47 degrees below zero in February, 1893; the following July it was 117 degrees above zero—a range of 164 degrees. On the Nebraska Sandhills and around Sheridan, Wyoming, it is normal, ten times a year, for the thermometer to rise or fall 45 degrees or more within twenty-four hours.[14]

Wind is the dynamic factor in a "continental" climate like this. Afternoon winds on the Great Plains *average* 12 to 14 miles per hour. The areas where the winds blow hardest are the two Dust Bowls of 1934: the inverted triangle reaching down from Canada through North Dakota to the center of South Dakota, and the Oklahoma and Texas panhandles.[15] Where the Front Range of the Rockies meets the Plains, nature has built a raceway for weather. Northers and chinooks follow one another down it. Not only do these cold and hot blasts condition the demand for moisture by plants (three days of a southwest wind can scorch a cornfield white in South Dakota, if the roots are dry), but they also determine the extent to which water soaks in or runs off. When the Plains are frozen shut, the result may be either drought or flood. Old-timers are right when they recall that an early freeze in the fall of 1885 kept the soil from soaking up late rain and winter snow. The drought of 1886 followed. The worst flood the Missouri can bring to Sioux City or Omaha comes from snowmelt on the Plains, when a chinook catches a thick blanket of snow on top of frozen soil. It happened in April, 1881, April, 1943, and April, 1952.

In this grand concourse of continental airmasses, it would be easy to assume that variations of climate would take place only on a grand scale. Yet in the Great Plains critical differences occur on a small scale and may even persist without evident cause. In twenty-four months, 1929–30, Mitchell and Scottsbluff, Nebraska, 8 miles apart, received 34 inches of rain. Scottsbluff got 17 inches each year; Mitchell had 14 inches in 1929, 20 in 1930. This close to the margin of tolerance, a 3-inch deficiency of rainfall is more than enough to ruin an unirrigated crop. Each town had hard summer rains of 1 to 2 inches, which left the other dry.[16] One of the heartbreaking experiences of the Dust Bowl years, as one of its victims, Kansas wheatgrower Lawrence

Svobida, records in *An Empire of Dust,* is watching thunderstorms deflected
from a single farm, not once but again and again, by some almost imperceptible variation in ground relief or soil density.[17]

Mingling its crosscurrents of moist, cold, or heated air, the lower atmosphere distributes a gradually moister and more moderate climate as it
circulates eastward. Within this general progression occur not only the chance
local variations of single storms and single seasons, but lines which divide
areas of quite different moisture *probabilities.* See Figure 3. Such a line follows the Missouri Coteau in North Dakota. Bismarck, which is on the line,
gets a few more subhumid years than semiarid—thirty to twenty-six in fifty-
eight years of record, with one completely arid and one humid year as well.
Across the Missouri, just thirty miles west of Bismarck, the likelihood of
dry years (semiarid or arid) is one-fourth greater. This sort of change in odds
is not easy for a homesteading farmer to find out.

Even when they have been measured, however, the climate probabilities
in the Missouri basin sometimes seem subject to change without notice. Consider the simple problem: What period of years represents the *normal* prob-

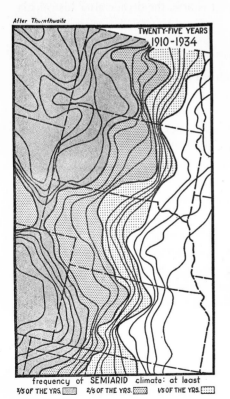

After Thornthwaite

TWENTY-FIVE YEARS
1910-1934

frequency of SEMIARID climate: at least
3/5 OF THE YRS.   2/5 OF THE YRS.   1/5 OF THE YRS.

Fig. 3. In the Great Plains portion of
the basin, climate is essentially a moisture risk. In the period 1910–1934, each
of the curved lines one crossed going
West added one chance in twenty-five
that the climate would be semiarid or
drier. Where the lines lie close together,
odds change in a few miles. The small
maps above show the extremes of variation in particular years.

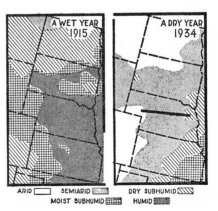

A WET YEAR 1915

A DRY YEAR 1934

ARID ☐   SEMIARID ▦   DRY SUBHUMID ▨
MOIST SUBHUMID ▤   HUMID ▩

ability of climate? Basin water calculations have, time and again, embarrassed their authors after a few more years of records came in.

Some have proved optimistic. In 1933, for instance, the Corps of Engineers, U.S. Army, transmitted to Congress the most exhaustive study ever made of the hydrology of the Missouri River. The 1,245-page document is familiar to initiates as the "308 Report"; [18] the Corps used it as the technical sourcebook of its present Missouri River plan. In it the Chief of Engineers gave the average flow of the river at its mouth as 96,300 cubic feet per second.[19] Sixteen years later, the average flow was reported by the U.S. Geological Survey at 70,290 cubic feet per second.[20] The Engineers had records of only four years, mostly wet.

On the other hand, some conclusions have already been proved pessimistic. At the close of the 1930's, J. B. Kincer, climatologist for the Department of Agriculture, examined all the Great Plains weather statistics. By using ten-year moving averages, he presented an underlying trend, beginning with the decade in which widespread gauge readings were available, of declining rainfall. The decade 1900–1909 was 8 per cent above average; the decade 1930–39 was 7 per cent below. Of course, the decade after his calculation thoroughly upset the trend.[21]

HAS CLIMATE CHANGED?

Are surprises still in store for weathermen and Great Plains residents alike? The Army surgeon at Fort Leavenworth recorded his rain gauge daily from 1836. He was a solitary scientist upon the frontier. Thermometers as well as rain gauges (adding the crudest measure of water need to the record of water supply) were read at Bismarck and a few other stations in 1877. Do the seventy-five years of recorded climate typify the mysterious centuries before? Geology gives no assurance. Ice ages are not surely behind us; our short perspective may conceal true changes in climate proceeding at the leisurely tempo of geologic time.[22]

Into this general obscurity four men have in the last decade thrown pinpoints of light. They read the prehistory of climate in the annular rings of the oldest trees. One was a merchant of seeds and, incidentally, a trained archeologist, Mr. George F. Will, whose father came from Harvard to the end of the railroad tracks in 1883 and established the business in the new town of Bismarck. Mr. Will discovered and read the record of two old oaks still surviving in a sheltered cove in the Missouri bluffs north of Bismarck and a cedar which sprouted above the Little Missouri, still drier country, sometime close to the year 1268. In Denver, the water rights engineer of the city-county water commission, Mr. H. L. Potts, found the oldest trees in the drainage of the South Platte, which supplies his city. One of them grew in the shelter of South Park, behind the Front Range of the Rockies, in 1339. Two other men interested in the fluctuation of rainfall for crops hunted tree rings for perspective. One of them, Mr. Harry E. Weakly, who now directs an irrigation experiment station of the U.S. Department of Agriculture in western South Dakota, published a tree-ring story of western Nebraska, near the junction of the North and South Platte. The other, Mr. M. A. Bell of the Montana Agricultural Experiment Station at Bozeman, finally found in a pine stump (the tree was felled in 1930) among the Bear Paw Mountains in the dry northern part of his state, a record beginning in 1579. The curiosity of these four men has stretched the limits of our knowledge about the water supply of the basin from seven decades to seven centuries. Taken together, this is what the tree rings show:

1. Series of wet years and dry years, like those of the forties and thirties, have followed one another since the fourteenth century. There is no trend through the centuries toward humidity or aridity, or toward greater or lesser swings between them. If we are emerging from or entering into another ice age, then, it is a matter of millennia, not of centuries. So much assurance we have. It is illustrated by the simple fact that there are these few sheltered areas on the marginal Plains where an oak, a pine, or a cedar could live for centuries.

2. But there is no discernible rhythm to the climatic swings. Above or below the average of the centuries they vary by pure chance or as a result of a number of periodic factors science has yet to determine. (Two ecologists thought they had discovered the eleven-year cycle of sunspots in Great Plains droughts, culminating in the dry year 1934. According to the sunspot cycle, 1936 should have been a wet year. Unfortunately, the Carnegie Institution's publication of their prediction in that year coincided with an even more general drought than in 1934.) [23]

3. At any one place in the basin, there have been wet periods and dry periods more persistent than the white man has seen. Mr. George Will's oaks, for example, enjoyed an unbroken wet spell from 1663 to 1702. And at the end of the fifteenth century, only three years of normal rainfall punctuated twenty-seven dry years.

4. How likely it is that a great drought, like that of the period 1928–41, may sweep the entire basin for a period of years is a more difficult question. We have tree rings from only four scattered locations in a half-million square miles. By the very scarcity of old trees the grassland hides its past. All we

know is that *five times before in seven centuries tree growth averaged below normal at all these places for at least ten years: 1343–53, 1408–22, 1467–83, 1731–41, and 1816–26.*

The moisture of the Missouri basin, we know now, varies radically through space, though nature left no markers of the change to the settler westward bound. We know, too, that it varies through time, without pattern of trend or cycle. For the first time, the tree-ring studies give us some assurance that the seventy-five-year sample man has recorded is a fair sample of basin climate. But they warn us, too, that the extremes man has experienced may come again, unheralded, and possibly some time a little worse.

Something else the tree-ring studies show. Each of the four men who made them worked independently, without support and without means of communicating his findings to the people of the basin.[24] In the office of the Corps of Engineers in Omaha, a young meteorologist put the four tree-ring records together. The Corps made practical use of them, but the collation has not been published.

Some day the time and money and foresight which are now devoted to exploring the geography of the basin's climate will be devoted also to discovering its history. The atomic age has already armed scientists with a revolutionary technique of dating ancient timbers by measuring the decay of radioactive carbon, which commenced when they were cut. Will, Weakly, Potts, and Bell, explorers of the prehistory of climate, may then join the company of Lewis, Clark, Pike, and Long in the record of the discovery of the Missouri basin. Meanwhile, the government of the United States, which commissioned, honored, and even published the reports of the nineteenth-century explorers, has devoted a mimeographed memorandum to the explorers of this scientific age.

SOIL

The record of tree growth is the record of climate years: the record the farmer reads contemporaneously in drought or bumper crop and the city dweller in full or empty reservoirs. Climate has left another record in the basin: a record of its millennial norms, of the changes of the ice ages. That record is the basin's soil. Even now, it is but partly read; yet it conditions vegetation and settlement as relentlessly as the seasonal fall of rain or snow.

Transition, east to west, which is the chief fact about the basin's climate, is the key also to its soil. Take the pioneer's perspective and move slowly up the river. Under 40 inches of rain, the middle of the state of Missouri is an extension of the Southeast. Upland soil is thin. The rain which in nature supports forests of oak and other broadleaf trees erodes the soil easily when the trees

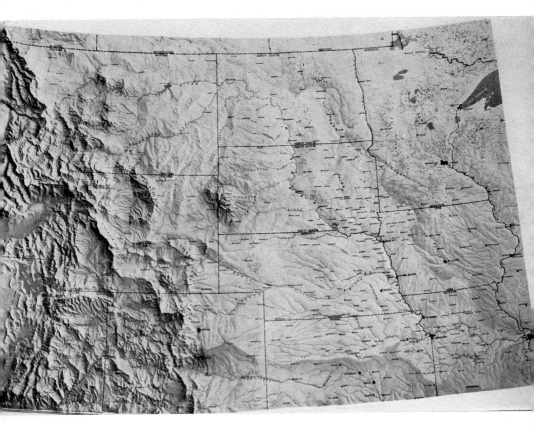

This is the shape of the Missouri basin, in which the frontier
of settlement made the transition from humid to arid land. Once across the river
into Kansas and Nebraska, the settlers came upon no natural barriers
to warn them droughts would occur. Nor, except where the Rockies are the divide,
does the form of the drainage basin itself command attention.
A basin that has to be given a lighter color to show up on a relief model
like this is bound to be something of an abstraction to the man on the ground.

—*River Basin Surveys, Smithsonian Institution*

This excavation at the margin of the Medicine Creek reservoir in southwestern
Nebraska has furnished important clues to the long prehistory of man,
animals, and climate in the Missouri basin. Twenty-five feet beneath the
modern soil surface, C. B. Schultz and E. M. Davis of the Nebraska State Museum
turned up fragments of extinct bison bones and flint scrapers on fire-blackened
hearths. Head-high from the base of the dig is another dark layer, once topsoil,
bearing flint weapons and tools. The workman on the right is excavating a still
later level of occupation—apparently a workshop where broken arrows and
spears were fitted with new points. The flints, sandstone grinders, and
ochre paints of a more advanced culture occur at the level of his head.
Radioactive carbon has fixed the date of the earliest human occupance at more
than 8,000 years ago. The abundant rivers of the humid glacial ages
repeatedly covered the earlier campsites with silt. The latest human remains,
however, were buried beneath five feet of loess—the residue of severe dust storms.
The site is on the boundary of what are now the subhumid and the semiarid
climates. The evidence is that much wetter, and much drier, climates had their
turns here since men first came; the suggestion is that climatic extremes
repeatedly drove men out.

are gone. The red and yellow color of the soil signals compounds of aluminum mixed with iron. More soluble, and fertile, minerals have been washed out. Lime is gone, and under the fermenting leafmold the soil is acid.

In the very midst of the oak, islands of prairie soil begin to appear, and westward the prairie expands. The trees are left behind in northwestern Missouri and Iowa, in eastern Kansas and Nebraska. The change is not sharp, but it is unmistakable. Prairie soil is black, deep, and neither acid nor alkaline. The blackness comes from decayed organic matter. The soil scientist, tracing the roots of knee-high grasses five to eight feet down, can see whence, in a few millennia of such occupance, the humus came. Soluble plant nutrients have not been leached away. Over the years, it is the best agricultural soil in the world. But once in a generation or so comes drought. Precisely why the forest gave way to prairie at any particular line in this middle western transition zone is a famous geographic riddle. Trees can be grown here and a good deal farther west. But those occasional droughts must have hurt them more than they hurt the tall grass in the ecological competition.[25]

At the roots of the grass, where the demand for moisture, year in and year out, begins to overtax the supply, soil scientists discovered, a quarter-century ago, a light-colored layer. A line through Sioux City, Lincoln, and Abilene approximates its eastern margin. That layer is calcium and magnesium carbonate. Above it the earth is still black with humus. But that layer signals soil whose base is perennially dry. The downward filtration of 25 inches of rain does not reach the upward seep of ground water under the capillary pull of the subsoil. In the perennially dry layer between, lime washed downward from the topsoil dries out and is deposited. This is the soil of the Plains.[26]

All the way west to the Black Hills and the outposts of the Rockies, the lime layer climbs nearer to the surface. From black, the soil shades to brown, then gray, finally light red in the Wyoming deserts. Humus declines, for the rain will support only hardy grama and buffalo grass, or in Wyoming, sage. Mineral nutrients abound (but sometimes mineral poisons, too, like selenium), and they tempt men with little wisdom to supply the lack of water from the rivers. After a generation of lush crops, the successors to these hasty irrigators find that the unaccustomed quantity of water has soaked the lime layer to the top. The salt fields are unfit for crops.

As precipitation sharply rises on the mountain slopes, the soil returns, here and there, to the conditions at the river's mouth: it is thin, acid, and leached. But higher in the Rockies it washes so rapidly off the steep slopes that climate has little time to transform the parent rock. Altitude classifies the conifers here: red cedar, ponderosa pine, lodgepole, fir, and spruce; and at the edge of the spruce are the moist meadows and the tundra of timberline. From this

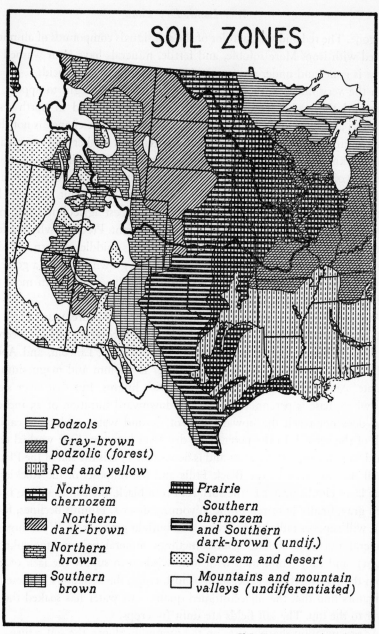

SOIL ZONES

Legend:

- Podzols
- Gray-brown podzolic (forest)
- Red and yellow
- Northern chernozem
- Northern dark-brown
- Northern brown
- Southern brown
- Prairie
- Southern chernozem and Southern dark-brown (undif.)
- Sierozem and desert
- Mountains and mountain valleys (undifferentiated)

U.S. Department of Agriculture

Fig. 4

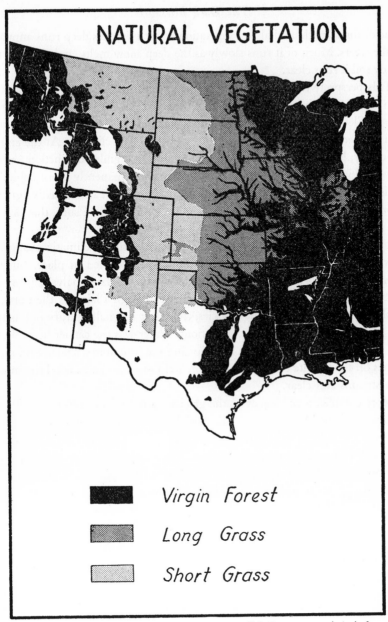

NATURAL VEGETATION

Virgin Forest

Long Grass

Short Grass

U.S. Department of Agriculture

Fig. 5

zone of forest, rock, and alpine vegetation water 10 inches deep runs annually to the rivers. Much of it runs slowly as the deep snow melts, and through the sandy soil it runs clear.

This perspective—climate manufacturing soil in place, with native vegetation as its chief instrument—is that of the greatest American soil scientist, Curtis Fletcher Marbut. He drew his theories from Russian scientists, who first studied continental plains under the transition of climates. At the end of his career, Marbut still concluded that "the most tangible" distinction among soil types was derived from permanently dry or permanently moist subsoil.[27] This is the distinction, invisible upon the surface of the earth as native grasses shorten imperceptibly from the black prairie to the brown Plains, that divides the Missouri basin.

There is another perspective on soil as formed under climatic change. It sees the soil formed in transit, as Marbut saw it formed in place. But the agents of transport, wind and water, derive, in the last analysis, from climate. Willard D. Johnson's explanation of the High Plains as the outwash of the soft rock mantle of the Rockies, though it is a half-century old, is still the most penetrating of such explanations. Water was the carrier here. Water has now largely finished the job of sluicing the limestones, shales, and sandstones off the granite core of the Continental Divide: even in flood the mountain streams run clear.

More complex is the legacy of the glaciers in the soils of the eastern Plains in Iowa and the Dakotas. Great glacial lakes, Lake Souris and Lake Dakota, received the layered sediment of glacier-fed rivers. Their dry beds are rich in minerals and poor in drainage. Deltas of glacial rivers leave their heritage of reworked sediment, much of it excellent for tillage. The deposits of the older glaciers were steeply eroded by the melting of the last ice sheet. There were five glacial stages in the Pleistocene epoch. The interims of heat which melted them turned the whole Plains into a Dust Bowl. Windborne soil filled in eastern Nebraska and settled, one hundred feet deep, against the ancient Missouri River bluffs of Iowa. This loess is among the most fertile, the most penetrable, and the most erodable of soils. Iowa farmers who watch black columns of it caving into the smallest watercourses compare its texture to that of sugar.

Meanwhile, the rivers carried on the job of moving earth downhill across the Plains. At the base of the mountains, the slope of the alluvial soil is steep and dotted only with sagebrush. It rains seldom here, but hard. "When it rains," said the director of the forest experiment station at Fort Collins, "everything goes out with a rush." On August 12, 1946, the Tongue River carried 12 tons of silt past Miles City, Montana, into the Yellowstone. On

August 13, it carried 55,000 tons. A single hard rain made the difference.[28] The Yellowstone, which receives the sediment of storms falling on the bare foothills of Wyoming, has always been the greatest silt carrier of the Missouri system.

The rivers work also from below. As the Missouri deepened its postglacial bed through the Dakotas, it accelerated every Plains tributary, and grand-scale gullying began. The Bad, the White, and the Cheyenne carry on that work today. They are small rivers, but frequently they are rivers of mud, carrying five to ten times as much sediment per gallon as the Missouri itself. The Badlands are the penultimate stage of that process which the geologists call valley trenching.

Silt from all these sources settles where the current slows. The Missouri never slows much below four miles an hour, and annually it exports 400 million tons of the soil of the Plains and foothills to the Mississippi valley. But in its preglacial course below Sioux City it leaves more sediment than it excavates. Its floodplain, one mile to ten miles wide, fills slowly in the process. What the river gives, it may, of course, recapture. The existence of the rich bottoms evidences their liability to flood.

Since the Pleistocene epoch, the substance and the shape of the basin have been the record of what climate has done to the bed rock. The essence of the climate is change. Change can be read through space; so Marbut read it. Or it can be read through time, in the alternation of the ice ages and the storms of dust and in the perennial work of the rivers. But the energies of climate process the rock through the mediation of plants. In the basin the greatest of these is grass.

Tall grass roots decaying through the millennia fertilized Iowa. But farther west, where the moisture balance is deficient, the marvelous capacity of grass is its power of recuperation. Toughest of all were the blue grama and buffalo grass, the cover of the Northern Plains when the white man found them. Consider the record of the Dust Bowl years. Grass measured by the Forest Service near Miles City, Montana, grew 13 inches in 1933, 1 inch in 1934, 15 inches in 1935. A year of 5-inch rainfall left it dormant, not dead. It sprouted from the living roots when the rains returned and matured its seed from the moisture of a single good rain. Individual plants may succumb if drought persists. But observations at the Hays, Kansas, experiment station show that the hardiest plants, taking advantage of moisture that sustained their neighbors, could survive all the droughts of the thirties. Blue grama and buffalo remained on 20 per cent of a well-managed pasture in 1939. In 1942, the sod was again complete.[29]

The resilience of the grass is great, but it is not infinite. The 80,000 square miles of wind-laid soil in the Missouri basin witness the failure of the sod, sometime in the Pleistocene epoch, to hold the Plains. Locally, that happened before the white man came, in climate which we have no reason to think different from our own. Of western Nebraska, an observer of tree rings believes:

It is probable that during some of the protracted droughts of the past the country approached an absolute desert in character, as in 1539 to 1564 when heavy filling of canyons by wind-blown soil apparently took place. In all probability the native grass cover of the country was very largely destroyed and great dust storms were doubtless common.[30]

James C. Malin has proved that the first traders and settlers in Kansas recorded dust storms long before the sod was turned.[31]

But equally convincing is the evidence that human uses of the grassland *can* trigger a new epicycle of erosion. It has happened in the loess hills of western Iowa. Valley trenching there, one hundred feet deep, followed the breaking of prairie sod. It can happen to the best stands of grama and buffalo grass too heavily pastured through dry years. An overgrazed range at Hays, Kansas, is still in annual weeds, twelve years after the drought. The resilience of the grass cannot compensate for the inflexible demands of fenced animals, and the ecological odds shift to thistle or to sage.

ECOLOGY

Men have an apparently incurable tendency to seek the sanction of "naturalness" for the behavior they think right. The facts related in the last two paragraphs have therefore been given contrasting interpretations by men of different disciplines and persuasions.

To the conservationist, unbroken sod is the key to "natural" behavior of water in its cycle. He reads into the meager facts an exaggeration of its powers. "There is no evidence that in historic times there was ever a severe enough drought to destroy the grass roots and cause erosion comparable to that which took place in 1934 and 1936," concluded the President's Great Plains Committee in 1936. But Professor Malin has produced such evidence. Of the silt-carrying tributaries of the Yellowstone—the Tongue, the Rosebud, the Powder, and most especially the Big Horn—Bernard DeVoto wrote in 1947, ". . . one reads with amazement descriptions of them written before the Civil War. They were comparatively clear streams, streams whose gradual, geological erosion of the land had not been accelerated—as it was when the cattle business came to Wyoming and Montana." [32] But since 1947, a three-year record has been kept of Big Horn silt. Half of it came from two small creeks, one-tenth of the Big Horn watershed. Forty per cent washed in from

the *banks,* not the grazed watershed of Five Mile Creek. Half-planned irrigation, not overgrazing, was at fault here. Muddy Creek contributed half of its
portion within three days following two July storms.[33] So few observations
were made of the basin in its primitive condition that it is entirely possible
that the rare heavy storms of summer moved dirt this way a century ago.
The partial cover which grass and sage are able to give these slopes in an
arid climate makes it probable.

On the other hand, cattlemen and farmers, who put the land to economic
use, engineers, and geologists are apt to see "nature" in the processes of soil
displacement. Erosion control, said a Bureau of Reclamation engineer, Glenn
Sloan, means "attempting to stop a geologic process and that is going to be
done only at enormous cost." James C. Malin, historian of the grassland in
use, sees not only erosion but flood control from this perspective:

In spite of great damage to man's improvement in the valley, especially urban development in flood bottoms (which never should have been made in the first place), the great
flood of 1951 in Kansas Valley was of great benefit, by and large, from the standpoint
of agricultural resources as reflected in improved productivity of bottom land.[34]

But this view, too, looks for "naturalness," though of the geologic kind, in a
context where man's improvements may represent the most important values
at stake.

We would do better to admit that all human occupance interferes with nature and that man cannot find in nature the tests of its desirability. That is
the truth in Bernard Shaw's quip that except for the first nine months of his
existence no human being manages his affairs as well as a plant. Whether
sod-breaking destroys the "natural" water cycle is not, therefore, a meaning-
ful question. What counts is whether it leads to results men want most, when
all the returns are in. That will be, Mr. DeVoto pointed out, a long time. And
it means, of course, results which nature can, in fact, be induced to yield. This
is the sense in which man can make his peace with nature.

Having seen the Missouri basin in the interplay of its processes, rock, water,
climate, soil, and vegetation, it is time to admit man upon the stage. The general course of history and the natural capabilities of the Missouri basin make
it enticing to preview at this stage what his role will *tend* to be. Man tends to
complicate his civilization. His role in the ecological setting will develop,
therefore, in two directions partly offsetting each other. Intensification of his
uses of the basin will set narrower limits to his tolerance of environmental
change. At best, corn will be less hardy than bluestem, wheat less hardy than
blue grama grass, and fenced Herefords less hardy than roaming buffalo.
Upon the floodplain his assembly plants and warehouses will be ruined by

floods that merely fertilized the cottonwoods or delayed the corn. On the other hand, his controls over his environment will increase. He will apply rotation and fallow and contour furrowing. Most rapidly he will learn to do the things which can be done to any river: to dam and dike and turn water into canals.

The Tennessee River, Franklin Roosevelt said with grace and substantial truth, "touches and gives life to all forms of human concerns." But on the broader stage of the Missouri basin the river is the creature of climate. Precipitation is here, as in all watersheds, the ultimate source. But wind and rain condition the Missouri in ways that are insignificant for eastern and for some far western rivers. The moisture balance in the topsoil controls the growth of plant cover beyond any possible extension of irrigation from the river itself. The plant cover controls the tempo of erosion and siltation. The moisture balance conditions, too, in human terms, the use which will be made in fact of river water to irrigate subhumid lands. Canals are not enough to put irrigation into use where bumper wheat crops grow, most years, un-irrigated. Temperature, as well as snowfall, controls the most devastating flood the basin can produce. A late, warm spring melting a heavy blanket of snow upon the Plains delivered just such a flood in April, 1881, and again in April, 1952. Trying to control the river, then, man will never quite control water in the basin. But control of the water as it falls, evaporates, and melts eludes this generation. Rainmakers promise much but measure nothing. Control via plant cover produces farm-sized miracles, but has yet to be tried on river watersheds. The impulse is to tighten control on the river itself to offset the vagaries of water at the earlier stages of the hydrologic cycle. That is fantastically expensive.

Conceivably, there is another way. Man might limit the demands he makes upon the basin's water processes. Beyond his power to control floods, he might keep his cities outside their path. Beyond his power to irrigate or cultivate dry, he might preserve the more resilient sod. But he would need to know the limits of his environment and of his own powers to transform it.

Now watch, with the ecologist's eye, as man enters the basin. From what direction does he come? From north or south within the zones of climate, or from the east across them? From the east the basin lies easy of access along the rivers. Only the gradual subsidence of the waves of grass keeping pace with the elevation of the plain marks the change from a safe to a fickle moisture balance. Far out over the Pacific, upper air currents ordain the changing climate in these inner plains; how, mankind has only begun to ask. Where sameness oppresses the eye, change is the fact of life to grass, tree, animal, and man. Of all changes, the least obtrusive is the change of climate through the years. Climate is a probability, working itself out without known pattern, over a period as long as a man lives. For years trends will appear. To doubt them, men must doubt what they have seen with their own eyes as far back as they can remember. Now and then, surviving Indians warned of cataclysmic droughts and flood. That, of course, was Indian talk.

Chapter 11

THE ENTRANCE OF CIVILIZATION

*Here is a suggestion that the successive inhabitants
perhaps entered the region during climatically favorable times only to be
forced out of it toward the east during periods of deficient rainfall,
which are marked by sterile overlying dust deposits.*
—Waldo R. Wedel [1]

THE FIRST PLAINSMEN AND THE FIRST SETTLERS

IN A POPULAR little handbook for the American Museum of Natural History,
the late Clark Wissler drew a classic picture of the harmony of man with
nature in the culture of the Plains Indian.[2] Wissler mapped this culture
throughout the Missouri basin, as well as southern Saskatchewan, Oklahoma,
and Texas. This was buffalo country. Buffalo sustained the Plains Indian in
every department of life: housing via the skin tipi, clothing, meat—fresh in
summer, pemmican in winter—and bone implements. The buffalo motif
figured in the mythology of the Plains Indian like the sea in Greek mythology.
From a center of thoroughgoing adoption among the Sioux in the heart of
the basin, Wissler found these culture traits spreading in diminishing intensity to outlying tribes. The Sioux proved their dominance in the same
amoral way that Western technology now invades Asia and Africa—by prevailing. There were some years, like 1862 in Minnesota and 1876 on the Little
Big Horn, when white men themselves, still clumsy in the warfare of the
Plains, found them dominant. Wissler's image, fixed in American lore, still
stands essentially true. The Plains Indian was, for three centuries after
Coronado found him in 1541, thoroughly at home on the Plains.

But in another conclusion, Wissler was quite wrong. The Plains Indian
as he was known to the advancing frontier was not the first human being
to occupy the Plains. The dawn of human settlement is always an elusive
event. In the Missouri basin, more light has been thrown on it since 1946
than in the preceding century. Radioactive carbon fixes prehistoric dates.
Archeology, under the joint sponsorship of the Smithsonian Institution, state
universities, and the dam-building agencies, is hurried by the deadline of
reservoir impoundment.

The earliest of known North Americans camped in the Missouri basin.

On Lime Creek, tributary of the Republican River in western Nebraska, charcoal from their fires is between 9,000 and 10,000 years old. They hunted big game, including a bison long extinct; their stone weapons are those of the famous Folsom man. How long their race remained we do not know. But after 3,000 years, men of their culture were still camping on the Lime Creek site, using weapons of unchanged design.[3] On Sage Creek near Cody, Wyoming, and at the site of Angostura Reservoir in the Black Hills a kindred tribe left spear points and a burned buffalo bone 7,000 years ago. At Signal Butte in extreme western Nebraska 6 to 8 feet of wind-blown soil cover a habitation of similar people.[4] In the last decade, the events of geology and the events of human culture have been brought onto the same calendar. The High Plains must have been a garden when these first hunters drove buffalo into its marshes to mire them down. It was watered by the retreating glaciers of the last ice age. But the searing drought that followed may have lasted a thousand years.

There are signs of intervening occupation, but the next people of whom we have extensive knowledge appeared in the basin after a gap of four millennia. They were relatively civilized: farmers, potters, hunters, and builders of houses. Apparently needing no defenses, they spread their houses out along most of the flood-safe terraces of the Republican, the Platte, the Niobrara. Under rain that now measures 23 inches they grew corn, squash, and sunflowers. And the surplus they stored underground against the lean years. Settling the river bottoms on the way west, by 1300 A.D. they had penetrated the short grass country. They lasted two centuries. Then, sometime near 1500, they abandoned their settlements and retreated eastward. Why? As we have noted, Nebraska tree rings record a great drought from 1539 to 1564, when the country approached an absolute desert in character. About this time Devils Lake in North Dakota had shrunk to a fraction of its nineteenth-century size. The hearth floors of the last aboriginal farmers of the western basin are found now by the archeologists beneath a foot of sterile, wind-laid soil.

The exodus must have begun about the time Columbus reached the Bahamas. It was over by 1541, when history, in the reports of Coronado, casts a flicker of light into the basin. At the basin's southern margin, in central Kansas, Coronado found disappointment at Quivira, the Eldorado toward which his Plains Indian guide had lured him. He encountered chiefly roaming bands of hunters "who live like Arabs" and whose sustenance "comes entirely from the cows, because they neither sow nor reap corn." These nomads harnessed dogs to drag their travois; otherwise we cannot be sure that they were much advanced over the ice-age hunters. Probably they had not even expelled the river-terrace farmers, but merely succeeded them when climate changed. But from European man they got the two instruments of dominion on the Plains: the horse and the gun.

From then on the contest is better recorded. It was not, as Wissler believed, entirely one-sided. In a hundred years the Plains Indian was mounted, in another hundred, armed. And his new technology routed or retrained every tribe in the basin. But in a hundred years, too, the farming tribes moved west again. This time they built stockaded villages against their mounted rivals. In three great tribes, Pawnees, Arikara, and Mandan, they carried the cultivation of corn, beans, and squash up the Kaw and the Republican, up the Platte and the Missouri to the vicinity of Bismarck. Pike, the Vérendryes, Lewis, and Clark visited their settlements and admired them. Until they, too, received the legacy of the whites, they held their own against the Sioux. But smallpox in 1772 and the shelling of Missouri River villages of the Arikara by Col. Leavenworth in 1832 tipped the scale. By then the Sioux themselves had only half a century left.

The 1950's are the dawn of archeological knowledge of the basin. But these things the emerging story of aboriginal man suggests. The most complex Indian culture was agricultural and hence, upon the Plains, riverbound. Even the Mandans did not try to break the tough grassland sod. The river valleys were perennially moist enough through the subhumid zone. Beyond that, the canniest aboriginal farmers could not survive the most extreme droughts of our climate era. As for the Plains Indian, it was chiefly a new mode of transport that gave him cultural initiative. In a climate of flux, it made him mobile. The buffalo, moving too, carried the Plains Indian economy where the climate suited. So, when the white man came, the basin held not one ideal type of culture but two. One was at home on the short grass, but it dominated only because of imported culture traits. The other was moving out of the woodland up the rivers; it never got to the headwaters, but it did perfect its own way of life. The values of these two cultures were as different as their ideal habitat, but neither asked more of nature than nature could supply.

THE IRRESISTIBLE TIDE

Four hundred miles up the Missouri its direction changes sharply. Through the state of Missouri it is an avenue westward. Settlement ascended that reach exactly as though it were an extension of the Ohio Valley, and in 1821, Missouri entered the Union. But the river's next four hundred miles lead more nearly north and south, and thus across the nation's line of march. It is at the bend, where Kansas City and her predecessors have been situated, that we can watch the civilization of the white American confront the Plains which lie in the basin's heart.[5]

In the year 1832, the visiting young French aristocrat De Tocqueville saw the moving edge of settlement as it reached the bend. "This gradual and continuous progress," he wrote, "of the European race toward the Rocky Mountains has the solemnity of a providential event; it is like a deluge of men rising unabatedly, and daily driven onward by the hand of God."[6] Before De Tocqueville's observation got into print, the "continuous progress" stopped. It did not halt at the Missouri bend, as Frederic Paxson maintained, "for half a century." But the interruption of a quarter-century (see Figure 6) was novel enough to call for historical explanation. It has been an enticing hypothesis, most vigorously put by Walter Prescott Webb, that the generation that reached the bend sensed the new risk of drought upon the Plains and hesitated. We need to know, therefore, what was happening at the blunted spearhead of invasion and what picture of the basin Plains was the common currency of that generation.

Between 1825 and 1850 there was a familiar and at the same time novel business at the Missouri bend. Up and down the river, which still served as a highway as well as a point of departure, moved the old American commerce in furs. Astor's American Fur Company, based at St. Louis with river outposts at Ft. Pierre, Ft. Union, and Ft. McKenzie, crowded out the poorer opposition.[7] In the process, river freight triumphed over land-borne freight. From 1821, steam moved on the Missouri River; soon it would reach out upon the basin lands. In 1850 the steamboat business began its greatest and final boom. In this respect the river was still what it had been to Thomas Jefferson, to the French from whom he bought it, and to its earlier Spanish possessors. When he asked Congress secretly (since this was still foreign territory) for an appropriation of $2,500 to explore the Missouri and the rivers to the west, Jefferson described the role of the river:

The river Missouri and the Indians inhabiting it are not as well known as is rendered desirable by their connection with the Mississippi, and consequently with us. It is, however, understood that the country on that river is inhabited by numerous tribes, who furnish great supplies of furs and peltry to the trade of another nation, carried on in a high latitude through an infinite number of portages and lakes shut up by ice through a long season. The commerce on that line could bear no competition with that of the Missouri, traversing a moderate climate, offering, according to the best accounts, a continued navigation from its source, and possibly with a single portage from the Western Ocean.[8]

But the river had to share the role. The business of the towns at the bend —St. Joseph, Independence, Westport—and of the Army's Fort Leavenworth demonstrated that the river was no longer, as it was to Jefferson, "the only easy communication across the continent, and so directly traversing part of it." Overland routes fanning out from the bend towns were now transcontinental; the river was not.[9] Many successors to Lewis and Clark had jumped off from the river route at or near the bend to blaze overland trails: Pike, the Astorians, Long, Jedediah Smith, Bonneville, Wyeth, and Fremont. From the head of steam navigation in 1821 William Becknell led his pioneer trading expedition to Santa Fe. He made money. Three years later a congressional appropriation provided $30,000 to mark and build a wagon road from Missouri to the United States border on the Arkansas. It was the work of the Senator from the new state, Thomas Hart Benton. The Missouri commerce under his protection extended alike to the newly emancipated Mexicans and to the Blackfeet at the Missouri River post, the fur trust adroitly named Ft. Benton. Quite clearly in 1850 the metropolis at the mouth of the Missouri was the capital of the western trade. But St. Louis traded more across than in the Missouri basin.

Eight years before, Benton championed his son-in-law's partly self-ordained mission to blaze the old trail (possibly of Hunt in 1811, certainly of Jedediah Smith in 1824) through the divide at South Pass. In 1842 the trail was pretty well worn. In 1839 Thomas Jefferson Farnham, a Peoria lawyer, got a remnant of the bickering band he had incorporated as the Oregon Emigration Society through South Pass to Oregon. They were the first of the settlers. Seventeen started; three arrived. But even through such individualists worked the nationalizing process. It was the avowed purpose of Farnham's Society to take possession of Oregon for the United States.[10]

By 1843 nine hundred settlers, including women and children, had crossed the eight hundred miles of Missouri basin plains from Independence to South Pass on their way to the Willamette Valley. Was it the American frontier settlers' habitual preference for timbered valleys that enticed them upon a passage as long, arduous, and risky as that of their forebears across the Atlantic? It was; but it was mingled in undiscoverable proportions with an insistent call which voiced through personal enterprise and vocation the purpose of a great nation finding what DeVoto called its "continental mind." "We will not cease," Bishop Soule told a camp meeting in 1833, "until we shall have planted the standard of Christianity high on the summit of the Stony Mountains." [11] Jason Lee, answering the call in the following year, had been escorted by Nathaniel J. Wyeth, a former ice merchant of Boston, whose aim was to carry the western fur trade by boat from the Columbia. Duty lay where commerce called, but hence where rival empires threatened. Americans who had shouted "Fifty-four Forty" in the campaign of 1844 would, as Jackson had put it, "expand the area of freedom" in the Southwest. The Missouri bend had by 1848 launched the conquerors of Oregon as surely as it had dispatched the Missouri volunteers under Col. Kearny upon Santa Fe and Fremont upon California.

In the year of peace with Mexico, Manifest Destiny disclosed its individual with its national rewards. The emigrant trains turned southwest at Wyeth's fort to the strike at Sutter's mill. But the Tehuantepec Railroad was completed in the following year, and the Nicaraguan route between the oceans in 1851. Scarcely less than those crossings, the Missouri basin beyond the bend was now an obstacle to be crossed—an obstacle separating civilization from the riches of the Pacific Coast. In 1853 Congress authorized the survey of routes for a railroad between the Mississippi or Missouri River and the Pacific Ocean. The question was now squarely before the nation. The basin as a region had been swallowed up in the basin as a route across the continent. Steam was upon the land, and Jefferson's river route was obsolete. Only one question remained. Where should the path of wealth, population, and political affiliation debouch?

The lower Missouri valley had a central position and a head start. When St. Louis held a Pacific railroad convention in 1849, support came from cities all the way up the Ohio valley and east to Philadelphia which would profit from the extension of the old keelboat and wagon route west.[12] The Missouri legislature had already chartered two railroads paralleling the lower Missouri, the Hannibal and St. Joseph and the Pacific of Missouri (St. Louis to Kansas City). For fifteen years, these railroads reached farther west than any others in the country.

The central position proved to be an unhappy one, however, as the sectional conflict deepened. In 1849, Thomas Hart Benton introduced his bill to extinguish Indian title so that settlement could proceed through a hundred-mile-wide strip from Missouri to California. He saw that a railroad would never be built through Indian country. A year later, he was defeated for re-election by Southern Rights Democrats in Missouri, led by Senator David R. Atchison. Promotion of the central route fell to Senator Stephen A. Douglas, a shrewder strategist from a less divided state. Two crucial roll calls in 1853 taught Douglas what he had to do. He had succeeded in blocking the southern course for the railroad through Texas. Southern senators had blocked organization of a trans-Missouri territory which, under the demarcation of the Missouri Compromise, would be free. To hold his party together, and to get his railroad, Douglas was willing to reopen the settled limits of slavery. His Kansas-Nebraska bill of 1854 picked up the necessary southern votes by repealing the Missouri Compromise. Onto the "slanting slab of prairie sod" Congress projected the national struggle over extension of slavery.

The men who carried the settled salient across the Missouri bend in 1854 were not thinking much about drought. Thirty miles west of the bend the crusaders of a new Emigrant Aid Society named their first town for their Boston philanthropist, Amos A. Lawrence, and a little farther up the Kansas River they built Topeka, both in 1854. Nevertheless, the initial advantage lay with the slavery forces, who had but two days' ride to make from the Missouri border. They named their capital Atchison. As Paxson concluded, the resulting bloodshed not only failed to deter settlers but advertised Kansas to thousands. In 1855 the territorial census counted 8,500 people in what a year before had been Indian country.

While the apex of the frontier was edging west in the Missouri basin after a stationary quarter-century, its northern flank was wheeling through the Iowa prairies and the pine forests of the Lake states. Pivoted on its bridgehead across the Missouri bend, it moved at a new pace upon a new basis of logistics: the railroad. From the southern tip of the Great Lakes the supply lines radiated. The spreading sector of rail communications matched the spreading angle of the prairie widening westward from Illinois. The prolific generation of the prairie farmers manned them both: the city hub and the prairie rim grew apace.

In 1854 the rim reached the Missouri basin, and the civilization which was to complete the occupation of the basin identified itself. While guerrilla warfare was beginning in Kansas that summer, the Council Bluffs and Nebraska Ferry Company entered the name Omaha on a plat of land it acquired in June from the tribe of Indian corngrowers of that name. The character of the founders is shown in the following sketch:

Among the early settlers were A. J. Poppleton, John M. Thayer, Andrew J. Hascom, Dr. George L. Miller, the Creightons, the Kountze brothers, William A. Paxton, Byron Reed, James M. Woodworth, James E. Boyd, and Joseph H. Millard. These were the men who made Omaha, most of them the sons of farmers or common laborers, who had seized upon the money-making opportunities of the West. They rapidly built up fortunes, some of which compare with the largest in America. These men were hardy, as the West demanded, and quite capable of taking care of themselves under any circumstances. They won their start in freighting, wholesaling, real estate, building telegraph lines across the continent, and cattle raising. With the fortunes thus gained they backed every enterprise that encouraged the growth of the city.[13]

There are no farmers on the list. Why should there be? These men were city builders, contemporaries of the founders of Lawrence and Atchison. The point is that they were frontiersmen performing the fateful task of moving the line of settled population across the Missouri River. To elect their senators and to sell their lots they crossed the last commanding marker placed by nature between a safe and an uncertain climate. Was it a calculated risk?

THE DESERT IMAGE*

Fifteen years ago, when drought again called the attention of the nation to the grassland, a Texas historian, Walter Prescott Webb, published the most persuasive historical explanation for the halt of the frontier. Looking out from his forests, the American of the generation before the Civil War pictured on his map of the continent a blank space before the Rocky Mountains. It was labeled "The Great American Desert." As long as he pictured it there, he would not settle in it. "The fiction of the Great American Desert," Webb wrote, "was founded by the first explorers, was confirmed by scientific investigators and military reporters, and was popularized by travelers and newspapers." [14] But this answer, like every fruitful hypothesis, leads to other questions. Who observed the desert? Why were they wrong? Why was their error spread? Did truth replace it before the frontier moved in? There is no longer much doubt among historians that in some form the idea of a desert between the Missouri bend and the Rockies prevailed among pre-Civil War Americans. It is to the ancillary questions raised by Webb's thesis that inquiry now turns.[15]

The first puzzle concerning the desert image as explanation of the halt is elementary: how could so many witnesses be wrong? For the Missouri basin was thoroughly familiar, in the second quarter of the nineteenth century, to thousands of Americans not on Webb's list. We have noted their coming and going through the towns along the Missouri bend: trappers, traders, missionaries, soldiers, and, finally, emigrants. Among them, they had firsthand knowledge of every climate zone and every season of the basin Plains. Chittenden is emphatic on the point. "There has never been a time," he wrote, "until very recently when the geography of the West was so thoroughly understood as it was by the trader and trapper from 1830 to 1840." [16] Who listened to these men? Not the makers of public opinion in the nation. For the railroad had moved the source of emigration out of the reach of the eyewitnesses to the frontier. And the informant of the emigrant now was the editor of his daily newspaper. It was in the "continental mind" that the desert

* The culmination of Bernard DeVoto's historical writing was a conspectus of all the westward exploration of North America from Cabeza de Vaca to Lewis and Clark. Through 278 years the goal was a water route to the Pacific. Leading not to the goal but to final disappointment, the Missouri River nevertheless extended the American notion of America to the Pacific boundary. How geopolitical realism mingled with wishful thinking in the earliest American views of the Missouri, long before settlement came to the fore, only readers of *The Course of Empire* can fully appreciate.

image grew. Walter Lippmann made his point about American opinion with reference to foreign affairs: "the pictures inside people's heads do not always correspond with the world outside." The diagnosis would have applied perfectly to the American view of the Plains a century before Lippmann wrote.

A good map of explorations of the West by Americans from 1803 to 1852 [17] records a tangle of routes radiating through the basin from the bend of the Missouri. Of all the scientific, military, and commercial expeditions, however, there is no doubt that four captured the attention of the nation: those of Lewis and Clark in 1804–6, Zebulon Pike in 1806–7, Stephen H. Long in 1819–20, and John Charles Fremont in 1842 and 1843–44. These men supplied the raw material for the desert image. Webb thought them simply wrong. But new evidence now suggests that they described the basin as it was. The new evidence comes from the prehistory of climate produced by the dendrochronologists.

If there remains from the pristine generation of social scientists a pure empiricist, one who finds in objective facts their own significance, let him read the journals of these explorers. Like other men, scientists or not, they reported the answers to the questions they asked. Yet how coincidentally the facts of nature confirmed their hypotheses! The three years 1804 through 1806 were like many other climate years in the basin, bountiful in one area and scant of moisture in another. Plant growth was above normal along the Missouri at Bismarck, Williston, and in the Bear Paw Mountains of Montana. It was above normal up the Platte to its fork. But in South Park, in the Denver area, it was at the lowest point in fifty years. Lewis and Clark, dispatched by river to find a river route for commerce, traveled in lush seasons. Their report is faithful to the facts they must have seen. It came to popular notice through the publication of the journals of Sergeant John Ordway of their party in 1807. Nowhere does he refer to dryness as the limiting factor in the value of the Missouri country. The word "deserts" shows up only once. He used it in describing the country above the mouth of the Musselshell River, in what is now west central Montana. Ordway's concluding statement about this area reveals how far he was from characterizing the Plains as a whole. "This country," he wrote, "may with propriety be called the deserts of North America for I do not conceive any part of it can ever be Sitled as it is deficient of or in water except this River, and of timber and too steep to be tilled." [18] There was nothing here from which to make a desert picture; but to Lewis and Clark, as the very casualness of Ordway's reference suggests, the question of suitability for settlement was a matter of curiosity, not of purpose.

Lewis and Clark were sent to find a water communication route. Pike was sent by land; and of his mysterious mission, we can best judge that it was to find a boundary. His report, received by the public three years after Ordway's, came in the full glamor of Pike's captivity by the Spaniards.[19] Its main impact was to advertise the sand dunes along the basin's southern flank. Pike's route lay mostly in the drainage of the Arkansas. But he made a side trip north to the Republican River through what is now Kansas. Where the river now crosses from Nebraska, he sojourned at a Pawnee village. History thus re-entered the archeological story of the reinvasion of the Plains by the river-farming people. This time they were few in number and concentrated for defense. Farther west, Pike left the peak to which he attached his name for a second short northward journey into the South Platte headwaters and on to the headwaters of what he mapped as the "Yellow Stone." It was more likely the North Platte. He encountered in this area, at least, climate which the tree rings show to have been exceptionally dry. He was not factually in error, then, in giving the first currency to the desert image. His errors as to climate are, indeed, negligible compared to his gross misplacement of rivers and mountains.

The change in the prairie country came, Pike concluded, at the headwaters of the Osage. That is about the 96th meridian—eastern Kansas. Even here, the change was not to sand but to uninterrupted grass. Of the country Pike wrote as follows:

The inhabitants would find it most to their advantage to pay attention to the multiplication of cattle, horses, sheep, and goats, all of which they can raise in abundance, the earth producing spontaneously sufficient for their support, both winter and summer, by which means their herds might become immensely numerous.[20]

The obstacle to population, Pike clearly said, was the lack of wood for building and for fuel. His widely quoted paragraph referring to "shifting sands" and distinguishing the western plains as fit only for "limited habitation" ended with a sentence, less noticed today, which identifies the limiting factor: "But possibly time may make the discovery of coal mines, which would render the country habitable."

Lewis and Clark had not returned to St. Louis before the fur traders were on their way up the river. For ten years the Plains were relatively wet and the rivers full. Then in 1816 began one of those rare extreme droughts which take in the whole basin. Until 1822 plant growth did not reach normal at any point where we have records; effects of the drought lasted longer. The limited evidence we have indicates consistently that *the decade centering in 1820 was as dry as the decade of the 1930's*. In this extreme of climate was launched the exploration that most directly stamped the desert picture upon the public opinion of the next twenty years. Major Stephen H. Long's assignment was significantly broader than that of his predecessors: "to explore the country between the Mississippi and the Rocky Mountains." For the first time, he had with him men of diversified scientific talent. The journals of the expedition were published by its naturalist (actually physician and botanist), Edwin James. Long's route, after he left winter quarters at Council Bluffs in the spring of 1820, lay directly along the Platte, the South Platte through the site of Denver, and south along the Front Range to the Arkansas basin. It was thus north of Pike's trail, except at South Park. But his conclusions were not different on the broad question of the habitability of the Plains. In fact, the corroboration of Pike added influence to Long's account.[21]

Long found in the grassland range enough for "incalculable multitudes [of wild animals] . . . yet the scarcity of wood and water, almost uniformly prevalent, will prove an insuperable obstacle in the way of settling the country." [22] James fixed as the zone for this description the area west of the 96th meridian, about the longitude of Council Bluffs and the boundary between Pike's zones of compact and limited population. But Long was wisely cautious of the line, claiming only that "a gradual change is observable in the general aspect of the two regions, which takes place in the vicinity of the proposed line."

Long noted tracts of sand along the Platte; in view of the climate of 1820, his description was surely not exaggerated. James used the title "desert" loosely for his account of the entire zone west of the 96th meridian.[23] But the man who creates a clear public impression is the man who writes a simple legend upon the apparently objective physical features of a map. Long, alone among the actual explorers, placed upon his map east of the Rockies (and in the zone where he had reported "ample pasturage") the absolute phrase "Great Desert." [24] By no means all the maps published before the frontier broke across the bend in 1854 followed suit. Webb cites four that did. There are at least a fifth and sixth. But there are ten maps published in the first half of the century which used either no categorization or some more neutral one than desert. Notable among the latter are the accurate maps of Albert Gallatin and of the U.S. Army Corps of Topographical Engineers in 1850.[25]

The year of the next influential expedition, 1842, was drier than normal, though less so than 1820. Note, however, the altered treatment of the facts by John Charles Fremont. At the forks of the Platte he noted the destruction of the grass and the "clouds of dust" raised by buffalo herds. But it was far to the west, at the 104th meridian (near the present Cheyenne) that he divided "the immense expanse of prairie, covered with the verdure of rich grasses, and highly adapted for pasturage," from the "sandy, and apparently sterile" region to the west. Only in these High Plains proper did Fremont conclude "that the barren appearance of the country is due almost entirely to the extreme dryness of the climate." For the first time, too, the climate observed is distinguished from the norm. Fremont noted the "unparalleled drought" in 1842. Known human habits were interfered with: the fur traders could not find enough water in the Platte to float their skins down; Indians had to resort to cottonwood leaves for horse fodder. The moisture of the basin was beginning to be read in time as well as space.[26] But it was not the scientists in the party that alone accounted for the care with which Fremont handled facts of aridity. The mission of exploration was changing. Fremont went to South Pass to scout the trail for emigration. His father-in-law and sponsor, Senator Benton, gave away the leading question of the expedition when he extravagantly appraised the Senate document in which Fremont's explorations were published. "This report," he stated, "proves conclusively that the country for several hundred miles from the frontier of Missouri, is exceedingly beautiful and fertile, alternate woodland and prairie, and certain portions well supplied with water." [27]

In all the explorers' reports the questions answered are the questions critical in the minds of their contemporaries. The supply of moisture for cultivation was not yet such a question. The fertility of soil and the availability of timber were. Looking out from the edge of his woods, the American pioneer asked first whether corn would grow where trees did not. Pike, though he disclaimed scientific knowledge on this point, felt called upon to speculate. Soil not protected from the sun by trees, he surmised, must therefore be barren.[28] But this question could be answered in Missouri and Iowa, in the oak openings. Long noted on his way up the lower Missouri that settlements were "most numerous in those parts . . . variegated with prairies and woodlands alternating." [29] The more serious question was the supply of timber to build the capital plant of civilization—fences, houses, towns—and to provide fuel through the long, penetrating winters of the Plains. Malin has closely connected the changing estimate of frontier Kansas with the need for wood and the discovery of an alternative fuel in coal. Webb did the same for fencing on the Plains. In 1811 a British naturalist, who got the endorsement of Thomas Jefferson for his exploration up the Missouri to the mouth of the Yellowstone, saw it all very clearly. The second edition of his book appeared in the year Long set out for the desert, but it appeared in London. In his book he noted that "accustomed to a profusion of timber, Americans do not realize how little will suffice. It is for this reason that the belief in America is, that the prairie cannot be inhabited by whites. . . . I must pronounce the soil to be excellent. . . . In time, timber would be raised." [30]

Men can deal with their environment firsthand without naming it. But
if they are to deal with it collectively, they need words. A generation of
woodsmen, therefore, groped for a label for the treeless lands. To the Spaniards and the French there had been no problem. Baron von Humboldt,
rigorously honest, drawing his map of New Spain in Mexico City in 1803,
inserted above the Platte the legend "Savannes qui s'étendent à l'Est de la
Sierra Verde." Southwest of the Platte he added, "Plaine immense où pais-
sent les Bisons (Cibola)."[31] Even to Pike, the simple designation "Plains"
had sufficed. But it did not suffice when the farm frontier had already occupied part of the level, treeless country and men needed to be warned about
the unmarked distinction that lay ahead. Plains seemed to include prairies;
as Bernard DeVoto has pointed out, there was a problem in semantics.[32]

In this ambiguity, the word "desert" fit. It had a conveniently dual meaning. It could stand for the arid region which, somewhere beyond the prairies,
ruled out agricultural occupation. But it could also mean deserted, though
habitable, wilderness. And in their emotions, as Henry Nash Smith has
revealed, Americans absorbed by the spectacle of the westward-moving tide
could not wholly give up the idea of the West as a garden of Eden, even
while they were speaking of its barrenness.[33]

Henry Wadsworth Longfellow acted his part in the symbol-making of his
generation, noting in his diary on December 17, 1846: "I see a diorama of
the Mississippi advertised. This comes very *a propos*. The river comes to me
instead of my going to the river; and as it is to flow through the pages of
the poem, I look upon this as a special benediction."[34] Two days later he
saw Banvard's moving diorama, "three miles of canvas." Not only the Mississippi but its tributary basins emerge from the fourth part of "Evangeline,"
which creates a beautiful, inconsistent, entirely expressionistic image of the
West.

> Far in the West there lies a desert land, where the mountains
> Lift through perpetual snows, their lofty and luminous summits.
> Down from their jagged, deep ravines, where the gorge, like a gateway,
> Opens a passage rude to the wheels of the emigrant's wagon,
> Westward the Oregon flows and the Walleway and Owyhee.
> Eastward, with devious course, among the Windriver Mountains,
> Through the Sweet-water Valley precipitate leaps the Nebraska;
>
> .   .   .   .
>
> Spreading between these streams are the wondrous, beautiful prairies;
> Billowy bays of grass ever rolling in shadow and sunshine,
> Bright with luxuriant clusters of roses and purple amorphas.

THE NATION MADE WHOLE

Why did a generation about to settle Kansas, Nebraska, and the slopes of the Rockies create its desert diorama? From the expedition of Zebulon Pike to the railroad surveys, the American people *needed* a desert on their western frontier. The motive, entirely apparent in Pike's conclusion, appeared even more transparently in the language of Long:

This region, however viewed as a frontier, may prove of infinite importance to the United States, inasmuch as it is calculated to serve as a barrier to prevent too great an extension of our population westward, and to secure us against the machinations or incursions of an enemy that might otherwise be disposed to annoy us in that part of our frontier.[35]

The evidence of this motive is persuasive. There was first the fear, rendered credible by the Burr conspiracy, that an overextended West would separate from the United States to form its own Mississippi Valley republic. This eventuality had, in fact, been foreseen by President Jefferson as a possible consequence of the Louisiana Purchase. He was not deterred, but he was moved to plan compact settlement to minimize the separatist tendency. There was, second, the practical concern with the defense of scattered settlements of which Long wrote and the more general preference, expressed by President Van Buren, for compact settlement rather than outposts on the "almost interminable streams of the West." [36] A few public figures from the Atlantic coast displayed the provincialism wrongly attributed to Daniel Webster in consigning the trans-Mississippi country to the savages. But the conclusive evidence that a desert coincided with national policy until it was supplanted by the imperative of Manifest Destiny was the decision to move the Indians there. Jefferson himself contemplated reserving for the Indian tribes all of the newly acquired Louisiana north of the Arkansas. "The rest of the territory," he wrote, "will probably be locked up from American settlement." Almost at once upon receiving word of the purchase he composed two drafts of a constitutional amendment for that purpose. This was never submitted. But he explained it this way:

The best use we can make of the country for some time, will be to give establishments in it to the Indians on the East side of the Missipi [*sic*], in exchange for their present country. . . . When we shall be full on this side, we may lay off a range of States on the Western bank [of the Mississippi] from the head to the mouth, so range after range, advancing as we multiply.[37]

When, twenty years later, Secretary of War Calhoun and President Monroe revived the Indian removal idea, the tentativeness had gone out of it.[38] And when Andrew Jackson carried out the removal of Indians to the country west

of the Missouri and pledged it to them "forever," the evidence was complete
that a pioneering generation had no desire to occupy the country they were
coming to picture as desert.[39]

When rivalry arose with Britain for the possession of the Oregon country,
and when the Plains Indians (crowded westward by the removal policy and
armed by the fur trade) began to harass our borders and our commerce,
the desert took on a new emotional meaning. Manifest Destiny found the
providential national boundary of Pike and Long peopled with migratory
hordes, a perpetual menace to civilization westward bound. First the Arabs,
then the Tartars of the Asiatic steppes became the analogues.[40] To such a
menace there could be but one answer: conquest. Furs could be traded across
a desert, but it was inconvenient to build a nation across one.

There was a little harbinger of the new historical climate in 1843 when Jim
Bridger, wilderness man par excellence, built a post just over the divide from
South Pass for the convenience of emigrants. "It was the first trading post
beyond the Mississippi ever built for this purpose," General Chittenden believed, "and its establishment marks the beginning of the era of emigration
into the Far West."[41] States on the Pacific would mean states in between;
transcontinental communications in a railroad era would mean population.
At last America knew what to do with her Louisiana Purchase.

Ideas do not quietly expire when their usefulness has ended. It was an
ironic lag of culture that just in 1850, as settlement edged across the Missouri,
the school texts came from the publishers bearing the words "Great American
Desert." The desert became a national stereotype just when it ceased to be
a national need. It was stereotyped, too, at a time when more and more eye-
witness accounts were coming in of the country across the Missouri. Railroad reconnaissance, begun by Asa Whitney in 1845 and culminating in the
careful though hurried Army surveys of 1853–55, produced some new facts,
though its more important effect must have been to reorient the nation's
wishful thinking from longitudinal climatic zones to transcontinental routes.
In any event, by 1854 the reports of emigrants headed across South Pass, of
agents and missionaries from the trans-Missouri Indian reservations, of Army
officers interested in communications with California as a result of the war
with Mexico (Kearny, Emory, Abert, Marcy), to say nothing of the cele-
brated accounts of the forty-niners, had punctured the desert myth with con-
tradicting facts. Even so, because the word desert was spread across some
maps, promoters of wholesale settlement would soon have their excuse to
exorcise it, substituting images equally immoderate and uncircumscribed—
prairies, granaries, fertile belts.[42]

While the popular image remained thus ambivalent, the most meticulous scientific interpretation of the moisture situation in the trans-Missouri West still did not command all the concepts which would have been necessary for the first settlers across the Missouri to understand their new environment. Such an interpretation we can examine in Lorin Blodget's excellent treatise on climate in America, published in 1857. Blodget gathered together all the scraps of weather observations concerning the unoccupied Plains. From these scant instrumental data he was able to map the "eastern limit of the dry plains" very nearly where the modern geographer marks the semiarid climate zone. He was the first to see that lower evaporation in the northern Plains would permit cultivation to extend a western salient along the Canadian border. To this extent, he anticipated the wheat belt of Montana. But this was not, as we shall see, the latitude in which the frontier moved. Finally, even this remarkably penetrating view of the moisture situation conceived its variation in *space* alone. Blodget missed the most characteristic feature of Plains climate for lack of a sufficiently complex theory of climate origin. It seemed to him that because the energy of the sun was constant, "all the changes we observe are periodic as belonging to the day and year, and nonperiodic in all other cases—the averages always returning to a line of the most absolute permanence." [43]

It took only three years to show that the scant available scientific evidence of moisture supply was being disregarded in the new advance. The population of Kansas had grown in five years from 8,500 to 106,390. Rainfall, according to the Fort Leavenworth gauge, rose from 24 inches in 1854 to 60 inches in 1858—a record unequalled to this day. In June, 1859, a drought set in which lasted through the following crop year.[44] Nineteen inches of rain fell at Leavenworth in the entire year of 1860. Farmers preoccupied with guerrilla fighting had accumulated no surplus. Now they starved. Many quit their claims and abandoned Kansas—one-third of the population, according to a contemporary historian.[45] Those who remained got, among much other charity, $50,000 of "famine," not drought, relief from the New York legislature. It was as if nature had contrived to enter it unequivocally in the record that the techniques and the policies of settlement which the nation had that very year elected were incompatible with the moisture conditions of the basin beyond the bend.

It was not climate or adaptation to climate that re-energized the transcontinental march. It was, for one thing, politics. The severing of the old ties of West and South which had defeated Benton was carried to its culmination in the affiliation of West and North. The states north of Delaware had not given Benton a single vote for his bill to reduce the price of homestead lands in 1828. Now they joined the Middle West (including four new prairie states) in electing a homestead President.[46] It was geography: the discovery of the fertility of the prairie, the lusty growth of the Pacific Coast, and the concept of America transcontinental. It was technology: the steel-faced plow manufactured by John Deere of Illinois in 1837, the railroads reaching out of Chicago in the 1850's as the steamboats had reached out from St. Louis thirty years before. It was economics: the beginnings of capital accumulation and the concentration of its power in the corporation which could build railroads and steel plows. An industrial revolution created a new demand for surplus farm commodities in the cities of Europe and America, while a revolution of transport brought the Missouri basin within reach.

An inevitable, an invincible, but a fleeting political alliance between the prairie farmers and the rising businessmen of the booming cities would now see that the gears meshed—that the railroads were built to the homesteads that would occupy the prairie that had been the desert. The homesteads would provide the freight for the railroads as they provided opportunity for a generation and a party and a nation. What now of moisture? In the year of the Kansas drought the Missouri basin was merged in the Mississippi. "The great interior region bounded east by the Alleghenies, north by the British dominions, west by the Rocky Mountains, and south by the line along which the culture of corn and cotton meets" spoke through Lincoln. In the Plains beyond the Missouri River the word was flesh. As Lincoln stated further in his Second Annual Message to Congress:

That portion of the earth's surface which is owned and inhabited by the people of the United States is well adapted to be the home of one national family, and it is not well adapted for two or more. Its vast extent and its variety of climate and productions are of advantage in this age for one people, whatever they might have been in former ages. Steam, telegraphs, and intelligence have brought these to be an advantageous combination for one united people.[47]

Chapter III

THE PLANNED FRONTIER

The frontier reached by the Pacific Railroad, surveyed into rectangles,
guarded by the United States Army, and recruited by the daily immigrant ship,
moves forward at a swifter pace and in a different way than the frontier
reached by the birch canoe or the pack horse.
—Frederick Jackson Turner [1]

WHEELS ON THE PLAINS

ON THE NIGHT of August 12, 1859, the people of Council Bluffs could have previewed their destiny. Abraham Lincoln, lately unsuccessful candidate for the Senate from a neighboring state, made them a Republican speech. On the same day, Lincoln sought out a twenty-nine-year-old railroad engineer named Grenville M. Dodge who had just returned from surveying a route westward up the Platte. According to Dodge, "We sat down on a bench on the porch of the Pacific House and he proceeded to find out all about the country we had been through, and all about our railroad surveys, the character of the country, particularly its adaptability to settlement." [2] There is more doubt about a local legend that citizens of the Bluffs took Lincoln up on Cemetery Hill to show him the "natural route" for the Pacific railroad stretching west of Omaha.[3] Bluffs on the Omaha side admit a very short view.

It was, nonetheless, the vision of the Platte leading directly west from the growing hub of Illinois railroads which Dodge believed Lincoln received in Council Bluffs. Perhaps both men were convinced already. Dodge, already a landholder in Council Bluffs, had taken up a claim twenty-five miles west across the Missouri, directly athwart the future rails. Lincoln had an interest, acquired from N. P. Judd, director of the Rock Island, in a valuable tract of land in Council Bluffs. Dodge planned to locate the railroad terminal on it.[4] We do know that Lincoln stopped off to make a speech at Council Bluffs partly because the steamboat on which he arrived from St. Joseph was delayed three days by an accident in the Missouri River. Lincoln disembarked to herald a new axis of communication by land. "Not one, but many roads," he said, "will someday center here." [5]

One hundred forty-nine steamboat landings were made that season at Council Bluffs. It was the peak in steamboating so far, but the future tipped its hand that night. Not the lower river, St. Louis to the landings at the bend, not the new rail route to St. Joseph already open from Hannibal, not the middle and upper river, but the rails directly west from the southern tip of Lake Michigan to San Francisco Bay would open the western basin to the second half of the nineteenth century.

The question of the sufficiency of water on the land was cut free of the question of water in the river. Lincoln inquired about soil and moisture in the Plains which his plan would settle. What could he find out? All the way from the Atlantic to the Missouri River each pioneer had answered these questions for himself. Now in 1859 the prairie President had met the rail-road engineer. At their next conference the President, preserving the Union, made it clear that he would name Council Bluffs the eastern terminus of the Pacific railroad. That was 1863; Chicago rails had not even reached the Bluffs, and would not reach them for four years. The planning was done for high stakes, and the odds were long. Would individual trial and error still suffice?

ALONG CHERRY CREEK, in the summer of 1859, the prospects looked good. It was the gold strike there which had drawn young Dodge into the business of freighting supplies up the Platte by wagon ten years before his railroad followed. But Cherry Creek and Pikes Peak were panned out in two years. Bannack City followed, at the headwaters of the Missouri; news of better luck at Alder Gulch evacuated Bannack. Thirty million dollars came out of the new diggings in three years, and Missouri steamboating had its last boom. The placer miners transplanted from the former Spanish colony of California a law to fix ownership in a flow of water. They transplanted, also, and improved upon, the vigilante method of administering laws in general. Since the mining camps of Alder Gulch in what is now Montana were, 1,700 miles by river and trail from their territorial capitol at Yankton, there was no alternative. What the miners could not do was to establish lasting communities and states. Colorado voted against statehood in 1860. The "Pikes Peak or bust" wagons were rolling back east with amended slogans. Montana had to wait for cattle, irrigation, and the Northern Pacific before getting statehood fifteen years after she became a territory.

Mining carried into the Rockies the customs and techniques of other mountainous, arid, and ungoverned places. Tenderfeet were educated by veterans of the California goldfields, such as James and Granville Stuart who made the strike at Bannack. As placer mining dwindled, and before machines were put to work on the hard-rock ores, a new industry invaded the basin: the raising of range cattle. It alone of all the enterprises of European man immigrated from a Plains climate. Walter Prescott Webb's interpretation emphasized the frustration of this Texas-bred economy by the attempt "to utilize the land after the manner of men in the humid timber lands." "No sooner," Webb wrote, "had the cattle kingdom been set up as a natural institution adapted to its environment than the forces of the Industrial Revolution began to modify and destroy it." [6]

But the junction at Abilene, in 1867, of the longhorn herds and the Kansas Pacific connecting with Chicago was symbolic in a way Webb underemphasized. The range cattle industry was itself the joint product of the Texas Plains and the urban-industrial era. From the former it inherited an extensive use of the land centering on water supply. Water holes fixed the actual right to property in the basin range, though the General Land Office, which owned it, missed the point. The herds were transient in a transient climate, though not transient enough to escape the blizzards of 1886 and 1887. Perhaps three-quarters of the herds perished in those winters and the dry summer between. But from the time it reached Abilene, the range industry was also a function of rail transport. The railroads not only carried cattle to eastern markets but brought them west to further overcrowd the free pasture. It was an industry capitalized by outside investors, some of the largest being Scotch and English, who turned it into the "beef bonanza." Until the cattle froze and starved, twenty years after the first drives, the industry had no way to control its own overcrowding of the range. Montana Territory gingerly endowed its Deer Lodge County with power to restrict range use to save grass for the winters. That was in 1866, before Montana had received either Texas cattle or the Northern Pacific. Wyoming tried self-control through its powerful Stock Growers' Association, but "the worst offenders were members of the organization itself, who overbought and endangered their own safety." [7]

The "natural" industry of the grassland had to learn the lesson of survival by initial failure. But where it held sway, in Montana and more especially in Wyoming, it learned more thoroughly than the homesteaders. Only in those two states did basin counties gain farm population when the ultimate climatic test came in the 1930's. When Montana cattlemen along Mizpah and Pumpkin Creeks, with advice and help from the railroad and the federal government, launched the co-operative grazing district in America, the range cattle industry was at last coming to be acclimated. Joseph Kinsey Howard tells that story, with much else about how men finally made themselves at home in his state, in *Montana: High, Wide, and Handsome.* [8]

The close of the Civil War, which loosed the Texas cattle drives, also reactivated the homestead invasion of the basin from the east. Two processes

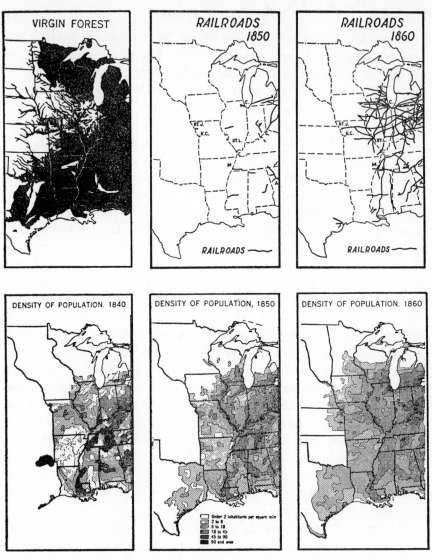

Fig. 6. The frontier crosses the bend of the Missouri River. Through 1850, settlement moved along the rivers, close to timber. In 1860 it had entered the grassland, supplied by rail.

Fig. 7 (facing). The frontier crosses the semiarid zone. Compare the shaded area (two or more inhabitants per square mile) with the lines of climatic risk and the growing network of rails. In this advance railroads not only supplied the frontier; they led the way.

mingled in the march of the frontier westward from its Kansas and Nebraska bridgeheads. On the one hand, this was a period of continuous retooling of agriculture by American inventors and manufacturers, of experimentation with new wheats, and of new systems of tillage by the first settlers themselves. Shannon has described the role of new machines in tillage; Webb has described their role in the occupation of the grazing country. Malin, in *Winter Wheat,* has revealed the vigorous ingenuity of farmers and businessmen in the new counties of central Kansas, adapting agriculture to the Plains. In these ways, men learned by trial and error how to make a living on new soils and in new climates.

But the frontier was pushed forward by another process which disregarded climatic variation, the process by which any Pacific railroad had to pay for itself. Writing about the railroad to his superior in Washington, the Surveyor General of Kansas and Nebraska fairly described the new motivation:

> This grand enterprise can in no way be better accelerated than by the early survey of the lands upon the contemplated route, as the settlers will be eager to precede the construction of the road. . . . When peace shall again be secured, Kansas will receive a large accession to her population, and, with the construction of this grand public highway to the Pacific, the hardy sons of toil will line the entire *central belt* of the republic with farms, towns, and cities, giving life to the trade and enterprise of the plains, and causing population rapidly to enter upon and readily reduce the rich lands to productive fields.[9]

Upon the basin Plains the belts of climate probability and of soils run generally north and south. The corridor through which the frontier moved ran east and west: the Central Belt of which Surveyor Delahay wrote. Compare the maps of population density in three post-Civil War censuses with the key map of environment, moisture probability (Figure 7). In 1870 the *moist* subhumid zone had filled up on a broad front by a population of two

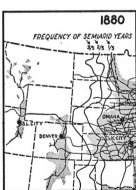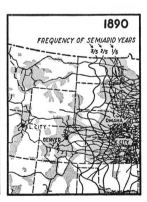

to six inhabitants per square mile (which the census regarded as indicating agricultural settlement). In Kansas alone had settlement gone beyond that zone, in the very area of the Kansas "famine" ten years before. In 1880 the *dry* subhumid zone was crossed, and feelers of settlement reached into semi-arid climates. But only in the latitudes of the Central Belt. Northward in the Nebraska Sandhills and especially in eastern Dakota nine-tenths of the nation's last subhumid climate zone lay empty. Minnesota, with all her wood and water, had 200,000 fewer people than Kansas, where drought had struck already. In 1890 the line of continuous frontier was at last interrupted; Frederick Jackson Turner had his text. The frontier closed in semiarid country, between Omaha and Cheyenne, between Kansas City and Denver. Meanwhile, dry subhumid lands farther north waited twenty years unused until Jim Hill's railroad and Henry Ford's car extended communications.

The Central Belt which ended the basin's continuous frontier was only secondarily a zone of relatively propitious climate. First it was the railroad belt. Its limits were fairly accurately described, in fact, by the Act in which Congress chartered the Union Pacific—"between the south margin of the Valley of the Republican River and the north margin of the Valley of the Platte River." [10] Do not think that it was the pressure of the earlier frontier salient up the lower Missouri River which alone pushed the frontier forward in this zone. Twice as many native Minnesotans and twelve times as many Iowans had moved into Kansas by 1870 as into all the Dakota territory.

Railroad building moved, after the Civil War, upon a new economic plan. No longer was it necessary, as Stephen A. Douglas had maintained in his arguments with Asa Whitney, to "progress gradually, from east to west, keeping up a connected chain of communication, and following the tide of emigration and the settlement of the country." [11] The Union Pacific was located within the Central Belt while its eastern terminus was nothing but a meridian of longitude (a branch was authorized to the 100th meridian, from some point on the Missouri River, which Lincoln fixed at Council Bluffs).[12] The western objective of the line was fixed, not at Denver, which as a mining oasis attracted the company's directors, but at the point in transcontinental topography where the highest level of the Plains met the easiest ascent of the Rockies. Dodge, now chief engineer of the road he had envisioned ten years before, discovered that point at Cheyenne. "That, of course," he said, "controlled the line from the Rocky Mountains east to the Missouri River." [13] Only after he had laid the track, in 1869, was Dodge called on by his directors to appraise potential earnings from the country the U.P. crossed. ". . . we had a road 1,086 miles in length, with few settlements upon it, and the country surrounding it, from our own observations, did not promise any

Westward Ho. The arrangements that moved three million people onto the Plains of the Missouri basin by 1890 were industrial, national and international. They were organized in cities a long way from the subtly changing environment.

But the Plains pioneer,
who battled blizzards and droughts,
and then the railroads and banks,
seemed to the nation, and often to himself,
more ruggedly individualist than ever before.
This is an original homesteader of
Pennington County, South Dakota.

—U.S. Department of Agriculture photo

Westward Again. Ruggedness was not enough in years like 1935. The photograph above was taken in Beadle County, South Dakota, in a twenty-six-mile wind.

—Lange, Collections of the Library of Congress

Some Dust Bowl refugees like this Nebraskan took up "stump farms" in Idaho. They moved west not to virgin soil, but to water.

great amount of railroad traffic." [14] Across the basin Plains the rails came first. The frontier followed.

It did not follow spontaneously. The Plains railroads, particularly those which could not depend wholly on subsidies of lands or cash, brought the techniques of induced colonization to a pitch of efficacy they had not reached since the first settlements were projected across the Atlantic. This is a phase of the basin's history about which we have learned a great deal in the last thirty years. [15] In Richard C. Overton's revealing account of the Burlington Road we see the members of a new profession, planners of land settlement, precisely analyzing the economics of their "tremendous colonization effort."

If 80 acres of land be taken as an illustration of your interests there [a railroad land commissioner wrote to his company], while it may be a fact that by holding that 80 acres for the next three years we can gain 50 cents per annum on the price (per acre) or $1.50 for the three years after deducting taxes, it should be remembered that that same 80 acres put into wheat would yield the road an average of $150 per annum on export and import freights. [16]

Most American histories describe the 13,444-acre wheat plantation promoted in the valley of the Red River, on the Minnesota-North Dakota border, by the Northern Pacific. It strangely fascinated a nation absorbed in giant machines and fearful for the family homestead. But the railroad soon found that it lost freight by such extensive cultivation. As it pushed its land sales into the semiarid climate of western North Dakota, it deliberately promoted smaller farms. The policy succeeded thoroughly. Northern Pacific land sales in 1886 averaged 257 acres per farm; in 1887, 180 acres. [17] It took half a century, ending in a Dust Bowl, for those prairie-sized homesteads finally to merge into the grazing units, twenty times that size, which the climate of the short-grass country demands.

Skillful press agentry brought the vision of fertile plains to city folk far from the frontier. On the "Indiana Editorial Excursion" of 1871, for instance, the Burlington brought newsmen from sixteen Indiana towns to Lincoln and the surrounding Nebraska country. A month later, "60 business men, farmers and mechanics from Indianapolis bought $25,000 worth of lots and lands in and around Lincoln." [18] The railroads went farther afield. They had their agents in Europe stimulating the flow of immigration from what the land commissioners happened to regard as the most likely nations. Sometimes this brought to the Plains colonies of settlers far more experienced with semiarid agriculture than any Americans. Land agent Schmidt of the Santa Fe attracted into Kansas a band of the Mennonites from the Russian Crimea who carried in their baggage seeds of Turkey wheat. It was Jay Cooke of the Northern Pacific who tried to get President Grant to sponsor the colonization on public lands along the railroad of other groups of these Russian Mennonites, who not only insisted on holding their lands collectively but refused to bear arms in defense of the United States. Senator Windom of Minnesota, stockholder in the Northern Pacific, introduced a bill to allow a collective land grant, but the Senate could not agree on the amount to be turned over to the collective farmers.[19] Many of the group settlements of Europeans succeeded, and some have proved more stable than the individual American settlement.[20]

As late as the years 1910 to 1922, Jim Hill populated the route of the Great Northern by employing his own agricultural experts to promote a particular technique of tillage. It was "dry farming" by which the soil was kept pulverized; the dust mulch was supposed to conserve soil moisture below. What happened to the homesteaders who took up 42 per cent of the area of Montana in this campaign, when the winds began to blow their pulverized fields, is a lively chapter in Joseph Kinsey Howard's *Montana: High, Wide, and Handsome.*

How carefully did the railroad executives who planned the settlement of Kansas, Nebraska, North Dakota, and Montana consider their climate? There is a partial answer in the record of the Northern Pacific. When the railroad was in the hands of Henry Villard, he commissioned Raphael Pumpelly, a Professor of Geology at Harvard, to conduct a survey of resources along the route. Pumpelly's expedition is remarkable not only because of its genuinely scientific mission but because its staff included the brilliant young soil scientist E. W. Hilgard and also W. M. Canby, who was to investigate "natural plants for grazing." After the survey had completed three years of field work, Villard lost control of the Northern Pacific. "I was ordered to stop the survey at once and disband the force," Pumpelly reported. It "was opposed by nearly all the officials of the roads, especially by those of the land departments, with whose schemes it interfered." [21]

The railroads made some positive contributions to the understanding of the basin environment. Weather records were kept by some station agents. Tree-planting in shelterbelts along the rights of way was widespread, though information was not kept on survivals. But in the main, executives of the roads shared and disseminated the popular misconceptions of the time. J. R. Buchanan, passenger agent for the old Elkhorn railroad, now part of the North Western, recalled that he "shared the common belief that turning up the moist soil would add to the moisture in the atmosphere, resulting in added precipitation, and so that each such effort and growing crops would aid in redeeming that portion of the arid belt, and I accordingly encouraged—even piloting some—colonies to go westward, where I knew there was excellent soil." [22] Jay Cooke went further. He was accused by General W. B. Hazen, a hard-bitten Plains soldier with an interest in weather, of bending the isotherms three degrees north to include the Northern Pacific right-of-way. Cooke thus coined the "northern tropical belt" and distributed large maps showing "The Continental Wheat Garden." "It is believed," wrote Hazen, "that these maps have been prepared purposely to deceive." [23]

American pioneers, even the schoolteacher and barber contingent, were not easily fooled. It was not long before the Northern Pacific Eden was popularly labeled "Jay Cooke's Banana Belt." The significant result of the railroad propaganda was more likely the tendency to conceive the basin Plains in terms of east-west zones, even if the descriptions of them be taken with a grain of salt. "The Central Belt," the "Gulf Stream of Migration," Charles Francis Adams' "Broadway of this continent" were stereotypes as clumsy in dealing with the basin environment as, thirty years before, the desert had been.[24]

The twenty years 1878 to 1898 were the years, according to the historian Arthur Schlesinger, in which America changed most rapidly from an agricultural to an industrial nation.[25] In those years there also occurred, as it happened, the climax in the settlement of the nation's most intrinsically agricultural frontier. It was not, of course, a coincidence. The rails that fed the cities also marketed the wheat and steers of a land ill-adapted to subsistence farming. Nor was it a coincidence that the settlement of the Plains became itself more and more a matter of speculation in townsites. In the detailed history of the Burlington, we see the railroads extracting the maximum return from their property by retailing city lots around their depots. In the skirmishing over the location of state capitals, an American proclivity which reached a climax on the Plains, we see competing railroads conducting free tours to the rival cities on their tracts (Pierre and Mitchell) not only for the legislators but for almost any South Dakota voter. We see Cheyenne created in 1867 from the open sagebrush by Grenville Dodge's location of a Union Pacific division point. To the holders of lots near the depots of any of the roads radiating from Chicago, their favored tract of short grass was an embryo Chicago. Fifteen Kansas towns, says the historian Fred Shannon, built streetcar lines in the eighties. In the nineties, one High Plains city totally abandoned in drought and depression had a $30,000 opera house.[26] "Your cities," cried William Jennings Bryan in his Chicago speech, "rest upon our broad and fertile prairies." He could not see to what extent the dependence was reciprocal, still less how much the settlement of the "prairies" depended upon the visions of their cities rather than of their fertility. Real estate booms are traditional incidents of the growth of America; on the basin Plains they came closer to being necessities of settlement.

What has been said here of the railroad applies in general to the process of industrialization. Machines provided not only the logistics of extensive agriculture but also the tools, typified in the combine and the tractor. "The whole culture of the western grass country is built on gasoline," wrote Isaiah Bowman.[27] If we are to have a symbol of the grassland, the cowpony dramatized by Walter Prescott Webb should yield, as Malin suggests, to the wheel.

The less obvious half of the story is the high fixed costs which the industrial revolution imposed on agriculture. After he passed the frontier of 1860, the farmer had to pay for, or do without, his water supply, lumber, fencing, fuel, and heavy wheeled machinery for extensive farming and transportation to market. He was selling on an uncertain world market partly because it was of tempting scale, partly because he had to. The machines which broadened the climatic limits within which he could grow wheat also tightened the financial strings on him when climate exceeded those limits. It was not surprising, then, that the farmers in the basin's heart rebelled with Bryan. But their revolt was nonetheless quixotic in its aim to cut those financial strings. It is a condition of the occupation of semiarid lands in an urban-industrial civilization that the plainsman make his peace with nature *and* with the planners of the economy, even if they reside no nearer to his floods and droughts than Chicago, Boston, or New York.

CLIMATE BY CONGRESS

An outline map of the United States hardly corroborates the thesis that the last frontier was carved out of wilderness by the undirected initiative of the pioneer. The bare boundaries of the states indicate that the original Atlantic Coast states were laid out on the basis of their human occupation: their variation in size and their accommodation to topographic features which interrupt communication reflect human history rather than simple geometry. As the frontier advanced, azimuths began to replace rivers and mountain divides as boundaries. Transport was easier, true, but essentially the last frontier was converted into states before it was settled. It was more artificially planned by the government of the United States than any other region. The only two perfectly rectangular states in the union, Colorado and Wyoming, cut straight across its most rugged and decisive terrain features. They were part of the Missouri basin's last frontier of settlement. In fact, from the edge of subhumid climate along the Missouri River to the Continental Divide, every state boundary is a pure Euclidian construct. The very shape of the last frontier was blueprinted in Washington.

If you will exchange the view of the map for a view from a country road in South Dakota, where it tops a long rise, you will see the results of abstract planning going deep into the fabric of human tenancy. Radiating from your vantage point will run the township lines, straight as the transit sights, across glacial moraines, watercourses, and soil types. Your road probably follows one of them, regardless of the extra grades and bridges. Fences, property lines, and corn rows do, too. The only interruption is but further evidence of the arbitrariness of the design: the General Land Office, running its survey lines at right angles upon a surface which, even on the Great Plains, is fundamentally spherical, had at last to offset them to accommodate the curvature of the earth.

"Square farming" is to this day the bane of the soil conservationist, who wants the plow to follow the contour and the field to mark the unit of soil quality.[28] "Square governing" adds to the cost and diminishes the usefulness of school districts in Nebraska (which, thanks to the surveyor's townships, now has more of them than any other state in the union) and counties in other states (until South Dakota has simply retired some of her counties from all the duties of self-government). But layout of the basin frontier by the General Land Office, upon the pattern which Governor Wentworth of New Hampshire developed for Bennington in the year 1749, and which the Northwest Ordinance extended to the true prairie land in 1787, has a deeper significance. It shows that with the railroads, Congress and the crude administrative agencies of seventy-five years ago fixed the pattern for filling up the part of the basin where local variations and exact local knowledge were most crucial.

The chief feature of the congressional plan was, of course, the Homestead Act. It was passed by the same Congress which gave statehood to Kansas in the very midst of the famine and chartered the Pacific Railroad. It was a prairie law signed by a prairie President, but it applied chiefly to the Plains. Upon a region whose climate required extensive agriculture, it stamped the 160-acre farm unit. The history of farming in the Plains has been a history of the enlargement of those inadequate farms—by the abandonment of some of them. The record is quite clear. North and South Dakota, which in their territorial days in 1860 averaged 215 acres per farm, actually got smaller farms by 1870 as a result of the homestead policy: 176 acres on the average. So did Nebraska and Kansas. In 1945, the average size of farms in North Dakota was 590 acres, in South Dakota 626 acres, in Nebraska 427 acres, and in Kansas 344 acres. The bare statistics mean that one-half to two-thirds of the homesteads were lost or sold out.

There were, as a popular commercial *Settler's Guide* informed the prospective homesteader, tricks to getting another quarter-section or, after 1877, another full section of government land.[29] Total fees for the first 320 acres amounted to eleven cents an acre, and for the added 640, twenty-five cents an acre. These facts multiplied the inducements to ownership, particularly on the part of those more interested in land values than farming, but left the concept of the quarter-section farm dominant. The speculator merely sub-divided. The Homestead Act, with these supplements, operated exactly like the railroad colonization policies, chiefly to get the land occupied as quickly as possible.

In this objective, all classification of the land according to suitability for cultivation was disregarded. Even the old law graduating the price of public land to the settler was abandoned just two weeks after the Homestead Act passed.[30] Mineral lands were reserved for special treatment; the miner had indeed carved out his own claim by 1862. The only other distinction in the farms Congress spread across the variable plains was that to the purchaser (as distinguished from the homesteader, who paid only filing fees) land within the limits of railroad grants was double in price. To Congress as to the public generally, not soil or climate, but the route of transport fixed the worth of the last frontier.

In the Homestead Act Congress expressed the philosophy of the gen-erous and equal prairie, and applied it to the marginal Plains. Eleven years later, in the Timber Culture Act of 1873, it legislated directly for the Plains.[31]

Congress decided "to encourage the growth of timber on western prairies" upon the direct recommendation of the Commissioner of the General Land Office. In the prairie states, he reported, settlement, by preventing prairie fires, "has resulted in increasing growth of timber . . . and a greater regular-ity and more equal distribution in the fall of rain." He cited the excessive droughts "so well remembered by the early settlers of Iowa, and prevailing a quarter century ago." Thus the bad year of Fremont's expedition, 1842–43, became evidence of amelioration. "If one third the surface of the great plains were covered with forest there is every reason to believe the climate would be greatly improved," he concluded. The very limitations upon the Plains environment could thus be brought to witness, in the words of this faithful expression of the philosophy of the last frontier, "the readiness of nature to second the operations of man in respect to climate, and other agencies affecting the productiveness of the soil." [32]

The significant section of the Timber Culture Act gave a quarter-section of public land, entirely independent of the Homestead Act, to the entrant who should "plant, protect, and keep in a healthy growing condition for ten years forty acres of timber." It was not necessary to live on the land. In ten years it had become so obvious that the law put a premium on fraud that even the Commissioner of the Land Office reported it, though he added characteristically, "At the same time, I am not inclined to recommend the repeal of a law of so beneficent an intention." [33] Over 100,000 claims had been filed under the law, of which 500 had been "proved up" by demonstrating growing timber. They covered 97,836 out of the 16 million acres entered. As an investigator commissioned by Congress commented, "The timber culture act can fairly be titled 'An act to loan to any person 160 acres of public land for eight years without fear, favor, or supervision.' " [34]

What had happened was the characteristic fate of conservation measures at the last frontier. The original Timber Culture Act, not fitting the Plains environment, had to be relaxed in fairness to the settlers who honestly tried to grow trees. Speculators poured through the loopholes. In 1874, Congress permitted the entrant to stagger his planting over three years, getting title in eight years. In 1876, after the trees which actually were set out in Kansas and Nebraska had been hard-hit by drought and grasshoppers, Senator Paddock of Nebraska got through an amendment giving entrants a year of grace for each year of grasshoppers and permitting planting to be accomplished by seeds and cuttings as well as young trees. This virtually thwarted inspection. Still the petitions for "relief" came to Washington. In 1878, ownership was permitted upon the planting of ten acres, instead of forty, per quarter-section. A year's extension could be obtained not only because of grasshoppers but because of what Congress called "extreme or unusual drought." [35]

Fraudulent use of the law prompted a New York congressman in 1883 to introduce a bill to stop the selling or disposing of future rights to a timber culture entry before the actual establishment of planting was "proved up" and to confine entries to residents of the county. But by this time a policy which could have worked, if soundly administered, only on the eastern Plains had come into vigorous use on the short-grass range. The Cleveland administration was cracking down on illegal fencing of the public domain by cattlemen. They needed fences to check overcrowding. Timber culture homesteads now provided them with a way to convert the range to private property for at least eight years. Cleveland's incorruptible land commissioner, Andrew Jackson Sparks, observed:

A "cattle king" employs a number of his men as herders; "cowboys" is the popular designation for them. The herd is located on a favorable portion of the public lands, where grass, water, and shelter are convenient, and each herder is expected and required to make a timber culture entry of lands along the streams. These entries often very nearly if not quite occupy all the watered lands in a township and render the remainder undesirable for actual settlement for farming purposes.[36]

A vested interest in someone else's good intentions makes a difficult combination to beat, and the New Yorker's bill failed in the Senate. Since the Timber Culture Act could not be tightened or repealed, Sparks set about to enforce it. He blocked issuance of final titles in those land offices where fraud had been the rule until claims could be investigated. "The response to Commissioner Sparks's order on the Nebraska frontier," writes a Nebraska historian, "was one universal protest and wail, prolonged and intensified as the months passed. . . . The universal business upon which all other business depended was the business of grabbing land." [37]

His order was revoked by the Secretary of the Interior, and Sparks resigned. His successor in the Republican administration was an Omaha judge who boasted that he had issued five times as many land patents in his first two years as Sparks. Nevertheless, the homesteader had been confronted openly with his rivals for the public domain, and in 1891 the act was repealed. Of course, an 1893 law added that title might still be obtained to entries commenced under the act if trees had been cultivated on them for eight years "without regard to the number of trees that may have been then growing on the land." [38]

The Timber Culture Act got into private hands ten million acres of public domain, three-quarters of it in the Missouri basin. It thus advanced what, during its life from 1873 to 1891, was a national purpose. But with regard to the added national purpose of adjusting the Plains environment to a forest-grown civilization, its net effect was disillusionment. Not that all planting failed. In 1934 the U.S. Forest Service found by spot check that Nebraska had one acre out of two hundred acres in groves, Kansas and South Dakota one acre out of three hundred acres, and North Dakota one acre out of four hundred acres. Some of the trees were over forty years old.[39]

The problem was rather that, by promoting what was beyond the potentiality of nature—alteration of climate—Congress designed failure into a program which might, with the attainable object of moderating the *effects* of climate, have worked. Since, moreover, the natural potential was assumed in the legislating of the program, there could be no thought of determining by experience just where or under what conditions trees could grow. When disillusion came in 1891, Representative Pickler commented, "This law lays down rules for the growing of trees for every climate in the United States." [40] When the United States again sought to sponsor large-scale tree-planting on the Plains, therefore, it found evidence of successes of timber culture. It could not learn from the mistakes.

That was in 1934, over forty years after the Timber Culture Act was discredited. In announcing the Shelterbelt program, Franklin Roosevelt still could not be scientifically sure that trees would endure the dry subhumid climate where he projected them in a great zone from Canada to the Gulf. But he could, and did, prepare for the program with a survey by foresters of the probabilities of survival and the likely results. The 44 million Shelter-belt trees of the 1930's were a calculated risk. So far they have lived remarkably well, and they have provided the shelter from scorching winds in summer and the catchment of snow in winter for which they were designed. But in terms of the vicissitudes of Plains climate, they are still young.

The Homestead Act assumed that the whole of the basin frontier was prairie. Still more presumptuously, the Timber Culture Act sought to make it prairie by the influence of man. It has been the popular assumption that these stereotypes, the desert in reverse, were projected by bureaucrats and congressmen unfamiliar with the area to which they proved unsuited. That assumption neither fits the facts nor rightly interprets the relation of the last frontier to its planners in Washington. The truth is that a citizens' meeting in Omaha petitioned Congress fifteen years before the passage of the act for inducements to tree-planting.[41] Nebraska senators introduced the Timber Culture bill, championed its liberalizing amendments, and when Commissioner Sparks, of prairie origin, tried to enforce it honestly, attacked him and drove him from office.

The interesting thing is that the Plains states were simultaneously expressing a very different approach. While their representatives in Washington were insisting on the most grandiose of public lands schemes, their state legislatures and agricultural officials were getting trees planted in practical ways. Sometimes they expressed the motive of improving climate. More often they were interested in the attainable, and worthy, goal of supplying windbreaks, fencing, and firewood. Local governments could apply the state inducements, tax concessions, with an eye to actual results. "Almost all the eastern counties of Kansas," the Forest Service discovered in 1934, "reported plantations successfully established in the years following the drought of 1860." Arbor Day was a Nebraska innovation. J. Sterling Morton arranged its first observance by resolution of the state Board of Agriculture in 1872.

As the frontier moved into new environments faster than it could adjust to them, two basic approaches to the resulting problems came into conflict. One phase of the clash occurred within the newly settled states; another took place in Washington. (This was, of course, a feature of government decisions; with the mild exception of Henry Villard, there had been no disagreement as to basic approach within the railroad corporations.) The conflict was essentially between those who, recognizing novel limits to the potential of the Plains, would adapt settlement to those limits; and those, on the other hand, who held that the resources of the frontier were limitless.

In Washington, there loomed over all the partisans of a scientific approach the one-armed, bearded figure of John Wesley Powell. His 1878 *Report on the Lands of the Arid Regions of the United States* remains a classic analysis of the environment of the Plains. In it he advocated many of the plans which have since been adopted in adversity because they were not adopted in foresight: 2,560-acre grazing units (the current average size of Montana farms is 2,533 acres), co-operative grazing districts, classification of the economic capabilities of the public domain, chartering of irrigation districts. More fundamentally, he offered a new image of the West. The margin of subhumid agriculture he slanted west of the 20-inch rainfall line at its northern end, taking cognizance of lower evaporation and concentration of rainfall during the growing season. He refined Blodget's concept of the wheat-growing potential of the north in opposition to the Central Belt. Moreover, the climate in this zone would fluctuate critically *in time*. ". . . the district of the country thus embraced will be subject more or less to disastrous droughts, the frequency of which will diminish from west to east. For convenience let this be called the Sub-humid Region." [42]

In Washington, Powell had opponents enough.* He had also a rival, Ferdinand V. Hayden, who though a scientist commissioned by Congress to conduct geological surveys of the territories was on record for the myth of the times. Rainfall in Nebraska had been increased, he reported, by "settlement of the country and increase of the timber." "I am confident this change will continue to extend across the dry belt." [43] Hayden received generous appropriations.

Ambivalence in public attitude and conflict among experts were also characteristic of opinion in the states nearest the edge of settlement. There were professors in the state colleges on both sides of the controversy. James C. Malin tells us, for example, that Professor Gale at Kansas State College had, by 1879, prepared a tree-ring calendar of rainfall going back to 1760. From it he concluded that settlement had not changed climate. "It remains for man, so far as he has the power, instead of indulging in quixotic dreams of cosmic revolutions, to counteract on the one hand unfavorable influence, and, on the other, make all possible provisions for the contingencies of the climate." [44] Against this sage observation, produced without much benefit of hindsight, place the words of Samuel Aughey, Professor of Natural Sciences at the University of Nebraska. In the very next year, he wrote: ". . . it is clear that rainfall is and has been increasing from year to year. As pioneers take up the government lands, and encroach on the plains the line of

---

* Powell's struggle to introduce science into government policy toward the subhumid and arid West is the central theme of Wallace Stegner's *Beyond the Hundredth Meridian* (Boston, 1954). Powell's character is evoked to the full in that biography; so is the character of the opposition—professional jealousy, western expansionism.

abundant rainfall also marches westward." [45] There is not much doubt that around 1880 the preponderance of popular opinion in the basin lay with Aughey. "Rain follows the plow" became the convenient concept when tree-planting could no longer keep up with the advance of settlement and thus explain improving climate. And yet, at the same place and time, the quiet, often ingenious trials and errors went on, adapting tillage to lower rainfall. Men like Gale could be tolerated on a state college faculty, though it was Aughey who received official commendation.

It was in Washington that the spokesmen for the frontier would not tolerate analysis of the concept of unlimited natural bounty. Aughey's dictum was part of a polemic called for by the Nebraska agricultural society and directed squarely against a "so-called examination of the unsettled lands west of the one-hundredth meridian." The survey thus prejudged was the most likely effort sponsored by Congress to fit its plan for land disposal to the conditions of the Plains. It was the work of the Public Land Commission of 1879, a response to Powell's report. The Commission, of which Powell was a member, was directed to classify the public domain as to its economic use, "having due regard to humidity of climate." [46] But Aughey's opposition was gentle compared to that of the representatives of basin states when the Commission reported its classification proposals to Congress. To Congressman Maginnis of Montana, scientific classification of public lands was sheer paternalism. Let these "scientific lobbyists" not interfere with the settler. "He is going to pick out his own lands with his own eye." Congressman Haskell of Kansas made it very clear that planning for the variations in Plains land was a sectional issue. It was opposed, with the exception of a representative from Illinois and one from California, by every member from public lands states. It was opposed unanimously by spokesmen for the Missouri basin where it would immediately apply. To Patterson of Colorado, Powell was "this revolution-ist." [47]

It is not enough, then, to ascribe the irrelevance of the Government's plans for settling the Plains to ignorance in remote Washington of a novel environment. In the new sciences integrated by Powell Washington possessed more accurate information than it had ever had of its unsettled territory. And opposition to the conversion of this information into policy came precisely from the spokesmen of the frontier itself.

Rather, we must admit that the climate of government had changed. Congress continued to plan the basic organization of the territories as it had done in the Northwest Ordinance. Indeed, it now planned, in company with the railroads, the economic as well as the political organization. It is true that the Old Northwest resembled the environment of the original colonies more than it resembled the Plains. But it is also true that the planners of the Old Northwest were at once politicians and observers of nature: Washington, the surveyor; Hamilton and Gallatin, resource planners; Gallatin, the realistic cartographer of the West; Calhoun, who submitted the only national development plan ever to come from the Corps of Engineers; and Jefferson, experimenter with patterns of colonization and scientific farming who, with his friend Madison, conducted the first simultaneous weather observations to determine variance at neighboring stations.

By 1862, the nation was clear about what William Gilpin so eloquently called its "untransacted destiny." Observation of nature was not needed to carry out the mandate implied in the phrase. The innovating minds were, as Henry Adams ruefully observed, at the service of business, such business, for example, as establishing the railroad belts. Not all of them; but for the scientist who sought to inform public policy, like Powell, or the politician who sought to effectuate informed policy, like Justin Morrill and Abram Hewitt, a great chasm lay between policy and science. Mark Twain, too, had an eloquent phrase, "the Gilded Age."

It was the peculiar lot of the Missouri basin to be settled finally in what was not only the Gilded Age but a period of climate when romance and reality coincided. For it was literally true, as a popular historian wrote of Kansas in 1885, that "meteorological changes have accompanied the settlement of Kansas." Early rainfall records are not wholly reliable and show many local variations. But on this point they agree. The six years beginning with 1880 were drought-free years for Dakota, Nebraska, and Kansas. The years leading to 1880 showed strong recovery from the low rainfall most pronounced in 1874.[48] For the oldest Kansas stations, Leavenworth and Manhattan, precipitation reached its all-time high in the period ending in 1880. That is in terms of five-year averages, which the sober observer might use to discount extremes.

At Leavenworth, the *increase* was 17 inches in sixteen years; at Manhattan, 12 inches in ten years. Certainly in 1860, and again in 1874, there was ample experience to contradict the myth of ever-increasing rainfall. But the railroad and homestead frontier was trapped by its own impetuosity. The census shows that two-thirds of the people in Kansas in 1880 could not have been there in 1870: allowing for turnover, the proportion would be much greater. So was it in Nebraska. Dakota Territory was, of course, entered too late for experience with the early droughts. Against this type of empirical evidence, a Washington geologist or a professor reading tree rings was a frail contender. The image of rainfall increasing with timber and cultivation was, like the image of the desert, founded on specific observed data. Unlike the desert, it was assailed contemporaneously by well-established scientists. The attack produced ambivalence in the frontier areas and conflict in Washington. It could not produce a public opinion of the nature of climate.

For that, it took catastrophe. Ten years after Powell's vain plea for a settlement policy adapted to subhumid climate, and after three states had been established in that zone under policies he had called irrelevant, one of the new states asked Powell to address its constitutional convention. In the incongruous setting of the Bismarck boom, the scientist who then headed the U.S. Geological Survey repeated the warning which for twelve fat years had gone unheeded.

You hug to yourselves the delusion that the climate is changing. This question is 4,000 years old. Nothing that man can do will change the climate. . . . The settlement of the country, the cultivation of trees, the building of the railroads—all these matters will have no influence upon your climate. You may as well not hope for any improvement in this direction. There's almost enough rainfall for your purposes, but one year with another you need a little more than you get.[49]

For the first time the founders of a frontier commonwealth listened to a warning that their land was not a paradise. They could shape their own destiny —within the facts of nature. Those facts not even empire builders could amend. In 1889 much of the western basin had still a year of illusion before the general drought began. But North Dakota, in the year of its statehood, received 12 inches of rain. Now that it was too late, the scientist would be heard by the architects of states.

THE UNSETTLED FRONTIER

Montana was so unfamiliar with emigration in settlement days that it didn't distinguish it from immigration and named a place where foreign settlers found gold Emigrant Gulch. Now it knows what emigration means.

—State highway historical marker near the town of Emigrant, Montana

Purposes are difficult to read. But the purpose strongest in all the plans, of the railroads as of the politicians, must certainly have been to populate the area of the last frontier, which overlay the basin. To populate meant, in an undetermined degree, to establish permanent tenure, to settle. In that sense the plans partly failed, and they failed to the extent that they were carried out. For in the quiet individual assessment which American families make of their parts of the country by moving in, staying, or moving out, for twenty years (as soon as the plans had been carried out) the Missouri basin has ranked lower than any other great area of the United States. Individual southern states—Arkansas, Oklahoma, and Mississippi—have sometimes shown losses proportionately greater but not so general or so long-continued as those of the last-settled states of the basin. The frontier is learning what emigration means.

There are (according to the 1950 census) 8,077,839 people in the 460 counties which best coincide with the Missouri basin.[50] In one-sixth of the nation's land, the basin has not much more than a twentieth of the people. The proportion has been falling steadily for thirty years. In 1920, as Montana's flivver frontier filled up, the basin had 6.9 per cent of the U.S. population. In 1930, it was 6.3 per cent; in 1940, 5.9 per cent; in 1950, 5.4 per cent. The decade 1930–40 was, of course, the one in which emigration assumed route proportions. The basin population actually dropped 40,000 in those ten years, while the country as a whole grew 7.2 per cent. More generally, the basin population increases, but much less than the whole country: in the last ten years, the increase has been 5 per cent for the basin, 15 per cent for the nation.

Missouri basin states, largely rural, have a higher birth rate than the rest of the nation. This fact would normally increase their population more than the national average if the emigration rate were not still higher. The telling figures are therefore those of *net migration*—out-migrants compared to in-migrants. These figures are not available by counties. For states, however, the Census Bureau published in 1946 an analysis of migration for the years 1935 to 1940, based on actual enumeration and containing information in great detail, not only on the origin and destination of those who move, but on their economic and social characteristics.

Relative to the 1940 population, net loss through migration was heavier in the Missouri Valley than in any other area of similar size in the United States. Four states of the Missouri Valley—North Dakota, South Dakota, Nebraska, and Kansas—were in the group of five states—the fifth is Oklahoma—which had a net loss through migration that amounted to more than 4.5 per cent of the 1940 population.[51]

The case of Nebraska, the only state wholly within the Missouri drainage, suggests the size of the net emigration. For each 1,000 people in Nebraska in 1940, 45 had entered the state in the previous five years, but 130 had moved out.

These years reflected the aftermath of the Dust Bowls—the Dakotas and Montana in 1934, Kansas and Colorado in 1936. It is not at all difficult to see why people left the basin states.

Item. Of 281 incorporated places in North Dakota, 54 had to haul in water by train or truck.

Item. In August, 1936, one out of every three farm families in the spring wheat counties—the last settled—was on relief.

Item. A sociologist of the state university of Washington interviewed migrants from the northern Plains. "The thing about which they ask first, and in which they are the most interested, is moisture. As long as there is rain in the district, they will buy stump farms."

The Dust Bowl has meaning as a name for an event, not for a locality. With the return of supernormal rainfall in the next decade and of war wheat prices, the eager question in the basin Plains was, "Will they come back home after the war?" The answer varied sharply from state to state within the basin. But 1950 census totals offer this general answer (we do not yet have net migration data): they did not come back as much in the basin as in the whole nation. Out of sixteeen states in the country growing at less than half the national rate, between 1940 and 1950, eight were basin states. One of these, North Dakota, had 3.5 per cent fewer people in 1950 than in 1940. In fact, North Dakota, along with Iowa and Montana, had fewer people in the basin drainage in 1950 *than thirty years before.*

Turning back from the last frontier may represent frustration of the congressional intent for the Plains states. But there are those who see emigration as a form of adaptation to the Plains environment. In 1936, for example, C. Warren Thornthwaite recommended: "The minimum reduction from the 1930 population consistent with a safe use of the land would be about 390,000 people or 95,000 families." [52] It is quite certain now that Thornthwaite's prescription has been filled. The growing size of wheat and cattle farms tells the story: the Plains is exacting the extensive form of agriculture to which it is, over the long term, suited.

Numbers cannot, however, measure the degree of acclimatization of the population on the Plains. Who is it that left and who stayed? The youth left for the new frontier in the city, extending the selective exodus that had begun in Montana fifteen years before. When city jobs became more plentiful as a result of war, their migration speeded up.[53] Those who left were not, moreover, those who failed to take advantage of the environment. They included some of those who demanded most from it. "The most prosperous farmers have migrated," concluded a study of Tripp County, South Dakota, in 1935, "and the least prosperous have been left behind." Here is part of the reason for the superior staying power of some European colonists on the Plains. They had seen worse.[54]

The census of migration in 1935–40 throws new light on the question of selection of population through migration. To take a very crude index, it demonstrates that those who left the center tier of the Plains states included more educated men and women than those who remained. That is true even if age be discounted. It is true for the farm population taken separately. And the heavier the net emigration, the more it is true. North Dakota is the extreme. In five years, North Dakota lost one college graduate from its farms for every two who lived there in 1935. That is three times the over-all loss of farm population. Contrast Colorado, which gained more farmers than she lost in 1935–40. Migrants from Colorado farms were not disproportionately well-educated people, and in-migrants included proportionately more college people than the 1935 population. In the states, therefore, where adjustment is most needed, the exodus took those who, theoretically, would have the most to contribute to the adjustment.

All this is inference from the wholesale data of census returns. What migration means to the actual process of adaptation to the new environment of the grassland we can better understand from intensive studies of counties and townships. Four such cases are available: twelve townships in western North Dakota, 12,000 families in South Dakota, three eastern Montana counties, and Dickinson and Saline Counties, Kansas.[55]

The South Dakota families were surveyed in the depth of the depression of the 1930's. They may have been too poor to move. In the other cases, great turnover was characteristic. In no case were as many as half the farm operators left in the same township at the end of fifteen years. During initial "settlement," the Kansas study revealed, only 43 per cent of the original farmers remained in the same county after five years. Stability increased as the townships grew older, but declined somewhat following the drought of the 1930's. A little over 60 per cent of the farmers remained in their counties in the five years 1935–40. If one appreciates the importance of the development of knowledge, and the passing on of experience by the men actually farming the new environment, the conclusion is unexpected but clear. Turnover means that the individual has seldom remained settled long enough to learn the peculiar variations of the Plains climate over the years. Instead, he has learned by what Malin calls "the folk process." We are driven increasingly to examine the community as the conveyor of knowledge.

"Civilization," wrote Isaiah Bowman, "needs continuity of effort in place." But the new logistics of railroad and motor truck which filled up the last frontier also put escape within the reach of every inhabitant. Individual experience will not be continuous. Continuity in an environment symbolized by the wheel requires many things, but among them must be a concept of the relation of man to the environment which is part of the culture, which can be passed down the generations. It is a problem not alone of unbroken scientific investigation. At the level of human motivation, it is a need for honored values of life that yield satisfaction in all the ineluctable conditions nature imposes.

THE PROBLEM of adjustment is not with nature and local institutions alone. In all the varied aspects of life controlled by national decisions, whether corporate or governmental, the people of the basin must work out, as well, a realistic picture of their role vis-à-vis the nation. Relative population decline challenges the old concept here as population mobility challenges the old notion of the settler learning how to farm the Plains through his individual trial and error.

It has been a long time since the old assumptions were spoken right out. The first Missouri River Improvement Convention, meeting in St. Joseph, heard them in 1881. "With the readjustment of the political forces of this country, under the tenth census, the center of power will be transferred to this valley," prophesied Senator Ingalls of Kansas, chairman of the convention. "We are able to enforce the just demand for the improvement of western rivers," boasted Missouri Senator G. G. Vest as he counted the new voters. The rules committee of a second Missouri River Convention was not too modest to define the question before the house as the "improvement of the Missouri River from the Gulf to Ft. Benton."

The Seventeenth Census gave less comfort to the empire builders than the Tenth. Its map of political power was simple and ruthlessly clear. It gave the Missouri basin states (omitting Minnesota because of its slight area within the basin) only 40 seats in the House of Representatives. Ten years before they had 42, and in 1930, 45. In 1912, when the membership of the House was fixed at its present total of 435, they had 54. Missouri basin states are, after the election of 1952, slightly weaker in proportion to the membership in the House of Representatives than they were in 1872. They have 9.2 per cent of the votes in the House; they had 12.3 per cent when Senator Ingalls spoke in 1881, and they had a little over 9.2 per cent ten years before.

What courses are open to a great area, one-sixth of the United States, when its political strength declines in one house of Congress at the ratio of 54 to 40? Suppose that it is of all sections of the United States that in which the frontier values are least modified and composed. One course is to commit its future to the two great sections which meet within the basin: the arid west and the Mississippi basin. By alliances with each it may use its undiminished strength in the Senate to modify their clashing interests while it enjoys their combined support in the House. The Missouri basin could thus avoid facing the decline of its political power. It would lose only its self-determination.

It might, on the other hand, rest its case upon the national interest in the development of the resources of a region. It might find its allies in policy and not in section. This course would involve a fight in the open: a fight first to determine what the basin wants, and a fight in Congress against those from all sections who oppose it. A certain risk in terms of votes would replace the risks in terms of objectives. But eight million people would have to decide how they would have a river serve them and justify their plan in the eyes of the nation. They would have to know their own minds.

Chapter I V

THEIR OWN MINDS

"WE FOLKS of the Missouri Valley," said an Iowa congressman colloquially, "are no different than they are in any other valley of America." [1] He was right, of course, about the overriding traits of Americanness. He was right, in another sense, about the wide range of cultures within an arbitrarily defined sixth of the nation. Aside from the melting pot of migrants from other nations and sections which is as characteristic of the Missouri basin as of any other extensive area, there is a mixture of economies and institutions here. Homesteader and slave, conquistador and voyageur, Texas drover and section hand, urbanite and Indian contributed their still unconsolidated character.

What is distinctive about the Missouri basin is solely the emphasis in culture which is the response to a transitional environment and a transitional history. In the view people in the basin take of their place in nature and in the progress of the nation, we find not a peculiarity of mind but rather an unresolved confrontation of some American peculiarities of mind which is remarkable. Diverse, inconsistent, even paradoxical, are adjectives which might be applied to any aspect of life in America. The interesting aspects of the thinking of basin people are that they cover real transition with constructed stereotypes, follow consistent ideals to frustration and reaction, act roles in which most of them sometimes, and some of them always, feel miscast.* Raw materials of great richness and variety seem to remain here unpatterned by some process of social learning into serviceable ideas. This was Bernard DeVoto's theme when, returning from a visit beyond the 100th meridian, he entitled his reports in *Harper's* "The Anxious West" and "The West Against Itself." [2]

---

* In Wallace Stegner's fine biography of John Wesley Powell, *Beyond the Hundredth Meridian*, one sees Powell's public career at last broken by these vested myths and inconstant sentiments. Near the climax of the story, when irrigation of the Great Plains was about to be put off for fifty years, perhaps forever, by the emasculation of Powell's irrigation survey, Stegner introduces Senator Gideon Moody of South Dakota, who "denied rainfall statistics and resented slurs against what had from its first settlement been a rich and productive wheat belt." Senator Moody's words were: "Our people in the West are practical people, and we can not wait until this geological picture and topographical picture is perfected."

After my own writing had been done, I came upon a phrase in Stegner's book that would have made an apt title for this chapter: "the unmodulated mind."

CONQUERORS

Like other Americans close to the process of civilizing the wilderness, people in the basin have an affinity for booms. Governor Sigurd Anderson of South Dakota was but doing his civic duty when he bragged before his Iowa hosts, who at a meeting of basin governors and aides had claimed the most productive cornfields in the universe, that his state supplied the seed. If there is any distinctiveness in the boom spirit which animates the Knights of Ak-Sar-Ben (Nebraska spelled backwards) in Omaha, or the reclamation association of any city to the west, it is only the limitless sweep of promise in proportion to fulfillment. "Where vastness in land and resources is an accepted fact," the Montana guidebook suggests delicately, "people are likely to be prodigal in measuring the size of their enterprises."

But there is a more tangible reason for the prestige of the booster and the ostracism of the "croaker." Whether or not he intended it, there was as much sober truth as sarcasm in the lampoon of an early investigator of the Nebraska boom: "the early activities of the settlers were directed mainly to the advancement of their civic interests, or in other words, to the sale of corner lots." [3] For if there were no boom in real estate prices, how else was the enormous capital outlay required to develop open plains into towns and farmsteads to be financed? This process Henry George first saw clearly. It was a characteristic process of city-building. But the peculiarity of the occupation of the basin Plains was its combination of the most exclusively agrarian production with urban motives and standards. Here its contrast with the subsistence frontier was complete. The last frontier was the place where raw land, to be occupied by a freshly urbanized civilization, had in a generation to be equipped with railroads and telegraph, not wagon roads; towns providing tractor service and elevators, not general stores alone; and schools. [4] What the settler was trying to do, economically speaking, was to take land the way geology left it and advance it into the twentieth century with the money available from its own appreciation in value. Only an unquestioned myth—the belief by all parties to the transaction in the limitless capacity of the Plains to flourish—could sustain that economic perpetual motion machine.

But the myth of the Plains, unlike the myth of the city subdivider, was predicated on a claim that could be verified: crop yields. Once or twice in a generation the farmer, not merely the speculator, saw that claim disproved, all the more devastatingly because it was by nature and not by human caprice. What was essential, then, was to find an explanation boding better for the future. Then speculation could revive. Tree culture or the turning plow would make it rain and, by converting western Nebraska or the Dakotas into Illinois and Iowa, correct what either God or the polar ice cap had overlooked. When that manifest destiny manifestly failed in the 1890's, the panaceas came. The basin was the happiest hunting ground for all their promoters. Irrigation was becoming a science in California when William E. Smythe, editorial writer on the Omaha *Bee,* turned it into a crusade. Hardy W. Campbell of Lincoln followed suit with his dust mulch "dry farming." Goodland, the Kansas town close to the Colorado boundary, became the capital of rain-making by magic in 1892–94. The local editor greeted as follows the formation of the corporation which got hold of the secret formula: "It is a happy hour for Goodland to know that she is not only the Mecca of the home seeker; the innermost chamber of these broad plains; the morning star among a hundred towns of western Kansas, but also that she holds within her grasp the scepter that even sways the clouds. . . . We are the people." [5] It is in the Missouri basin, sixty years later, that contemporary rain-makers have so thoroughly blanketed with contracts the Rocky Mountain front and foothills in Colorado and Wyoming that Weather Bureau scientists privately complain they have no control areas left to discover whether the seeding of clouds by portable silver iodide generators has affected precipitation.

In those parts of the basin where drought was endemic, the gamble, not the boom, became ideal. "The chief occupation was mining," wrote James Bryce about western Montana, "an industry which is like gambling in its influence on the character." "There is still grass on 'them thar hills,' even if gold in them is hard to find," added the American National Livestock Association from Denver in 1938, *"if and when it rains."* [6] "The western Kansas farmer is a gambler . . . ," said William Allen White a year later.[7] "Last Chance Gulch" Montana prospectors called their mining camp before they renamed it Helena and made it the capital. There was an element of finality about many of the gambles in the basin, insofar as it was the last frontier.

"Bonanza," the word of the Spanish prospector who struck it rich, got attached to the beef business as it moved in from the Southwest. It was also applied to the culture of wheat as, via the Northern Pacific's Dalrymple farm, it moved into the basin from the northeast. The Missouri basin is, indeed, the place where it became a common-sense matter to describe homesteading itself as a gamble. "The government bet a quarter section against the filing fee," went the saying, "that you couldn't live on it for five years." But this was, of course, the cynical view of the cattle rancher, only in retrospect accepted as an accurate description of family farming by the homesteader himself. What changed the sober process of sweating out a living into a gamble, and quietly loaded the dice in the gamble of the cattle game, was the unforeseeable change in climate probability. The point is very difficult to grasp even now. Ladd Haystead, an agricultural journalist who is himself a native of the Great Plains, thus describes the outlook of the High Plains wheat farmer: "Uncle Bill knows there have been droughts in the area ever since 1800. The average is two or three out of every five years—and the natives demand only one good year in five to make a profit!" [8] Does the wheat farmer know that the average number of droughts in five years may be halved in one generation and doubled in the next?

But whether by subduing the wilderness, even its climate, to his way of life or by outguessing its chances of occasional conformance, the hero of the last frontier was the lone conqueror of nature. He went ahead of civilization. There is no better portrait of the pioneer of the Plains, saliencies unrounded, than Mari Sandoz' portrait of her father, first settler of the flats along the Niobrara. She recalls a neighbor saying:

Old Jules is crazy, but a lot of people listen to him. . . .

You never saw him lean over his shotgun on the hill overlooking the Running Water and his orchard. His daughter took me up to him, resting there after a hunt. He pointed out what he saw in the country the day he came. There was something of the prophet who remains to make his word deed. He is rooted in a reality that will stand when the war and its hysteria are gone, a sort of Moses working the soil of his Promised Land. . . .

But it's a good thing too that you never had to live under Old Jules's roof or join fences with him.[9]

The later comers are always stale and flat by comparison. We look back to the giants in the earth.

ADAPTERS

These themes are the dominants. But side-by-side with the booster, the gambler, the individual conqueror of environment recur the recessive types, those who succeed as well, perhaps better, but whose example does not get passed on. There was the folk experimenter, the man who recognized limits in his new environment and set out to discover adaptations. Tracing his methods and his influence in his own farming community has been the contribution to American history of James Claude Malin. Read his transcription of the speech of T. C. Henry, king of winter wheat in Kansas, to the Dickinson County fair in the year 1870:

. . . We discover an arrangement of the laws of nature here, unlike those to a considerable extent that we have been accustomed to in the Eastern States—and I am persuaded that the methods and practices in farming that are suitable to those states, are in very many respects out of place and not adapted to the peculiarities of this locality and this climate. . . .

It behooves him [the farmer] then to study the nature, condition and quality of his lands; observe closely the great laws about him that have shaped the local and climatic peculiarities of his geographical position. . . . He must read and reflect, experiment and discover new methods of overcoming the obstacles and hindrances that arise about him. In this great work we want for leaders men whose examples and precepts will excite the enthusiasm and secure the confidence of their fellow laborers in this field of agriculture.[10]

There was the man who refused any longer to gamble with resources which he sensed were not wholly his own. Granville Stuart, pioneer cattleman in Montana, had come to the state prospecting for gold. This was his reaction to the terrible winter of 1886: "I never wanted to own again an animal that I could not feed and shelter."

There was the organizer of collective effort in an environment which occasionally overpowered even the unaided giant. It was along the Cache la Poudre, where it joins the South Platte, that Horace Greeley sponsored a native, secular collective settlement. It was the first such colony to succeed since Americans occupied the Atlantic coast. There was an element of appropriateness to semiarid irrigated agriculture in his collective design which a religious hierarchy like the Mormons had discovered, but which was recessive in the outlook of the Plainsman. Looser collectives, however, controlled economic life, because even as they were repudiated in theory, they worked. The Farmers Union in North Dakota is, to the outsider who knows the West from books, an incredible example. Its 316 local grain co-operatives are second in number only to those of Illinois; its co-operative oil and gas business is surpassed in the state only by Standard Oil.[11] But anyone who thinks that organization to master a vast environment is a Scandinavian import peculiar to the country from Minnesota west to Montana should investigate the operations of the Wyoming Stockgrowers Association. Except in California, where the irrigated plantation is individually, not collectively, managed, it would be hard to find in rural America equivalents for the locally originated public power districts of Nebraska, the water conservancy district in Colorado, the grazing district in Montana, and the state business enterprises of North and South Dakota.

AUTONOMY IN APRON STRINGS

When the basin populace thinks of its regional role in the nation's history, it calls up an image which blends easily with the image of the self-reliant conqueror of nature: the autonomous region somehow embodying the destiny of the United States. All the old symbols of the distinctiveness of the last frontier contribute to the vividness of the image: the remoteness and irrelevance of Washington-made law, with its corollaries, the vigilante and the squatter-sovereign; the successful improvisation by which the wheat farmer or cattleman cheated the Land Office to amass a farm of practical size; the rejection of traditional ways of farming and the folk-invention of new ways that worked.

But there was, and is, an even more powerful symbol of autonomy. Recall the voice of this part of the country at bay, in the speech of William Jennings Bryan: ". . . we reply that the great cities rest upon our broad and fertile prairies. Burn down your cities and leave our farms, and your cities will spring up again as if by magic; but destroy our farms and the grass will grow in the streets of every city in the country." The last frontier remains, in the minds of its settlers, the last stand of the land-owning, free-standing farmer as against the dependent life of the city. Walter Prescott Webb reflected the mind of the Plainsman when he wrote in 1931, "It is in the West that rural life has remained dominant over urban life." [12]

Independent of the city, basin people tend to view themselves as independent of the United States government, too. The view comes from motives a good deal deeper than party politics. "Bold, independent, self-reliant, full of energy and intelligence, they do not need to rely upon the arm of a paternal government to carve out their own fortune." [13] This is the role which the United States designed for its pioneers. Representative John H. Baker of Indiana, speeding the homesteader westward with these words into the unclassified domain of 1879, was already voicing a cliché. Clichés are, of course, the stuff of public attitudes.

But independence of government may not, in the dominant view, divorce one from his city, county, or state. The man who thinks of himself as an individual face-to-face with nature may also think of himself as a member of a local government face-to-face with Washington. This is the significance of the powerful allegiance to the irrigation district, or to the state government in its capacity of water adjudicator.

Beneath the stereotyped views, contrasting attitudes run deep but inarticulate. The rancher who thinks of Wyoming as autonomous reads the fate of his enterprise in Herefords in the market reports of the Chicago *Tribune*. The local chamber of commerce, hard upon the heels of a resolution demanding independence from eastern finance and management, continues, as Ladd Haystead points out, "looking for that wealthy Easterner, that out-of-state capital, that new branch." The docility of the Montanan paying a transportation premium in the price of gasoline refined in his own city or of the Colorado consumer buying beet sugar made in his own state at the nation's highest prices fits poorly with the assumption of economic independence. [14]

In action, the basin citizen accepts dependence on decisions made by federal as frequently as on those made by corporate bureaucracies. It is important, of course, that the local agent of the federal or corporate program move into the basin. Consider, as a revealing instance, the reaction of the editor of the Omaha *World-Herald* to the great federal relief operation by which roads were opened and cattle fed during the severe blizzards of 1948–49.

The people in this region of wide open spaces and independent spirit are not quitters. They don't give up easily. But there is a limit to human endurance. . . .

"Our best hope," said the Governor [of Nebraska], "is that nature will give us a break. Man is not big enough to do the job alone. . . ."

What the situation called for was organization, with one man to run the whole show and accept the complete responsibility. . . .

This meant that the Fifth Army, with headquarters in Chicago, would take over. It meant also that General Pick would be the man in charge. . . . And in every community he found people . . . were glad to accept a central authority in the emergency. . . .[15]

What happens in emergencies, of course, is that the hero battling nature, though he be a federal hero, neutralizes the expectation of self-reliance. General Pick was a skilled leader, but nowhere else in the United States would military command be so unquestioningly accepted. And this is the area where natural emergencies are chronic.

But in and out of emergencies, Washington is the effective governor of many basin economic enterprises. Wool and beet sugar with their indispensable tariff subsidy, wheat for the national stockpile and the world market, public irrigation, grazing on the public domain: these are businesses which have to meet a roll call, not a payroll. Their organized managers do not hesitate to call on Washington for help even against rival industries within the basin itself. There is something characteristic about the picture drawn by William Allen White of the venerable and loved Senator Capper, then leader of the congressional farm bloc, sitting all day long before 1,200 of his constituents in Topeka, vainly attempting to secure from them a consensus of the views of the barnyard cattleman and the Plains rancher, of the subsistence farmer and the wheatgrower west of the 100th meridian, of the irrigator and the orchard and truck farmer.[16] The allegiance to local government, in contests with Washington, seldom implies submission to local or state government of the rival claims of industries within the basin. The Wyoming stockmen had their business thoroughly organized on an interstate level, had brought about the formation of the American Livestock Association, and were lobbying for the formation of the U.S. Bureau of Animal Industry at a stage when they were settling their disagreements with the homesteaders of Johnson County by hiring a small private army to shoot them.

In the light of the history of settlement of the basin some of the inconsistency is resolved. Every entrant into the Missouri basin felt (often legitimately in the context of national opinion) that in pursuing his self-interest he was automatically achieving the nation's destiny. The history of the basin could be written as a succession of awakenings to the dissonance within this assumed harmony of interests. The fur trader, the director of the land grant railroad, the pre-emptor, the claimant of timber culture and desert land entries, the buffalo hunter, the locator of gold, the speculator in townsites, the bonanza wheat farmer, the grazier of the public domain—each has in his turn seemed to be the instrument of the nation's purpose when he entered the basin and a despoiler of the nation's resources before he was through. What could be more natural than for the industry under attack to turn to its subsidizers and planners in Washington for defense? And why should not the interests fight it out in Washington, where their campaigns had been planned?

Even in adversity, the two images—individual master of nature and embodiment of the nation's destiny—could powerfully reinforce one another. Even if the individual settler failed to conquer his environment, other "peaceful soldiers" would go on to triumph. Even if some form of exploitation was assailed as contrary to the national interest, it could always be answered that it was a "natural" use of resources and therefore bound to serve the historic American purpose. But not always or for every man and woman; and when the two images came in conflict disillusion followed more bitter than America had yet seen.

THE COST

There was always, as Nicolay and Hay noted in their life of Lincoln, an undercurrent of melancholy on the frontier. But only when the Missouri basin was reached in the midst of the unconfined boom did it find a voice. Vernon Parrington detected here "the first note of the tragedy of the frontier" in American literature.[17] Hamlin Garland sounded the note in *Main-Travelled Roads*. In his *A Son of the Middle Border,* and much later in Mari Sandoz' *Old Jules,* it received definition. For Hamlin Garland, the individual cost of the national destiny emerged in contrast to the richness of Old Jules's European culture, but also in contrast to the dimensioned, rooted life of the older Wisconsin and Iowa frontier. On the Plains, the autobiography of the pioneer became not merely epic but tragic. The novelist, sensitive to the life of thought and emotion as well as of action, perceived the tragic note at once. Willa Cather and Ruth Suckow traced it in the lives of women at the edge of the prairie. A generation of pioneers sensitized by contact with a life richer than that of the log cabin received the onslaught here of natural forces too powerful and too mysterious for the human will to command. This is the tragedy of Rolvaag's *Giants in the Earth*. The born pioneer Per Hansa falls before them, made vulnerable by the heritage of an ancient culture embodied in his wife Beret. From its complexities the endless plain provides no shelter.

Against these chords the romance of the cowboy plays an optimistic obbligato. The literature of the cattle and sheep business is not quite of a life where never is heard a discouraging word. Yet it is romantic, and the reason throws much light on the problem of finding the source of the abiding morale of this area. Those who wrote the classic accounts wrote of an occupation, not of a life complete in its generations, its causes, and its expectations. Its analogue was the literature of the sea, pre-Melville.*

What the eyes of the novelist saw as intrinsic the eyes of the Plainsman opened to episodically—in times of drought and cheap wheat. The conflict between manifest destiny and individual fulfillment which produced tragedy in the characters of Antonía, Per Hansa, Old Jules, and Dick Garland produced the stormiest revolts of American farm politics in the seventies, the nineties, the years before and after the first World War, and the 1930's. This is no more the place for analysis of the Populist movement and its counterparts than for literary criticism, but there are competent analyses,[18] and they point up two conclusions.

Nature "failed" and prices failed in the genesis of these revolts. The assumed conformity of individual fortune and national purpose was shattered throughout whole states. Recessive attitudes welled to the surface. Collective action and government intervention became the slogans. "Government paternalism," in the language of the opposition, has never been more thoroughly espoused by a major American party than by the Populists (government railroads, communications, credit, commodity stabilization). But the one stereotype which none of the middle western protest movements ever relinquished was the notion of the independence of their own area. Economic relationships which it was necessary to organize they therefore sought to revolt from. This is the serious significance of Mary "Yellin" Lease's exhortation to raise less corn and more Hell. Of the later Nonpartisan League in North and South Dakota, Professors Saloutos and Hicks said, "It stressed the role that the gov-

---

* And yet where the open-range cattle industry confronts the climate of the northern Plains, not in fiction but in reporting, tragedy appears. The legendary ticket to fame for the cowboy painter, Charlie Russell, was a sketch on the back of a postcard showing a single steer surviving the winter of 1886–87. He called it "The Last of Five Thousand."

ernment could play in aiding the farmers, but at the same time it proved the futility of a single state's acting alone." [19]

The tough fact is that in practical political terms the Populists failed. Frederic L. Paxson called it the first failure of a frontier revolt since Washington rallied the backwoods against the Tory adherents of George III.[20] In any case, the frustration of a vast aggrieved area of the nation, an area of farmers, is remarkable. It is difficult to escape the explanation that the population of the basin states, even when it conceived itself united upon a crusade, never fully understood its own powers and wants. It did not understand them because its organizing conceptions of nature and of its role in the larger progress of the nation were tailored to other frontiers: the prairie and the Far West. Lacking a conception of the geographic core of their area, lumping it in a single term "The West," even the insurgents could not define their own needs. Always partly sharing the image the nation held of them, they could not organize the raw materials of grievance into a program. Isaiah Bowman's formulation is precise: "The earth has never gone back on man, but man has found himself entangled in *the unpredictable* effects of his own system. What really happens is that knowledge at the moment of strain is not great enough to control the forces of nature and of systems of government combined." [21]

DARK GLASS

What sorts of knowledge are needed? There are three kinds at least: information about common resources and problems, knowledge translated into technically sound courses of action, intercommunication of the plans and responses of others in the basin "public." The problem of the basin states has been the lack of all three. Information has been retarded because a low premium was placed upon accurate measurement ("We are getting so dry," wrote a correspondent to a Kansas newspaper, "it is almost impossible to tell the truth.") [22] and because records of nature must be kept over a long time span in order to be reliable. Moreover, in spite of such almost unique historical research as Malin's, it remains largely true, as the North Dakota Agricultural College recently pointed out, that "most of the history of the state was 'recorded' only in the minds of the men and women who made it, and no sustained effort has ever been made to secure it from them. . . . We are not quite sure what is happening to us as human beings, or to our institutions." Raw data as to resources and desires can be translated into useful opinion and even individual decisions only in terms of what is technically and economically feasible. But with the important exception of the agricultural technicians on the staffs of the state colleges, experts and professional people of all sorts are too few in the basin area. Their careers lie in cities, and cities lie outside or at the edges of the basin.

It was one of John Dewey's profound insights that a public cannot come into being unless citizens can exchange reactions with all those who may be affected by a social problem.[23] It is precisely the holding up of this sort of mirror to its own responses that the communication system of the basin fails utterly to do. Richard Baumhoff, the very exceptional correspondent of the St. Louis *Post-Dispatch,* has shown some of the specific shortcomings.[24] Dailies published within the basin simply are not read as much as dailies elsewhere. Particularly is this true of Sunday editions, which might have space for explanatory material. The Minneapolis *Sunday Tribune,* for instance, outsells any other Sunday paper in North and South Dakota. But since it is published more than one hundred miles outside the watershed, it reports almost no opinion upon watershed development. An opposition press, which might kindle public interest in rival plans, is a rarity. A second daily newspaper is published in only seven basin cities out of the fifty-two with over 10,000 population. The extreme case is Montana, where Baumhoff documented the legendary "copper collar" with a letter from an official of the Anaconda Copper Mining Company acknowledging stock ownership or majority control over seven Montana newspapers: morning and evening papers at Butte and Missoula outside the basin and dailies in Billings, Helena, and Livingston inside. The New York *Times,* with William Blair stationed in the basin, and the *Post-Dispatch,* with Baumhoff assigned to cover all water development activities in the area, have given fuller and more comprehensive accounts of basin plans than any newspaper printed in the watershed. With some notable exceptions, the basin press is paying for its lack of independence and vigor by losing influence to radio. But radio does not communicate the public mind.

It is one of the unanticipated consequences of the very richness of mass communications, radiating from the great metropolitan centers, that the people of the basin, whose institutions were so significantly planned from outside, should also see their own reactions to those plans through the eyes of New York and Chicago journalists. Of that synthetic New York and Hollywood construction, the Wild West, enough has already beeen said.[25] And a great furor arose when the U.S. Department of Agriculture sought, through "The Plow that Broke the Plains," to propagandize within the basin its oversimplified image of the High Plains as permanently threatened by tillage. But the opposing stereotype of Plains agriculture as a gamble is received unquestioned from the *Saturday Evening Post,* which entitled its article on the postwar plow-up of the High Plains "The Great Plains Hits the Jackpot." [26]

Unlike Greece, or England, or the subdivided Atlantic Seaboard where the least-questioned concepts of American life germinated, the Missouri basin is a more than man-sized domain. It was never occupied completely as a home, but always partly as a route. So, as with its weather, the basin gets many of the concepts by which to lay hold on its emerging factual data from outside, from the clash of extraneous forces within its vast theater. Vicissitudes, extremes, unresolved conflicts, and uncertainties result. There is, of course, no lack of imagination and perception within the basin population. There is only a transmission loss from one innovator or adapter or interpreter to the next, from one generation to the next. Leaders in basin state politics know that in terms of votes their sheer power declines. Not quite knowing their own minds, they are tempted to attach themselves to the stronger of the movements which impinge from outside. There is much impetus to gain, and of the self-determination which it costs the basin never quite got the taste.

Chapter v

ABUNDANT-WATER PLANS

*Of all the variable things in creation the most uncertain
are the action of a jury, the state of a woman's mind,
and the condition of the Missouri River.*
—Sioux City *Register*, March 28, 1868.[1]

WHEN MAJOR Stephen H. Long embarked with his exploring party of Army
engineers from St. Louis on June 5, 1819, he came close to being the first man
to navigate the Missouri by steam. The steamer *Independence* had made a
successful round trip to the town of Franklin a month before, only twelve
years after the *Clermont's* first voyage up the Hudson. Long found the Missouri difficult. The first of his four boats, honored with the name of ex-
President Jefferson, sank on a snag at the mouth of the Osage River. Two
more made so little headway against the swift current that they wintered
at the bend, near what became Atchison, Kansas. The fourth boat was a little
75-foot stern-wheeler designed for the Missouri, to draw 19 inches of water.
She was named the *Western Engineer,* and she made 635 miles, almost to
Council Bluffs, before ice stopped her. Major Long failed in his mission to
test the navigability of the river up to the mouth of the Yellowstone and
plant a fort there. He took a land route the next year and later announced
its aridity to the nation. But the *Western Engineer* served one purpose. It had
a pipe rigged out over the bow painted like a serpent with a red mouth.
When exhaust steam from the cylinders hissed out of this apparatus, the
Pawnees were duly impressed. Even then, navigation on the Missouri was
something more than a means of transportation.

It cost too much. Light, expensive cargoes alone made it pay. These the
fur trade offered, and it was at a river post of the American Fur Company,
named Ft. Lisa after its great voyageur, that the *Western Engineer* wintered
in 1819. Astor's monopoly turned to steam in 1831 and in the next year in
its side-wheeler *Yellowstone* finished the voyage on which Major Long set out.
The Santa Fe trade, too, made steamboating pay on the lower river.
The Santa Fe Trail began at the head of navigation, Old Franklin, Missouri,
until the river undermined the town and swept it away; then the Trail began
at Independence, Leavenworth, and Westport. But the best enticement for

traffic on the river was gold. The year of the Pikes Peak rush, 1858, saw the height of Missouri navigation. Three hundred six boats arrived at Leavenworth that year; St. Louis newspapers announced more sailings up the Missouri in 1859 than for the upper and lower Mississippi combined.[2] Five years later the strike in Alder Gulch carried the boom in river traffic all the way to Fort Benton. By 1867, 10,000 passengers and 8,061 tons of freight were disembarking at the foot of the great falls in the Missouri.[3] The low proportion of freight is significant. It cost twelve cents to ship *a pound* of freight to Fort Benton from St. Louis and five to ten cents to Leavenworth.[4] Insurance cost an additional 6½ to 8 per cent of the value of the shipment.

The reasons are not hard to find. In 1896 Chittenden listed 295 steamboat wrecks on the Missouri, 193 of them caused by snags. Readers of Mark Twain's *Life on the Mississippi* will recall that the superior skill, and pay, involved in piloting on the Missouri River enticed his mentor, Captain Bixby, from the Mississippi. These "ornate and gilded" experts, he reported, "if they belonged in the Missouri River in the heyday of that trade (Kansas times), . . . got nine hundred dollars a trip which was equivalent to about eighteen hundred dollars a month."[5]

Adventure received its economic challenge the very year Captain Bixby changed rivers, for in 1859 the first railroad reached the banks of the Missouri. "The struggle between the steamboat and the railroad lasted just about twenty-eight years, or from 1859—when the Hannibal and St. Joseph railroad reached St. Joseph, Mo.—to 1887, when the Great Northern reached Helena, Mont."[6]

In 1867 there were seventy steamboat arrivals at Fort Benton. Ten years later Fort Benton received the last boat ever to carry commerce through from St. Louis. The next year Congress was prevailed upon to undertake permanent channel improvements. It is not the only illustration of an industry calling in the government doctor when its disease became chronic. Hiram Chittenden was to have an official role in the efforts of the Corps of Engineers to restore a commercially attractive waterway. Yet looking back on the episode he wrote: "Even at that time the fate of Missouri River navigation was to most men as clear as the flash of light in the night. It was dead beyond the hope of resurrection, at least within another century."[7]

THE MISSOURI RIVER COMMISSION

Before 1852 the United States carried on what might be called first-aid work for the benefit of Missouri River navigation. Snags were removed from the river as early as 1838. In that year the Corps of Engineers had two snagboats operating west to the bend. They pulled 2,245 snags and cut 1,710

Navigation flourished on the untamed Missouri as long as there was no safer, cheaper transportation. The Indian fight in this old illustration is mostly melodrama, but the snags and the current are real.

The *Benton*, commissioned in 1875, probably carried more cargo (250 tons one trip downstream) and certainly completed more runs to Fort Benton than any other mountain boat. In 1876 she supported the campaign against Sitting Bull on the Yellowstone. Yet it is not entirely unfair to show her here partly sunk. For like other Missouri River boats she was snagged and went down several times before she was finally wrecked on the Sioux City bridge in 1897.

1934

1936

1939

Making the river constrain itself. Three photographs of Rock Bluff Bend, twenty-five miles below Omaha, looking downstream. In 1934 the river had the run of the floodplain. Applying their eighty-year-old technique, the Army Engineers drove rows of wooden piles out from the concave bank, ending at the smooth curve they had designed for the bend. Slowed as it passed through the piling, the river dropped its silt. Five years later willows had sprouted on the new land. The Engineers were extending the permeable dikes from the opposite bank to narrow and thus deepen the channel. In 1939 the works were still vulnerable to severe floods. By 1942 a continuous stone lining along the right bank had secured the bend.

overhanging trees. The limited scale of these operations is apparent, however, from their total cost: $49,335.53 in fourteen years.[8] In 1852 the first appropriation for channel improvement amounted to $40,000.[9] Sixteen years passed before the second appropriation, of $25,000, was made. Both were used in the lower river, Kansas City to the mouth. In 1876, $25,000 was appropriated for the Kansas City to Sioux City channel and $20,000 for the river above Sioux City. Beginning in 1878, Congress made five annual appropriations far exceeding the total of the preceding forty years. All these appropriations singled out specific localities for improvement, the number in each act growing until by 1881 the five bills contained forty-three individual items for thirteen localities. "The means were inadequate at nearly every point, nothing could be finished, and the incomplete work was an easy prey to the destructive forces of the river. At the same time the supervision of so many works, so widely scattered, required a large and expensive staff." [10]

Meanwhile the general optimism of the Missouri basin frontier in the early eighties produced a vociferous demand that the United States revive the failing river commerce. In 1881 three hundred delegates attended a Missouri River Improvement Convention at St. Joseph. They were buoyed up not only by a sense of emergent political power but by the discovery of what seemed to be two keys to the solution of the problems of river development. Major C. R. Suter, for six years the officer in charge of the work of the Corps of Engineers on the Missouri, had demonstrated the technical solution to the problem of stabilizing a silt-laden stream. The Mississippi River Commission, composed of engineer officers and competent laymen, held out the hope that the administrative problem might be solved—the problem of log-rolling at the expense of the general waterway.[11] The real impulse that spurred on the move for systematic improvement was well described in the memorial which the emissaries of the convention took to Congress the following year. Reviewing the experience of 1878, when a tow of three barges was induced to call four times at Kansas City to pick up wheat, the memorial concluded:

At the time these barges thus carried from Kansas City to St. Louis 208,516 bushels of corn and 44,198 bushels of wheat, the rail rate between the two cities was thirteen cents per bushel on wheat and eight cents per bushel on corn. The rate at which the barges carried it was five and a half cents per bushel, or $8,537.65 on the four shipments. But this is not all; the barges while making such a saving to the owners of the grain, and while running empty one way, made, at the rate charged, a profit of one hundred per cent.

Could we successfully employ barges on the Missouri River, between Kansas City and St. Louis alone, so as to realize this saving in the cost of marketing our crops, it would make a vast difference to the people of the Missouri Valley.[12]

In 1884 the convention's proposal prevailed. Congress placed all of the functions of the Corps of Engineers on the Missouri River under the supervision of a Missouri River Commission. The act creating the Commission charged it with two principal duties: "to superintend and direct" the improvement already authorized on the Missouri and "to consider, devise, and mature such additional plan or plans, and all such estimates as may be deemed necessary and best, to obtain and maintain a channel and depth of water in said river sufficient for the purposes of commerce and navigation." The Commission functioned under the direction of the Secretary of War. Major (later General) Suter was appointed chairman. Two other engineer officers and two civilian engineers were members.

The Suter technique of stabilizing the river was at once adopted by the Commission. With minor changes, it has remained in use to this day. The hydraulics of a silt-laden stream within soft, erodable banks are interesting and complex. Major Suter understood the general principles; the full long-term effects are almost as little known to the modern engineer as to him. A river of this kind meanders. That means that its current must speed up on the outside of the bends. At higher speeds, the water cuts faster and transports more silt. There is, moreover, a spiraling of the current which helps excavate the concave bank to disproportionate depths. But as it straightens to cross to the opposite side of the floodplain, the stream loses speed. Silt settles to the bottom. In the "reaches" in which this occurs sandbars always cause trouble. The two requirements of engineering are therefore to guard the outside of the bends and to narrow and deepen the reaches. The first, Major Suter did with revetments, or protective linings of willow trunks, lumber, stone, or brush. The second, he ingeniously effected by running out into the reaches rows of vertical piling, not to dam the river completely, but to slow it at the edges so that the siltation would occur there and the flow be concentrated in the middle of the reach. The river could thus be made to build up its own ordered channel. The design was such that all bends were trained to smooth and even arcs, not straightening out the river, but avoiding the dangerous cutting involved in sharp hooks.[13]

From the first the Commission was bothered less by engineering problems than by political and economic ones. They came from interests—individual, corporate, and municipal—desiring protection of their property along the banks more than facilities for through transportation on the waterway. "Naturally the persons holding these views have most frequently and most vigorously made themselves known to the Commission," observed its 1885 report.[14] By 1897 the complaint which had led to the creation of the Commission thirteen years earlier was recurring:

The progress of the work for systematic improvement of the river by continuous work by reaches . . . has been seriously interfered with during the past year by the requirements of the river and harbor act of June 3, 1896, which specified numerous localities, separated by many miles, where work was to be done, notwithstanding the fact that the amount of money appropriated was largely reduced from that of previous years.[15]

By 1900, this process provoked the chairman of the House Rivers and Harbors Committee, Theodore E. Burton of Ohio, to schedule a hearing to permit congressmen from the Missouri River districts to show cause why appropriations for the river should be continued. He frankly raised the question with them whether bank protection was a legitimate river and harbors expense. To this Representative Gamble of South Dakota made reply: "My home is at Yankton. . . . My own concern is as to Yankton." Representative Burke of South Dakota was equally frank: "Mr. Chairman, in what I have to say I shall confine myself entirely to my own city, which is Pierre." Representative Shackleford of Missouri "was very much alarmed a moment ago by the announcement of this committee that it was being seriously considered whether they would not abrogate the Missouri River Commission." Hence his testimony is all the more interesting. "If we would bridle our constituents and persuade them not to ask for a diversion of funds and then all try to get as large appropriations as we could out of this Congress, I believe with those appropriations within a few years the opinion of this committee would be very much changed with regard to the navigation of the Missouri River. . . . But if there is to be any diversion, do not, for God's sake forget Murrays Bend." [16] Of fifteen Missouri basin congressmen who appeared, none made any general defense of the Missouri navigation project or of the Commission. The Committee's report was unfavorable. Two years later the Missouri River Commission was abolished, its plant scattered or liquidated, its unfinished channel works exposed to the depredations of the river.[17] Between one-third and one-half of the channel works were destroyed in the next ten years.[18]

The nature of the Commission's demise left an obvious doubt whether the responsibility for failure lay with it or with Congress. The Rivers and Harbors Committee report implied, according to the Commission, "that the money appropriated by Congress in the interests of navigation . . . has been used without Congressional authority for objects other than the improvement of navigation." But these objects had been specifically directed in the appropriations. Moreover, "the Commission has never been called upon by Congress to express its views as to the propriety or necessity for these legislative allotments." [19] To the commission form of organization the final report attached no great importance, but it commented: "The public has more confidence in and respect for such bodies, which are, therefore, better able to resist undue pressure that individuals might find it hard to make headway against. Such pressure has not been wanting in the past history of the Commission. . . ."

THE TEN-YEAR PLAN

The decline of interest in the Missouri River Commission coincided with years of low water in the river, of agricultural depression and population loss. By 1908 all this had changed. A renewed wave of settlement swept over the Great Plains. The district engineer estimated the 1908 population in the seven states bordering the river at 21 per cent greater than the 1900 census showed. There was water in the Missouri and grain in the elevators. Jim Hill had begun building his empire of homesteads in North Dakota and Montana. In 1906 and 1907 farmers could not get cars enough to load their wheat, corn, and cattle, and Hill himself declared the railroads could not handle the load unaided.[20] Transportation already seemed to be the bottleneck of a new wave of prosperity when Theodore Roosevelt joined his Inland Waterways Commission in their famous voyage down the Mississippi. He was heard by unprecedented crowds from Keokuk to Memphis. The concept of the "waterway," a national birthright to be preserved and enhanced, became a cardinal point of the conservation movement. Gifford Pinchot's astonishingly successful crusade to arouse the nation to save its forests was founded on the constitutional power of the United States over navigation; it therefore necessarily fanned the hopes of waterway advocates.[21]

In 1901 the National Rivers and Harbors Congress was founded, partly as an alliance between Atlantic and Gulf navigation interests, partly as an expression of the world-wide interest in water transport which accompanied the demonstration of new engineering techniques.[22] At its meeting in 1906 the Rivers and Harbors Congress unanimously advocated a plan whereby the United States would issue 200 million dollars of bonds to finance a comprehensive and systematic development of rivers and harbors independent of the vicissitudes of annual appropriations. Once more the confidence of people in the Missouri basin that their river was not beyond the capacity of American engineering skill and governmental leadership was aroused by the object lesson of a great national navigation project successfully begun. This time it was the Panama Canal, at last proceeding satisfactorily under Col. Goethals.

In this spirit seven hundred politicians and businessmen convened at Sioux City in 1908 for the Missouri River Navigation Congress. There was less emphasis than in 1881 upon the dawning political power of the basin. Instead, delegates were appraised of the kindred movements for improvement of the upper Mississippi and the Ohio. In a remarkable speech, both intelligent and forthright, Congressman Edgar C. Ellis of Missouri singled out the fundamental obstacle to development of the river for navigation. It was particularism, the failing which had killed the Missouri River Commission. He proposed to substitute three principles to be observed by those campaigning for a waterway. First, bank protection projects must give way to through navigation. Second, the engineer or commission in charge must have a free hand to select the works necessary to provide navigation. Third, the waterway must be completed in continuous lengths, working up from the mouth of the river. "The first work, you will readily perceive," he told the delegates, "will be to shape public sentiment right here at home. . . . It must be demonstrated that benefits are to be general; that advantages are to enure to all classes and to all communities." [23] The convention elected Ellis president, and "cheerfully" left "to the national government to determine just where beginnings shall be made and how it shall be carried forward."

This time Missouri basin shippers were not content with resolutions. Heeding the optimism of the Sioux City convention ("the channel of the river was never better than it is today"; therefore "the way to navigate is to navigate"), they set about getting boats on the river to demonstrate their sincerity. The leaders of the campaign were Walter S. Dickey, Kansas City brick and tile manufacturer, and Col. William Rockhill Nelson, redoubtable publisher of the Kansas City *Star*. Kansas City businessmen, with some help from other cities, organized the Kansas City-Missouri River Navigation Company in 1912. They publicly subscribed its capital of about $1,202,000. The Company grew out of five years of experience in the operation of steamboats between St. Louis and Kansas City.[24] There might have been some warning against single-purpose development in the admission that the flood of June, 1908, destroyed the line's St. Louis terminal and damaged that at Kansas City.[25] But the Company later built "probably the most complete inland transfer wharf in the U.S." at Kansas City and a modern warehouse at East St. Louis.[26]

Members of Congress were impressed enough by this tangible evidence of faith to overcome the skepticism of 1900–1902. By act of July 25, 1912, they adopted the recommended twenty-million-dollar project to assure a six-foot channel from Kansas City to the river's mouth.[27] Here was the second authorized plan for Missouri River navigation. It substituted for piecemeal treatment of the whole river a plan for through navigation on the most likely stretch, as Congress declared, "with a view to the completion of such improvement within a period of ten years." Thereupon maintenance was estimated to cost but $500,000 a year. The lessons of the late Missouri River Commission seemed not to have been lost upon the Corps of Engineers or Congress; the authorized document "emphasizes strongly the absolute necessity of continuous and systematic work." [28]

The 1912 plan had, of course, the benefit of the Commission's work with channel stabilization, which it pronounced effective in the main. It drew on some French and German experimentation with open-channel improvements. But at one point it was defective technically. Although it found that federal irrigation projects alone in the headwaters would divert an aggregate of 14,000 second feet of water,* it flatly declared: "The low-water flow during periods of navigation is sufficient to render unnecessary a discussion of reservoirs and forestation as an adjunct to the improvement." [29] The calculation of channel characteristics was based, remarkably enough, on the mean monthly discharge for twelve years, 1879–90, a period ending eighteen years before the date on the survey report and omitting the striking decade of low flows that had intervened.[30] The reason is simple enough: the Corps of Engineers did not measure the normal flow of the Missouri River from 1890 to 1922.[31] As it turned out, the amount of water dependably available was a serious matter about which to be ignorant.

But more immediate problems were glaringly evident at the end of the allotted ten years. According to the Chief of Engineers, the waterway was 35 per cent complete. "The work is not as yet sufficiently advanced," he reported in 1922, "to secure a dependable depth in excess of 3.5 feet at low water." [32] But a 35 per cent channel did not, of course, yield anything like that proportion of the anticipated navigation. The Chief of Engineers reported that 176,550 tons were hauled on the lower river in 1922. It is well to look closer at the figure. Of this total, 159,227 tons consisted of sand, gravel, stone, and cement which "moved but a short distance" and would have been barged without channel improvement. Another 14,047 tons were brush, piling, trees, and miscellaneous materials used in the river improvement itself, There remained 3,276 tons of grain, building materials, livestock, iron and steel, and unclassified freight theoretically creditable to the through navigation project. But even these commodities actually moved very short distances: except for 26 tons of unclassified freight, the haul averaged 8 to 17 miles. People called it "a navigation project only by courtesy," an officer of the Corps reported privately.[33]

Whose fault was it? The Chief of Engineers explained in 1922 that "the appropriations and allotments for this district have been small and insufficient to effectively carry on the systematic improvement. . . ." [34] It is true that only half the estimated 20 million dollars had been appropriated to the

---

* Cubic feet per second: the standard engineering measure of rate of flow. One second foot of water flowing for twenty-four hours will cover an acre to a depth of two feet.

Missouri River plan by 1922, and of this but $7,380,579.60 was for new construction. On the other hand, the War Department got 57 million dollars of unearmarked money between 1914 and 1920 from which it could have made additional allotments to the Missouri. Of its lump sum of $42,815,661 for 1922, it allotted but $100,000 to the lower Missouri River.

But whether Congress or the Chief of Engineers, or both, made the decisions, it is not hard to see why expenditures fell below the plan. The first reason is that a war intervened. The second is that the national economic benefits of the waterway were cast in doubt almost from the beginning. In 1915, after $6,250,000 had been invested in the project, Congress ordered it reexamined.[35] The study was made by Lt. Col. Herbert Deakyne, District Engineer. Ten years later, a congressman from Missouri was still referring to it as "the black eye" to Missouri River navigation. Col. Deakyne simply did not find evidence that enough commerce would materialize to justify improving the river. He proposed that the United States fall back to its program of 1824 and spend $40,000 to pull snags out of the river.[36]

Deakyne was an engineer; he got support from a young professor of political economy at the University of Chicago, H. G. Moulton, who sought in vain to testify in the public hearing. Moulton estimated, in a written statement, that barge traffic enough to offset the cost of the Kansas City–St. Louis waterway would amount to four million tons per year. That was a million tons more than all the freight carried on all the railroads between the two cities in the preceding year.[37]

There Deakyne's support ended. In the public hearings, local protestations filled 280 pages of the printed record. In Washington, the Board of Engineers and the Chief of Engineers reversed their district engineer. They advocated going ahead with the 1912 plan, but they brought forward only two answers to Deakyne. The first was the confidence in future traffic demonstrated by the investment of the Kansas City–Missouri River Navigation Company. Their innocence as to the ways of the boom mentality was all the more interesting because Mr. Dickey, president of the company, had himself testified, "We were of the opinion that the use of the river would encourage appropriations. . . ." Two years later, the company sold out to the wartime government and thereby ended for twenty years the attempt to carry on through commercial traffic on the river. The second reason why the Board of Engineers advocated the 1912 plan was that the Panama Canal now left the Missouri basin on the periphery of cheap transportation and without any other means to restrain freight rates than water competition. It was an interesting line of argument from a strictly engineering body without professional or legal competence to plan transportation economics. It was an argument, moreover, that would fail unless water competition to the railroads actually developed. By 1922, it so obviously could not develop that the Chief of Engineers ceased estimating the saving possible by water shipment as compared to rail shipment.

On the heels of the Deakyne report, the predictable happened. Congress began inserting in appropriations (which gave little real promise of gaining through navigation) specific bank protection projects. Vermillion, South Dakota, and St. Joseph, Missouri, got revetments. Moreover, money continued to be frittered away on the "navigation" project above Sioux City and on a separately authorized improvement of two lower tributaries, the Gasconade and the Osage rivers in Missouri. The 1912 plan turned out not to be comprehensive after all.

The second effort at planning, so like the first in results (for that matter, so like the timber culture scheme and all of the other national plans for a region of boom spirit and limited resources) was incisively analyzed in 1930 by an officer of the Corps. The report has never been published. Actual construction under the 1912 plan, he wrote, "consisted largely of revetments."

Until quite recently the driving force behind the appropriations for Missouri River Improvement was primarily this interest of land protection and there was no organized and consistent body of public opinion so vigorously advocating large-scale navigation. The Administration was therefore forced into the policy described above, and district engineers had to build accordingly.

The majority of the works still stand, and have become integral parts of the comprehensive improvements. But even so, the policy was bad for the interests of the river in the long run, and for two reasons. First, as soon as the politically powerful areas had received their protection, they lost interest in the project and pressure for appropriations diminished correspondingly. Second, while a considerable fraction of the total work actually got done, there was almost no improvement, even local, in the navigable channel, since, roughly speaking, at any given stretch only half the works needed for a controlled channel were put in.[38]

EXTENSION WITHOUT PLAN

In 1922, the first Director of the Budget, Charles G. Dawes, used the powers which Congress had delegated to his office a year before to cut the estimate of the Corps of Engineers for rivers and harbors from $42,800,000 to $13,500,000. The ten years of the 1912 project were up, and there was "an increasing feeling, in Congress and elsewhere, that the Missouri River could not be developed."[39] What followed, therefore, was a little surprising. It was immodestly but not inaccurately described by the president of the Mississippi Valley Association two years later. Commenting on Mr. Dawes's action *"arrogantly* and *arbitrarily"* reducing the request of the Chief of Engineers to one-third its original size, this accomplished lobbyist reported: "A fight in Congress, largely abetted by the MISSISSIPPI VALLEY ASSOCIATION, resulted in the passage of an amendment to the bill, by a vote of 2 to 1, increasing the appropriation from $13,500,000 to $42,800,000, the full amount asked for by the army engineers." [40]

Having suffered this "rebuke and defeat," Mr. Dawes resigned and shortly began his mission to Germany to scale down reparations. His domestic Dawes plan had run afoul of a new political alignment reviving the old log-rolling technique. The Mississippi Valley Association, born under the competitive threat of the Panama Canal and the hope created by the Federal Barge Lines of World War I, had become a political power.[41] Its first meeting was held in 1916. The new focus of political impetus for river improvement was signalized that year when the office of the American section of the Permanent International Association of the Congresses of Navigation moved from Detroit to New Orleans.[42] When shippers of the Missouri basin convened in the future to promote their waterway, it would be under the aegis of the Mississippi Valley Association. They had caught sight of a coalescing sectional and economic force which offered alliance and which appeared to make it unnecessary to clarify their own designs.

The possibilities of the new approach appeared at once. Without any suggestion of re-examining the status or justification of the expired ten-year plan, $1,200,000 of the generous 1923 appropriation was allotted to the lower Missouri. It was more money than had been available since 1913. There had not been the slightest revival of the flagging basin-wide interest in navigation. Instead, bank protection, which had been ruled a local, not a federal, concern twenty years before when Theodore Burton was chairman of the House Rivers and Harbors Committee, was now frankly accepted as the objective. The intent was to require matching of Corps of Engineers expenditures by the riparian owners who were benefited. A 1915 law permitted the Secretary of War to do this. In any event, as in 1912 local funds were offered eagerly for a few years. From 1923 through 1927, landowners supplied $1,355,000. In the quarter-century since, only $300,000 more has been forthcoming. The reason again is simple—economics. Revetment at $100,000 per mile would have required all abutting lands four miles back from the river to pay thirty dollars per acre in order to meet the Secretary's terms (75 per cent local support). But the river valley is usually too narrow to provide four miles of protected land; where it is wide enough, landowners removed several miles from immediate danger were not inclined to contribute. In short, the contributory policy failed. It left a negative reaction to the idea of U.S.-local co-operation which is not entirely justified. For it never included an economic assessment of the benefits of what was intrinsically a dual-purpose project, navigation of regional and national benefit, and bank protection as a benefit to the landowner.

Instead, landowners quickly discerned a new opportunity to get the United States to defend the crumbling banks. Secretary of Commerce Herbert Hoover addressed a Missouri River Improvement Conference in Kansas City on October 19, 1925. He proposed a great trunk waterway from Chicago to New Orleans. Crossing this channel, he said, "I visualize an east and west waterway from above Pittsburgh to Kansas City, 1,600 miles. . . . These great trunks can ultimately be deepened to nine feet. . . ." And in a list of waterways "we need diligently to complete" he added the upper Missouri. The very next year Congress wrote the Hoover vision into the rivers and harbors bill. The most controversial feature of it was the Lake Michigan–Illinois River channel, which was needed to complete the Chicago–New Orleans trunk. On circumstantial evidence, it appears quite likely that the extension of the Missouri waterway up to Sioux City was the *quid pro quo* for support of the Illinois project by basin congressmen. Evidence can only be circumstantial, for there were no roll calls on the decisive votes. But opposition to both measures came from the states—Wisconsin, Michigan, Ohio, and New York—which might be injured by diversion of Great Lakes water into the Illinois. An Ohio congressman addressing a rally against the Illinois waterway listed Nebraska, North Dakota, and South Dakota as the only states not on the Great Lakes which might yet be won to opposition. The other side apparently operated on the same premise, for an Illinois congressman went out of his way to link the two projects together: "The whole system would be absolutely worthless without that connection. . . ." The House cast 117 votes to extend the Missouri waterway, 118 for the Illinois measure. Both carried.[43]

The other noteworthy aspect of the authorization was its specific limitation to 12 million dollars of the money which might be spent on the Kansas City–Sioux City channel improvement. Tough-minded Congressman Burton immediately pointed out that the latest survey report, then eighteen years old, estimated the project would cost 50 million dollars. In a few days the reason for the limitation appeared. After the House had approved the extension, and the day before it came up in the Senate, the Corps submitted a new survey report finding the Kansas City–Sioux City waterway not feasible! The limitation served strategically to reassure the Senate that it was not wasting too much money. There was now, in addition, a new argument to direct against the Engineers' finding. "The question as to whether there is sufficient commerce to justify the improvement is not an engineering problem. That is a problem about which we should have the views of the Secretary of Commerce, and Mr. Hoover has spoken in no uncertain terms regarding this problem." It was, of course, easy enough, the year after Congress enacted the twelve-million-dollar authorization, for the House Committee on Rivers and Harbors to report innocently, "It is insufficient to complete the project adopted, and was therefore, inconsistent with and repugnant to the terms of the project. . . ." Congress was asked to eliminate the ceiling, "simply a correction of what amounts to an error in the last bill." [44]

Congress did not at once comply, but its commitment was nonetheless decisive. Herbert Hoover's two axes of navigation had become a political as well as a geographic alignment. The waterway below Kansas City, which under the impetus of a deliberate ten-year plan had but once received an annual appropriation above two million dollars, now never got less than that, except in the two war years 1944 and 1945. The extension to Sioux City fared almost as well. The indication was that a systematically conceived program with a chance of completion fared worse in the politics of rivers and harbors than a nebulous project without engineering endorsement, but twice as long and with good connections.

ENGINEERS AGAINST RESERVOIRS

In 1844, six years after the Corps of Engineers began to pull snags from the river, a flood occurred whose crest appears to be still unmatched from Kansas City to the Mississippi. This counterpart to the 1951 Kansas flood emptied into a Missouri River itself moderately full. In 1881, the year of Major Suter's first report on channel improvement, a blanket of snow which had drifted to a depth of fifty feet in places melted suddenly in the upper basin. Ice had not yet cleared the river. The ensuing April flood was unequaled at Sioux City, Omaha, and St. Joseph until 1952. In 1903 the Kansas River flooded at the time of the Missouri's June rise. The crest was three feet lower than in 1844, but damage was far greater. Sixteen of seventeen bridges on the river were destroyed; property damage in Kansas City was 20 million dollars.

Congress did not regard these great floods as federal problems anymore in the Missouri basin than elsewhere. It is remarkable only that in 1903 the Corps of Engineers, engaged for twenty-five years in permanent channel stabilization, did not measure the flood flow.[45] The Missouri River Commission had done that in the minor rise of 1892, and its records are of great value in designing flood-control structures today. Nature has a way, however, of disregarding jurisdiction. Even in 1903 the Corps was charged with clearing the river of obstructions to navigation. In two weeks the flood restored to the river as many snags as the Engineers found when they began clearing it in 1838.

Unfortunately for any awakening of wider interests which such incidents might have occasioned, the Corps of Engineers began about this time to feel itself on the defensive in professional and political battle with the proponents of two flood-control panaceas: forests and reservoirs. Both approaches to flood control had long since reached sufficient prominence to be advanced in public debate. That forests would reduce floods was a corollary to the proposition that they would increase runoff in times of drought. Debate on the forest reserve act of 1891 made much of this point. Floods on the Missouri in 1887 were noted as following destruction of headwater forests by fire.[46] Even earlier, Representative Atkins of Tennessee connected reservoir storage for irrigation in the headwaters of the Missouri and the Arkansas with flood control on the Mississippi.[47]

Theodore Roosevelt made these vague notions a very present possibility. "The storing of floods in reservoirs at the headwaters of our rivers," he said in his first message to Congress, "is but an enlargement of our present policy of river control under which levees are built on the lower reaches of the same streams." Congress promptly passed the Reclamation Act toward which these words were directed. The President's forthright advocacy of unified administrative control over all aspects of water development succeeded no better than have the revivals of the idea by his successors. But it served to identify schemes of flood storage with threats to the autonomy of the Corps of Engineers on the rivers. "It is not at all strange," wrote a participant in Roosevelt's conservation crusade, "that . . . the engineers of the army, having in charge our river improvements, should fail to welcome the larger movement in which their work was sought to be absorbed." [48]

Within the engineering professions, the controversy began with reference to the Ohio River. The chief hydrographer of the U.S. Geological Survey, Maxwell O. Leighton, published in the *Preliminary Report* of Roosevelt's Inland Waterways Commission a carefully calculated scheme of reservoir storage which, he urged, would entirely control floods on the Ohio and would make much cheaper the project of channel improvement.[49] The Chief of Engineers replied that reservoir storage of floods had been officially rejected for the Ohio in 1870, but that the Corps had since accepted the method for particular watersheds and had in fact installed reservoirs to supplement navigation flows in the upper Mississippi.

The objection to the storage-reservoir method [he wrote] has not been due to lack of suggestions by the United States Engineer Corps so much as the fact that Congress, representing the general public, has been reluctant to enter upon an enterprise of such magnitude in cost and such great extension of federal powers as would result from extending river and harbor improvement so as to include the other improvements. . . .

He destroyed the effect of this disclaimer, however, by expressing his own view that "flood protection and prevention is largely a local matter." [50]

The controversy in its technical phase was transferred to the Missouri basin by Hiram Martin Chittenden, who knew the basin as well as any living man, having been a district engineer in the Corps, historian of Missouri River navigation, and secretary of the Missouri River Commission. General Chittenden's shrewd observations contained some deserved rebukes for the hasty generalizations of forestry advocates that denuded slopes had *caused* floods. On reservoirs, he was wrong: "It must not be expected that the character of works for river regulation can be materially changed by means of reservoirs, forests or soil wash prevention." His argument revealed that he based this view on economic as well as engineering considerations. The illustration which he chose is worth full quotation.

In 1903 the great flood of the Kaw River [Kansas] brought up the reservoir question again. Ex-Senator Burton, of Kansas, advocated the plan very urgently, stating in a speech at Kansas City that he "would have tens of thousands of reservoirs beginning at the headwaters of the stream and coming right down." A Board of Engineer Officers was appointed to investigate the practicability of providing against future disasters such as this flood had caused. The reservoir idea had made so deep an impression upon the public mind that a specific consideration of that feature of the problem was requested. In its report the Board found adversely to the scheme on the ground that its great cost, conservatively estimated at $11,000,000 and the annual loss from the withdrawal of the necessary lands from occupancy, conservatively estimated at nearly $600,000, would not be justified on the ground of flood protection alone. Owing to the character of the country, this last consideration was particularly strong. The only real justification of so extensive a system in a country so largely devoted to agriculture would be its use in irrigation and power and if it became necessary for these purposes, doubtless a portion of it would be built.[51]

Here are reflected two handicaps of the Corps of Engineers in approaching multipurpose watershed development. The general public, whose reluctance to accept reservoirs Col. Bixby had taken for granted, turned out to be highly interested in broad schemes, even ill-prepared ones, presented boldly in times of crisis. But a systematic development employing reservoir storage inevitably creates certain local damages which must be balanced against benefits to different economic interests, possibly in other Congressional districts. Here again, as in the case of navigation, the Corps, which disclaimed the job of economic planning or political advocacy, made its essential recommendations upon economic and political grounds.

Congress had left President Roosevelt's Inland Waterways Commission penniless. But progress moves in devious ways, and in 1909 Congress created its own National Waterways Commission by a clause in the rivers and harbors act. The chairman of this body of six senators and six representatives was Theodore Burton, the same man the President had appointed to head the Inland Waterways Commission.* In November, 1909, the new Commission inspected the Missouri River from Kansas City to its mouth. Its preliminary report of the following January squarely tackled the two problems of multiple purposes and national versus local concerns.

Thus far in the United States no reservoir system, intended to be operated for several purposes, has been adopted. . . . The position of the Corps of Engineers who have supervision over river improvements has been that an increased depth of a stream could be secured much more cheaply by the use of dams, diverting walls, and other devices than by constructing reservoirs at the headwaters, and in this view the engineers have in general been right. . . . When, however, the improvement of a stream is considered from the standpoint of all its beneficial uses, as well as the prevention of damage by floods, the policy of constructing reservoirs may become, in particular cases, more feasible.

And as against the Chief of Engineers' view of flood control as a "local matter," the Commission of congressmen and senators was impressed

with the increasing unity of our national life and the growing necessity of securing for human needs the maximum beneficial use of the waters of every stream with all its tributaries as a unit. In the nature of the case so comprehensive a policy could be successfully administered only by the Federal Government and consequently the eventual desirability of Federal control is easy to predict.[52]

In spite of the finding of the congressional Waterways Commission that rivers must be considered with a view to all their uses and potential dangers, members of Congress got no further than had Theodore Roosevelt in achieving unified administration. Until the nation became preoccupied with the war, Senator Newlands perennially introduced and argued for his bill to create a river regulatory commission empowered to bring into harmony all federal water-use programs. It failed. As yet Congress could deal with new concerns of river development only by a process of atomization. In 1915 the House created its separate Flood Control Committee.

Climatic variance was not kind to Chittenden's viewpoint in Kansas. In the absence of long-term runoff data he could not have foreseen a series of extraordinarily wet years. They quickly made his approach to flood control appear inadequate. The superflood of 1903 was followed by a smaller one in 1908, and another in 1909. The wet year 1915 produced the remarkable phe-

* Formerly chairman of the House Rivers and Harbors Committee, Burton was in 1909 elected to the Senate. After his term he served once more in the House.

nomenon of five successive flood stages on the Kansas River and the Missouri between May 30 and July 21. In 1915 the Kansas legislature petitioned Congress to reopen the question of reservoirs for flood control plus irrigation. In the fall of 1915, Governor Capper invited Senator Newlands to Topeka to address a conference of state officials and citizens interested in his scheme for co-ordinated treatment of the waterways. They endorsed the Newlands Bill. But more significant, they set about getting facts about the flood danger from the Kansas and its tributaries and from the Arkansas River system. Finding that the Corps of Engineers kept no records of this nature, they turned to the United States Geological Survey to aid state efforts. In Washington Senator Charles Curtis, later Vice President, succeeded in attaching to the rivers and harbors bill a remarkably farsighted amendment which had been recommended by the state engineer to aid in getting information about Kansas floods. In July, 1916, therefore, the Chief of Engineers received this congressional directive:

State of Kansas, floods in: Investigate the flood periods of the Kansas River and its tributaries, the Cottonwood and Neosho Rivers in the State of Kansas by an examination of the territory and from data already gathered by governmental, State, private efforts, and by the Board of Engineers of the War Department, and to devise some general plan which will best guard against the recurrence of floods and diminish their damaging effects upon the lower valleys of the Kansas, Arkansas, Missouri, and the Mississippi Rivers.[53]

There was obviously room in this loose mandate for the Corps to consider flood control as one of the purposes of its surveys of the Missouri River system. Instead, it waited a dozen years until a great Mississippi River flood precipitated a nationwide demand for action. Kansas fell back upon her own resources, and in 1917 the legislature created the first administrative agency in the United States charged with the conservation of all the potential uses of water. The Kansas Water Commission was directed to work out in conjunction with federal agencies a "plan for the complete development of each watershed in the State in order to secure the most advantageous adjustments of the interests involved in matters of floods, drainage, irrigation, water power and navigation." [54]

The Commission never had enough money to attain that objective. Its appropriations never exceeded $9,000, plus a small annual grant from the U.S. Geological Survey. With these funds it established fourteen stream-gauging stations in the Kansas River basin in its first year, thirty-one throughout the state by 1922. The Secretary of the Commission, Professor H. A. Rice, preached stream gauging in the language of every water user: farmer, power-plant operator, municipality, irrigator, factory owner. Thus he kept the program going through years when there were no floods. In 1918 Professor Rice read a paper before the Kansas Engineering Society which suggested how inadequate had been the estimate by the Corps of Engineers of the absence of interest in flood control among farm people. "Destructive floods have occurred so frequently, especially in some of the smaller watersheds, that the most optimistic farmers are disheartened . . . . the psychological effect of such crop failures is readily apparent." Far from finding flood-control measures antagonistic to agriculture, he found that the two were interdependent. When ten years after its creation the Kansas Water Commission was reorganized as the Division of Water Resources, it was located in the Agriculture Department.[55] Even the "tens of thousands of reservoirs beginning at the headwaters of the streams," so obviously visionary to Chittenden in 1912, became the program of state and national government in twenty-five years.

NEW TECHNIQUES, NEW POWERS

In 1927 the flooded Mississippi River burst through its levees. A national catastrophe created a demand in Congress for plans comprehending all of the techniques of river control and all of the uses of river water. Section 10 of the Flood Control Act of May 17, 1928, directed the Chief of Engineers to survey each of the major tributaries of the Mississippi from this comprehensive point of view.[56] The act created a noteworthy change in the activities of the Corps of Engineers on the Missouri River. Measurement and experiment were instituted upon engineering questions on which there had been no new information since the years of the Missouri River Commission. For instance, the silt in the river, which had been estimated twice before, 1879–90 and 1905, was sampled daily from 1929 to 1932. Nine decades after it performed its first work on the river, the Corps began preparing hydrographs, continuously plotting the flow of the river beginning at its mouth.

Two more things happened at the time this scientific approach was taken. Reservoirs for flood control had become accepted civil engineering practice. The Missouri also began to exhibit one of its extremes of low flows. The Corps was compelled to admit that the minimum flow of the unregulated river at Kansas City was only half what had heretofore been assumed.[57] Reservoir storage therefore became an obvious necessity for navigation itself.

The economical location for navigation storage was in the upper Missouri, unfortunately too high to lend itself to the quick control necessary to cut the peaks off lower river floods. The best site was, in fact, Fort Peck in eastern Montana. The question was whether to build a large dam there of 6,400,000 acre-feet * of storage, which would supply a six-foot channel; or a huge one with 17 million acre-feet, which would permit a nine-foot depth; or none at all, and abandon the navigation project. The district engineer equivocated in his recommendation, but the Missouri River division engineer did not. He rejected a six-foot channel as incapable of economic use both because it would require transshipment of commodities from the deeper Mississippi River barges and because powerful boats required by the Missouri current needed deeper draft for economic operation. But he could not discover the evidence of forthcoming commerce necessary to save the cost of a nine-foot channel: 210 million dollars including the larger Fort Peck and the completion of the channel work.

Once more, the engineer on the spot was reversed in Washington. In September, 1933, the Chief of Engineers recommended that Fort Peck be built "to the maximum practicable capacity." But he also recommended that the existing (six-foot) channel from Sioux City to the mouth "be vigorously pressed to completion." This was the one combination of projects for which there was no justification in the record. The only use of the maximum Fort Peck storage was for nine-foot navigation; and the six-foot channel had been found even less feasible commercially than the deeper project. In any event President Roosevelt authorized the greater Fort Peck dam two weeks later as a National Industrial Recovery Act project. Congress made no decision at all until 1938, when it adopted the dual recommendation of the Chief of Engineers. It thus prepared itself for a second *fait accompli*. For water was backing up behind the enormous earth barrier—water that would suffice, if put to no other use, for deep navigation. The expenditure had already been incurred. That very year, therefore, the Chief of Engineers reversed himself and proposed the deeper channel. Congress inserted it into the rivers and harbors bill of 1940. It seemed to the President at this juncture, however, that "the nonmilitary activities of the War Department should give way to the need for military preparedness." He took the politically unorthodox step of vetoing the entire bill.

Meanwhile, the Corps was learning that the disasters caused by floods evoke popular insistence upon specific projects as navigation never does. In May, 1935, a cloudburst sent a flash flood, behaving much like a tidal wave, down the Republican River in Nebraska and Kansas. In the middle of the night there was no warning; 105 people drowned.[58] New York state had a somewhat similar flood that summer. New England suffered the next year. In 1936 Congress passed the first nationwide Flood Control Act. It made

* An acre-foot is enough water to cover an acre one foot deep.

these recommendations: (1) that the prevention of floods on navigable streams or their tributaries was a national purpose under the commerce clause of the Constitution; (2) that local interests benefited by local protection works (as distinguished from dams, reservoirs, and channel improvements) be required to pay for lands, easements, and damages involved; and (3) that the Department of Agriculture be authorized to engage in water-flow retardation and soil-erosion prevention as flood-control activities. Flood control was now on the same basis of political support and project authorization as the improvement of rivers and harbors.

The 1936 Flood Control Act authorized local protection at cities in the lower path of the Republican–Kansas River flood—Kansas City, Topeka, and Lawrence. It added levee projects which had been found justified in the 1933 study: Belle Fourche in South Dakota; Saco, Harlem, Glasgow, Forsyth, and Wibaux in Montana; Marmarth in North Dakota. The estimated cost was $145,383,000. The Corps of Engineers designated this "the general comprehensive plan for flood control in the Missouri River Basin." [59]

Only in the next five years, however, did the growth of flood-control planning become extensive. In 1937 another Mississippi Valley flood occurred. The Missouri tributaries close to the mouth could have held back a few feet of the crest. So in 1938 Congress authorized nine reservoirs upon these tributaries, including three which would also help protect Kansas City.[60] In 1941, even in the midst of the prewar defense effort, Congress authorized two more major projects. One was a series of agricultural levees along the Missouri from Sioux City to Kansas City. They had been found uneconomical in the comprehensive study of 1933, but a flood in the meantime had overtopped the locally constructed dikes. And the 1941 act carried the first authorization of reservoir storage for flood protection at the very headwaters of the Missouri system, Cherry Creek Dam, and a second minor dam to protect Denver. In five years, not only had the Corps taken on a new function as costly in dollars as its century-old navigation effort, but it had cast off the last geographic limit to its hydraulic responsibilities within the Missouri basin. The country had scarcely awakened to the magnitude of the expansion—except for Fort Peck and Kanopolis, appropriations were not yet requested—when the war came and suspended public consideration.

The metamorphosis of engineering control methods was revolutionary enough. Multiple-purpose projects (involving not only flood control and navigation, but because of their high heads, power as well and, depending on their location, irrigation) raised a whole series of new problems of calculating benefits, repayment, and the mediation of competing needs and uses. The Corps was suddenly drawn into the planning of a geographically boundless series of local projects—levees and floodwalls—which need have no relation even in theory to the mainstem navigation. But in addition, something had happened as obscure to the engineering perspective as the swings of the climatic probabilities. The government had, with the evidently firm sanction of the American people, cast off the two unseen limits to federal river improvements: the balanced budget and the strictly construed Constitution.

The effect of the new dimension of federal spending was so great on the Missouri waterway that it is fair to say that only during the period of emergency relief appropriations has the channel stabilization project shown real likelihood of completion. Unfortunately, the war intervened before the final stone paving could be laid down. The new meaning of the Constitution, established by the Supreme Court in the Appalachian Power Company and Denison Dam cases in 1940 and 1941, took off the last geographic limit to the work of the Corps within the basin. Those two decisions removed all doubt as to the constitutionality of combining other engineering purposes with navigation in reservoir construction. Under the commerce clause of the Constitution, the United States could now develop any tributary of a navigable stream which would affect its navigability, even if the dominant purposes were flood control, power, and other water uses. The national planning power leaped from the main channel to the watershed.

The power to capture public attention and to influence the unfolding of economic life in the basin was correspondingly unprecedented. At Fort Peck, the Corps found itself, almost involuntarily, building the largest earth dam in the world, with the largest reservoir since Hoover Dam. Willy-nilly, it would soon be generating cheap electric power at that dam. Industrialization, irrigated agriculture, recreation, the encouragement or discouragement of urban expansion in flood areas, the value of agricultural real estate—all came suddenly within the capabilities of its projects. But the agency remained the same (except that its leaders were whisked into overseas combat as the new responsibilities appeared), the lobbies remained the same, and the congressional committees remained the same. All had entered a new world of techniques and powers for using abundant water. But it was a world they never made.

SCARCE-WATER PLANS

▲▲

FIRST IN TIME

EAST IS EAST and West is West in nothing more than in the law of waters. Until the forty-niners went west, Americans (in the provincial Yankee sense) had just become conscious of a crystallizing legal doctrine that any owner of land along the banks of a stream is entitled to have its natural flow come down to him undiminished. Justice Story and Chancellor Kent, protecting established New England mill sites, discovered their precedents in England, but contemporary English judges, completing one of the strange reflexes of the law, got their name for this superficially simple interpretation from Story and Kent: "riparian rights."

When the initiates of the Sacramento came east across the Divide to prospect on Cherry Creek, they imported a very different rule. The man who makes first use of water owns it as against anyone below or above. He can take it from the channel, send it where he pleases, and use it up entirely. That is the "appropriation doctrine." The Denver People's Courts began applying it at once to the Spanish and Indian prospectors as well as to the men from the states who had lived under a different law. A rough and ready hydraulic measure, the "miner's inch," [1] became the unit of property in what had never been Anglo-Saxon legal property before, the flow of a stream. Certainly in this respect the process of civilization leaped across the Missouri basin. When it re-entered from the West, it showed a lasting change.

It was a change born in arid climates. But its specific origins are dim. The situation and spirit of the prospector show clearly enough. He needed a claim to water, as to ore, which was clear and simple against his neighbor without waiting for the judge. He needed to divert the water to where the gold was. As the California courts soon discovered, he was not concerned with the fate of the owner far below who had been accustomed to navigate the river or irrigate from its waters. Being himself a squatter in the eyes of the United States courts, he could scarcely, in any case, put forward a legal claim based on ownership of the banks of the stream. But there is also in the appropriation doctrine an unknown mixture of Spanish tradition. It had carried over in the former Spanish colony of California the un-American decree promulgated upon the European settler as well as upon the native irrigator in Mexico: "We command," the Spanish sovereign had said, "that the same order which the Indians had in the division and distribution of waters, be preserved and practiced among the Spaniards to whom the lands are entrusted and assigned. . . ." [2]

As to the translation for irrigated agriculture of a law which Americans first used in placer mining, we need to know more about the influence of the object lesson of that remarkable oasis the prospectors saw west of South Pass, the Mormon settlements. Highly organized application of artificially diverted water fitted their theocratic hierarchy as neatly as it fits the new Zion of the Israelis today. The unfettered individualists, whether American woodsmen or Arabs, can scarcely fail to have received some lesson, contemptuous though they were. In any case, irrigation was soon practiced at Army posts and by the earlier Spanish settlers along the South Platte. The miner's law became the law of the farmer under the ditch.

This is not to say that the basin states where irrigation is practiced all maintain the same appropriation law. The variant of the doctrine which they adopted and its intermingling with the earlier riparian rights reflect with striking faithfulness the water facts about a transitional region. [3] Montana recognized no riparian rights after 1865, even for domestic and stockwater uses. Gold had been discovered in 1863. Colorado repudiated riparian rights *ab initio;* Wyoming, drafting her constitution late, never recognized them. In the middle tier of states, appropriation law has been superimposed on riparian law. Thus in Nebraska water could be taken by prior appropriation, beginning in 1889. The riparian owner, however, retains his rights provided he uses the water. By an interesting specialization of the law, South Dakota protects navigation rights from appropriation. Kansas clearly subjected riparian rights to appropriation only in 1945. [4] Before that her law reflected the preoccupation of her southwestern irrigators with diversions from the Arkansas and of her northwestern irrigators with pump irrigation, and the interest of eastern and central Kansas in riparian ownership as well as diversion. [5]

To the student of the common law, or to the easterner encountering the speed and resilience with which the precedents of the Thames and the New England millstreams were quietly supplanted by the practices that worked on the Sacramento and the Platte, here is one of the remarkable vindications of a system which has room for local initiative in the growth of law. [6] But to the state water engineer in the western basin the problem is more complex. When his problems are considered, it becomes plain that the one humid-culture tenet which the western water lawyers have never given up is the notion that a mere legal doctrine, however acclimated, can dispose of a human problem so thorny as the just distribution of water. "Here is a land," runs the inscription around the base of Colorado's capitol dome, "where life is written in water."

When the appropriation doctrine was applied to farming in the basin, it was applied not to collective hierarchies like the Mormons', but to individual units embodying the independent homestead tradition. The result was an immediate problem of overappropriation. Montana, where arid climate and the homestead influence most thoroughly overlap, felt the problem most keenly. Montana left each appropriator to file his claim with the county clerk and subjected it to test only if a competing user wished to sue.[7] Not long ago, Mr. D. P. Fabrick of the Montana Conservation Board found only three of sixty-odd appropriators along Willow Creek getting any water at all at the end of the summer season. Montana has been forced to begin inventorying her water supplies to discover which of the prior claims had any realistic hope of fulfillment.

Farther east on the Plains, the problem has been the familiar one of changing reaction to changing climate. Nebraska's difficulty is typical. In 1917 the state engineer secured the co-operation of managers of irrigation projects along the Platte in reporting gauge heights, discharge measurements, and canal flows as in fact they were required to do by state law. In the following season he was able to report twice a week on the discharge of the river. But three years later he admitted that "results . . . fell short of our original intentions. . . . When there is plenty of water, project managers become very indifferent to state regulations." In the relatively good water year of 1926 the state engineer reported that his funds "were used up entirely at the end of August which necessitated the dismissal of our regularly employed Hydrographers. . . . This action resulted in a break in our record of a long period of years of the flow of streams, especially the Platte rivers." On the eve of the great drought of the thirties, he was still pleading for the investigation of water resources "year after year." [8]

It was not long, moreover, before the doctrine "first in time, first in right" began obviously to protect vested interests as against any higher development of the economy. Wyoming, drafting her constitution upon the experience of earlier states, prudently added to the familiar appropriation formula the proviso "priorities for beneficial uses shall be given the better right." That has now become part of the customary, if not the statute, law of the states having the appropriation doctrine. But the decision as to what is a more beneficial use is one for which the attitudes of the mining tradition provide no base. Wyoming, with a fairly simple and tightly controlled economy, has been able to legislate a priority of industries. Interpreting it and keeping it up to date as industrial uses expand are another matter. The Nebraska state engineer confessed in 1940 that he could find no means of defining beneficial use even among competing irrigators.

A determination of what is beneficial use . . . is susceptible to such varied opinions that for practical purposes it is no limitation at all . . . . if the minimum amount of water was used to produce a maximum crop, the available supply would go much farther. This can be accomplished of course, by the proper co-operation within existing irrigation projects or by the establishment of a definite legal limit.[9]

One of the serious shortcomings of western water law, which creates problems for Missouri basin irrigation, is that it positively encourages overapplication of water to land under the ditch in order to maintain a maximum legal claim. That wastes water; it may also exaggerate the problem of waterlogged soil.

The third problem unsolved by the appropriation doctrine concerns the limits of the area within which it is to be applied. Does an appropriator have the right to divert water into the watershed of another stream at the expense of future claimants within the original watershed? This, of course, puts the logic of appropriation to the severest test in comparison with the rationale of the riparian ownership doctrine. It is a test which in Nebraska, for example, has never been met. An important unit of the Missouri basin irrigation plan and an important improvement in the economic use of water from the Platte await action of the state legislature to permit irrigation with Platte water of level lands straddling the divide of the Republican River watershed just to the south.[10]

But the rival claims of watersheds within a state are easy to resolve in comparison to the rival claims of two or more states. The doctrine of prior appropriation was itself a state product, adopted at different times and with different degrees of completeness by different states. The downriver states, Iowa and Missouri, have not, of course, adopted it at all. Hence it has provided no strictly legal answer to the question of apportioning the flow of a river between the states it waters.

The U.S. Supreme Court is available, under our Constitution, to decide such a question. There has developed in the western states a profession of water lawyers accomplished in trying water rights cases both within and between states. But some of the most eminent members of that profession recognize that while an interstate suit over water rights may keep a lawyer in business for a lifetime and put his son through law school, it will seldom apportion the available water quickly, cheaply, and clearly enough to permit the best use of the river. This is the illustration supplied by a member of a leading Denver firm of water lawyers:

In *Wyoming v. Colorado* suit was filed in 1911 and a decision was not reached until 1922 after the case had been argued three times. The decree which was entered was modified in the same year so as not to prejudice a certain Colorado diversion. In 1931 Wyoming alleged that Colorado was allowing excessive diversions, and Colorado's motion to dismiss was overruled. In 1936 final hearing was had, and an injunction issued against further violation of the decree by Colorado. In 1940 the matter was again brought before the Court as Wyoming sought to have Colorado adjudged in contempt for violation of the decree. The petition was denied upon a showing that Wyoming had acquiesced in the excessive diversions during the period in question.[11]

The latest dispute between Missouri basin states to be decided by the Supreme Court was *Nebraska* v. *Wyoming*.[12] Filed in 1934, the case was decided in 1945. But even before the Supreme Court issued its decree, the U.S. Bureau of Reclamation began planning a new reservoir which made still more water available for use and for dispute. On Nebraska's complaint, Congress blocked construction of the new Glendo reservoir until the additional dispute could be settled.[13] That has now been done. But it was done out of court, by negotiation of interstate agreement to an enlarged Bureau of Reclamation project. The Supreme Court merely approved a stipulation by the states and the Bureau modifying its 1945 decree.[14]

States in the Missouri basin have, since *Nebraska* v. *Wyoming* was litigated, consistently sought a cheaper, prompter, more durable way of apportioning interstate flows. The method which now commands the greatest confidence is the interstate compact. It is not new to basin water-development history. Colorado and Wyoming agreed to a compact prescribing their rights to South Platte water in 1923.[15] In nine years, 1943 to 1951, three more interstate rivers were included in compacts apportioning their waters: the Republican River in Colorado, Nebraska, and Kansas, 1943; [16] the Belle Fourche in Wyoming and South Dakota, 1944; [17] the Yellowstone in Wyoming, Montana, and North Dakota, 1951.[18] Congress has authorized compact negotiations among the states concerning the Cheyenne (of which the Belle Fourche is tributary), the Little Missouri, and the Niobrara.

These are striking accomplishments: the agreements have been reached without the bitterness that characterizes lawsuits and with a finality which court decrees in this field lack. But the very prestige attached to interstate compacts makes it important to note what they have *not* accomplished. They have not discovered clear principles of distributive justice which water users in two or more states will accept as determining their water rights. To be sure, the Yellowstone compact expresses the adherence of Wyoming and Montana to the doctrine of prior appropriation. But the very fact that the compact took nineteen years to negotiate and ratify shows how far that doctrine was from composing the competing claims. Prior appropriation has little logical force in deciding the distribution of water which becomes newly available by construction of a federal reservoir. But the prospect of hitherto unappropriated water being available behind federal dams was precisely what occasioned the controversy and motivated the settlement in all the recent cases—those of the North Platte, Republican, Belle Fourche, and Yellowstone Rivers.

Secondly, the compacts have not succeeded in defining the relative shares of stored water to be used for irrigation as against navigation or hydroelectricity, or the respective claims upon storage space of irrigation, hydroelectricity, and navigation. They have not defined the powers of the states relative to those of the United States in developing and controlling these uses. Only once, in fact, has a compact attempted that vastly more ambitious task. In 1942, Colorado, Nebraska, and Kansas sought to write into the Republican River compact a limitation upon the use outside the watershed of water stored in it. That would have prevented the Army Engineers from operating Harlan County reservoir to aid navigation on the lower Missouri. But the federal Constitution requires that interstate compacts have the consent of Congress, and President Roosevelt vetoed the resolution of consent. The states had to content themselves with a congressional declaration of intent to respect the priority of irrigation and other "consumptive uses" within the basin, not a legal limit to the federal commerce power as it might infringe upon scarce-water uses. This is the approved wording: "The United States . . . shall recognize, to the extent consistent with the best utilization of the waters for multiple purposes, that beneficial consumptive use of the waters, within the basin is of paramount importance to the development of the basin. . . ." [19]

No state government, if it be responsible at the polls, can voluntarily sign away to another state an interest in water which any group of its citizens feel is theirs. That is why compact negotiations have taken almost as long to settle as Supreme Court cases. The national average time required for interstate river compact negotiations is, in fact, eight years and nine months.[20] And settlement comes when a new potential of water use is opened up by the plans of a federal agency, which has been free to make those plans from a national or regional, not a state, perspective.

IN THE WEST, including the semiarid portions of the Missouri basin, water has become the most vital of properties. State laws, different in each state, have evolved for the appropriation of that property, so that its consumption may be assured against the claims of others. But though the Supreme Court may by the most strained analogies ultimately decide interstate water rights, and even refer to a "federal common law" to do so, there is in fact no system or principle of United States law apportioning scarce water. The disputes between Colorado and Kansas, Wyoming and Montana have been worked out almost exactly like the disputes between the United States and Mexico or Canada.

No doubt this would seem an anachronism to George Washington, Alexander Hamilton, and James Madison. For it was the perennial nuisance of trying to control an interstate river, the Potomac, by agreement among sovereigns which precipitated the Annapolis Convention of 1775 and thus the movement to frame a constitution for the United States. The interstate river problem the founding fathers encountered was navigation. They subjected it firmly to federal control. The interstate problems of scarce water are more urgent by far than those of navigation. And in the meantime, the national power has been radically expanded, not least in the constitutional definition of commerce and navigation. But, imbued with the homestead philosophy, lacking concepts to recognize the arid, semiarid, and subhumid environments, lacking any unit of organization and planning larger than the state but smaller than the West, Congress made no attempt to create scarce-water law, still less to reconcile it with the rapidly expanding federal abundant-water law.

What is remarkable about this, aside from the accidental twist of constitutional history, is that for the last half-century Congress has been building up in the West, and in the western Missouri basin, a vast agency and vast physical works for using scarce water.

OF, BY, AND FOR THE WEST

The United States, projecting its public land policy westward, conceded at once that it had no workable law to convey water rights in the mountain and Pacific Coast states. "Whenever, by priority of possession, rights to the use of water for mining, agriculture, manufacturing, or other purposes, have vested and accrued, and the same are recognized and acknowledged by the local customs, laws, and the decisions of courts, the possessors and owners of such vested rights shall be maintained and protected in the same." [21] Significantly, this clause was part of the act relating to the disposal of mining claims. In 1877 Congress made its first attempt to afford irrigated homesteads to settlers. The Desert Land Act recognized the rule of appropriation of water for beneficial use as the law of the arid states and territories to which it applied. In the basin, these were Dakota, Montana, Wyoming, and by later amendment, Colorado. In its administration the General Land Office theoretically required the entryman to show title to a sufficient water supply to irrigate his 640-acre claim.[22] As a device for bringing homesteads under irrigation the Desert Land Act failed, just as the Timber Culture Act failed to produce groves on the treeless prairie.[23] If the states were attempting to administer water appropriations with weak, localized administration, the United States tried to do it with none at all.

Eleven years after this futile irrigation law passed, and after his prophetic but unheeded survey of the arid regions of the United States, John Wesley Powell received an unexpected opportunity to bring about the actual use of the domain for irrigated farms. By joint resolution of October 2, 1888, Congress authorized the Secretary of the Interior through the Geological Survey, of which Powell was now director, to survey sites for reservoirs and canals for the purpose of irrigation in the arid lands. He was authorized also to select tanks for the storing of storm water. The Secretary was empowered to reserve these sites from entry.[24]

Powell received $350,000 for the first two years of the irrigation survey. In that time he had located 181 reservoir sites. The Secretary, on his advice, withdrew 547,000 acres of land for future irrigation projects, including not only reservoir and canal sites, but the irrigable farm land below them.[25] It is of interest to note that some of the topographic maps used in the planning of reservoirs for the present Missouri basin plan—the only such maps of large areas in Montana available in 1943—were maps produced by Powell's survey in 1890.

The most startling product of this survey, however, and one that has remained unnoticed even by the later backers of the project, was his proposal for the stabilizing of subhumid agriculture on a grand scale by the diversion of the waters of the Missouri River east to the valley of the James. A year after his Bismarck speech, he made his proposal before the House Committee on Irrigation:

I do not believe that the Missouri will ultimately be wholly used in the arid region. I think a part, and a very considerable part, can be used in the subhumid region . . . and that North and South Dakota will ultimately be benefited thereby to a large extent. It seems probable that the waters of the Missouri can be taken out at the great bend. . . . We now believe that the lands in here can be covered if we can get across or through the divide.[26]

But this was only one project in Powell's vision of a Missouri basin development for the fullest use of water which the technology of his time commanded.

To store up the water of the Missouri and its main affluents for the purpose of irrigation is to diminish the volume of that flood of the Lower Mississippi which is most destructive by reason of its occurring in the heart of the farming season. Moreover, the great difficulty of the problem of the Lower Mississippi arises from the fact that the river normally makes a deposit there, thus clogging its course and giving to its channel an unstable position. The principal source of the sediment is the Missouri River, and it is carried forward during flood. . . . For every acre reclaimed to agriculture in Montana another acre will be reclaimed in Louisiana; and in general, all lands redeemed by irrigation on the Great Plains will be equalled by the lands redeemed from floods in the great valley of the Lower Mississippi.[27]

It was a comprehensive view of irrigation serving the co-ordinate purposes of flood control and silt control, a view of the Missouri as part, but not creature, of the Mississippi system. Its technique was the multiple-purpose reservoir. This the Corps of Engineers officers in charge of the Missouri and Mississippi—the respective commissions were then at the height of their prestige—specifically rejected for fifteen years, only to accept after eighteen more. Its scope was the river basin, the watershed interacting with the channel, and its approach was the foresighted employment of existing public powers and programs to serve widening purposes. In the ten years since Powell's *Report on the Lands of the Arid Region,* much of that region had been settled in ways he had warned would fail. Now drought had brought that failure. Even at this late date, Powell thought the government could provide for permanent settlement of some arid land by using the new technique of irrigation from storage reservoirs.

But canals and reservoirs required detailed, accurate surveys; the worst of the drought was over before they were complete. Moreover, Powell knew enough about the total available water supply to warn that only 20 per cent, perhaps less, of the land beyond the humid zone could ever be irrigated. For the boom mentality of the West, that was the last straw. A senator from an arid state charged that two-fifths of the United States could not be settled unless the irrigation reservation law of 1888 was repealed.[28] The Republican Party had successfully made its attack on Andrew Jackson Sparks a campaign issue. Commissioner Groff of Omaha was boasting of the facility with which his administration of the General Land Office was parceling out the domain to settlers. It was the representatives from the basin states, along with other members of the western bloc, who again chose the phantasm of an unimpeded boom instead of the reality of permanent settlement.[29] The resolution of 1888 was not repealed; in fact, in 1891 Congress appropriated $325,000 for the irrigation survey. But Congress reopened to entry the lands subject to irrigation from the reservoirs, thus actually reducing the existing project reservations to 385,000 acres.[30] This relaxation incidentally converted

Powell's reservoir surveyors into locating parties for speculators. These had but to buy or homestead the land so situated as to be watered by these reservoirs and wait. In 1894 Powell resigned the directorship of the Geological Survey. Within a decade, westerners began to find their Reclamation Fund being dissipated to purchase sites which the government had recently given away.

By the time of the demise of the Powell surveys, there was in progress among the irrigation enthusiasts of the dry years a sharp controversy concerning the desirability of a direct federal program to build irrigation projects. During the early 1890's the proponents of state construction with federal subsidy had the upper hand. In 1894 the Carey Act, named after the senator from Wyoming who had been a leader of this wing of the irrigation movement, offered federal lands to the western states, up to a million acres each, on condition that they would bring them under irrigation and settlement.[31] The states were free to develop projects themselves or to bring about development by private colonists. The act had the support of the western bloc.[32] Like land grants to individual settlers, however, irrigation merely by grants to the states got few farms permanently under the ditch. By 1910, 2,500,000 acres were included in Carey Act projects. Ten years later the acreage had dropped to 1,100,000, and well over half was in the single state of Idaho. Wyoming is the only Missouri basin state which got more than 100,000 acres of Carey Act lands. By no means all of it is actually irrigated.

When the drought reached its peak in 1896, the proponents of irrigation by direct federal action for the first time carried a resolution in the National Irrigation Congress. Aside from the desperate need for water on farms in the western states, it was becoming apparent that the irrigation projects capable of development by private enterprise or unaided colonies of settlers were running out. Irrigation would continue at its going rate of expansion only with federal aid more direct than the land subsidy of the Carey Act. Five years later this view had found its champion in Theodore Roosevelt. His first annual message to Congress contained a strong argument on the point.

The pioneer settlers on the arid public domain chose their homes along streams from which they could themselves divert the water to reclaim their holdings. Such opportunities are practically gone. There remain, however, vast areas of public land which can be made available for homestead settlement, but only by reservoirs and main line canals impracticable for private enterprise. These irrigation works should be built by the National Government.[33]

The definition of the region in which federal irrigation was to be authorized passed through an interesting evolution. The General Land Office suggested a description including lands between the 100th and the 121st meridians.

This conventional concept of the arid region would have excluded from federal irrigation the land of subhumid climate which Powell had proposed to water by a Missouri diversion, and with it most of the prospective irrigation of the Missouri basin plan of today. Congress chose the politically simpler definition in terms of state boundaries. States were included in the region for irrigation if they lay wholly or partly west of the 97th meridian. The basin states of transition climate in the North Dakota to Kansas tier were thus included, those to the east excluded.[34]

In a more basic way, also, the Reclamation Act signed by President Roosevelt on June 17, 1902, represented a regional rather than a national program. The act required that water for use on federal irrigation projects be appropriated under state law. A U.S. Circuit Court, refusing to transfer to the federal courts a suit contesting a water right claimed by the U.S. Bureau of Reclamation, thus found that "by the terms of the act the rights of the Government as an appropriator of water are governed by the laws of the State and are no greater than those of any other officer." [35] Only in 1944 did the United States lay claim in the courts to ownership of nonnavigable water in the public lands states insofar as it had not been appropriated. Intervening in the suit *Nebraska* v. *Wyoming* for allocation of North Platte water, the federal government contended:

The Reclamation Act does not itself relinquish ownership of non-navigable, unappropriated water, nor does it relinquish control over such water to the states. . . . Even if that were not so the United States would still be owner of project water rights by appropriation. . . . With Federal proprietorship in such instances goes control by Congress pursuant to the Federal Constitution.[36]

But the Court avoided adjudication of the claim as unnecessary in the North Platte case, and Nebraska demonstrated, by securing the amendment of Bureau of Reclamation appropriations to limit construction of the Glendo project on the North Platte in Wyoming, that the legal position of the United States with respect to the states might continue to be an academic question as long as the policy of the United States in matters of water rights continued to be defined subject to the veto of any state acting in Congress.

At first sight it seems astounding that the United States should embark upon a program which in its first forty years cost a billion dollars and which was foreseen in debate even in 1902 to be potentially very large, without exercising its constitutional powers to make that program as likely of success as possible. When the Reclamation Act was under debate, the decision in the Rio Grande Dam Co. case had but lately confirmed the power of Congress to control the building of a dam for irrigation on the unnavigable tributary of a navigable stream. In 1902, under the Presidency of Theodore Roosevelt, federal constitutional powers were in any case considerable.

But to take this view is to misunderstand the whole motive of the Reclamation Act. Its success would not be judged in terms of successful irrigated farming or advantageous use of the rivers. The object was the peopling of states with the sons of toil, the traditional purpose of homestead legislation. This much national purpose the Act expressed, and the Bureau of Reclamation is entirely accurate historically when it claims the avoidance of land monopoly and the wide distribution of ownership as the constant threads in federal land policy from the date of the Homestead Act. "When it was proposed at the turn of the century to develop the arid West," Mr. Ickes told a Senate Committee in 1944, "Congress deliberately carried forward those principles which it had established for the settlement of the Ohio and Mississippi Valleys two generations earlier." [37]

Some years before the Reclamation Act was approved, an Australian visitor to the United States who made a study of our irrigation projects was shocked at what he found. With few exceptions, irrigation works in western America were constructed by private persons. "Not only has the Government spent nothing on them, but it has known nothing of them. They have been constructed entirely outside the law." [38]

The lack of concern with the laws and economic situation of the arid states could not be overcome in a few years. The truth is that the Reclamation Act at the time of its passage was a device to secure to the West the financial and administrative power of the federal government without clearly raising the question of the wisdom of the irrigation enterprise as a national policy. The tactic was explained by Senator Pettigrew of South Dakota on the last day of the 1901 session:

We have tried for years to secure an appropriation for this purpose directly out of the Treasury, and although the Senate has always favored it and we have passed appropriation after appropriation, the other House has always refused. . . . Now we propose that the region itself shall furnish the money, that the proceeds from the sale of public lands in the arid and semiarid land States shall be devoted to the reclamation of the desert lands of those States.[39]

If this was the price of acquiescence by the East, it was also the unqualified choice of the reclamation states themselves. They had recently and reluctantly accepted direct federal construction of irrigation works within their boundaries, and they had no intention of subjecting these works to the votes of superior numbers of congressmen from the humid land states.[40] "The Menace of the Arid Lands" was the title of a speech delivered before the Farmer's

National Convention at Macon, Georgia, in 1902. Competition of irrigated farms with the established agriculture of the East was one of the principal arguments against the reclamation bill, and western congressmen were sensitive to the charge.[41]

If as a national issue a majority of the House of Representatives would oppose irrigation by the federal government per se, then the solution was to free reclamation entirely from the need for congressional or Presidential action. A separate and presumably self-replenishing fund, with project authorization entirely in the hands of the Secretary of the Interior, and operating under state law at the point where it might have conflicted with the state interests—it is difficult to think of any way in which Congress might have created a more autonomous regional program. Reclamation, said Frank A. Barrett, Congressman from Wyoming, in 1947, "is really a development program for the West. It is our baby." [42]

ELEVEN PROJECTS

The Missouri basin had 4,410,385 irrigated acres in 1939 (located as Figure 12 shows), more than any other river basin in the United States. One-fifth of the nation's acreage and one-sixth of the investment in irrigation projects were located in the basin. But an overwhelming proportion of basin irrigation was, and is, performed by individuals and partnerships, co-operatives, irrigation districts unconnected with Bureau projects, commercial water companies, states, and other local enterprises. At the time the present basin plan was launched, the Bureau of Reclamation was the sole water supplier for 530,670 acres—one out of eight irrigated acres in the basin.[43]

The Bureau of Reclamation had eleven completed projects in the basin at the end of its forty-second year. Seven of these were authorized in its first four years, 1902–6. Three, plus six additional projects still under construction in 1944, were authorized in the last dozen years—1933–44. A single project, Riverton in Wyoming, was authorized during the intervening twenty-seven years, 1907–33. It had been started partly as a private project, partly by the Office of Indian Affairs when it was turned over to the Bureau of Reclamation in 1920. In this same period two projects begun by 1906 were abandoned. The question of evaluating the federal reclamation program in the basin therefore takes on two aspects. How well adapted to the basin were the nine original projects, of which two were abandoned and seven now exhibit some forty years of experience? What were the innovations of the recent projects immediately preceding the Pick-Sloan program; did they solve the problems which had halted the growth of the early program?

The two early projects abandoned as failures were the old Buford-Trenton

—Bureau of Reclamation   1947   1956

Reclamation—traditional habitat. In 1910 Buffalo Bill Dam, east of Yellowstone Park, began storing the water of the Shoshone River for one of the earliest of the Bureau of Reclamation projects. In 1947 Leslie Bovee and his wife took up Unit No. 55 on the Heart Mountain extension of that project. They moved into a war-surplus building, planted a shelter belt in front of it, began irrigating. Now the Bovees have a modern log house, a row of trees above roof level, and a good crop of irrigated hay. Here and there in the arid portion of the basin, the Pick-Sloan plan could reassemble the traditional ingredients of federal reclamation: water stored economically in a mountain gorge, hydroelectricity as paying partner, irrigable sagebrush land, pioneering settlers.

—L. C. Axthelm, Bureau of Reclamation

Reclamation—the new environment. East of the mountains, and except for the main river, there are no inexpensive dam sites. Water for irrigation has to be stored behind long dams on land already in use for farms and roads. There is too little fall to produce power. Dams on the Plains usually help control floods, but if built primarily for that purpose by the Bureau of Reclamation or the Army (as was Harlan County Dam on the Republican River, above) they weaken the inducement to farmers to sign repayment contracts for irrigation.

Most of the Pick-Sloan irrigation was planned for subhumid country like this. It proposes to make perennially prosperous corn, alfalfa, or sugar beet farms out of larger, usually prosperous, wheat farms. That is a proposition very different from settling a desert, and it is not clear that federal reclamation law and administration are adapted to it. In the lower picture Earl Mues and his son siphon into their fine field of corn water from the Cambridge Canal, which leaves the Republican River just above Harlan County Dam.

project in North Dakota and the adjacent Williston project. A going project which is conceded to have "serious repayment problems" is Belle Fourche in South Dakota.[44] All three were authorized in the attempt to comply with Section 9 of the Reclamation Act (repealed in 1910) by distributing projects among the states in proportion to the contribution which land sales in the states made to the Reclamation Fund.[45] The origin of the early Buford-Trenton and Williston projects is illustrative.

During the summer of 1903 Mr. F. E. Weymouth was sent out by the Reclamation Service to try to find a project in North Dakota. Although a thorough reconnaisance of the entire state west of the Missouri River was made, nothing was found that would appear to make a feasible project except the Lower Yellowstone Project, of which about one third was in North Dakota and two thirds in Montana.[46]

But North Dakota had "contributed more money to the Reclamation Fund than any other State or Territory to which this act applies." [47] A project had to be found within her borders. A scheme was devised involving the technically questionable device of a barge-mounted pumping station to shuttle between the Buford-Trenton and Williston canals raising water from the Missouri to each in turn. A steam electric plant in Williston provided the power. The projects were opened by the Secretary of the Interior in April, 1908. "On July 3, 1908, the water user's association, by a vote of 1014 yes to 6523 no, declined to adopt the necessary bylaws as furnished by the Secretary of the Interior covering the levying and collection of assessments, which they obligated themselves to do when they signed the contract for the construction of the project." [48]

The projects were briefly revived after the first World War. Dry years, coinciding with a national impulse to provide homesteads for veterans, prompted a futile experiment under a new repayment contract. In 1926 both Williston and Buford-Trenton were finally written off the books of the Reclamation Fund at a combined loss of $630,518.[49] The year before, the Secretary of the Interior had published a fitting comment: "The political pressure to have works built in the different states frequently determined the location of many of the projects." [50]

Between the years 1925 and 1932, Congress considered at great length a reclamation project urged by a Wyoming senator in his own state. Then called Casper-Alcova, it has since been named for him the Kendrick project.[51] In 1930 the Secretary of the Interior transmitted to Congress a report which upon application of arithmetic showed that the project would require more than one hundred years for repayment at the highest rate farmers could afford.[52] In July, 1933, President Roosevelt authorized construction of the project from emergency funds to be repaid under the terms of the Reclamation

Act. The *Engineering News Record* commented: "According to common reports, the truth is that the project was not selected or adopted for its economic soundness, but was placed on the list of federal public works for allocation from the PWA emergency fund at the instance of a Senator representing the State." [53]

Like the Corps of Engineers, the Bureau of Reclamation did not possess, at the time it embarked upon its eleven projects in the Missouri basin, all the facts which proved to be needed for success. In the beginning, it lacked facts governing the most elementary engineering assumptions. Thus at the time of the authorization of Belle Fourche, the consulting engineer wrote to the chief of the Reclamation Service: "The limit of the project is the available water supply, upon which the data is very meagre, consisting only of measurements since last June." [54] How relevant a caution this was appeared forty years later, when the Bureau presented its comprehensive plan:

The Belle Fourche project was originally planned for approximately 80,000 acres, but run-off during the past 12 years has proved to be an inadequate supply for so large an acreage. By the construction of the Keyhole Reservoir of 276,000 acre-foot capacity, the water supply for the Belle Fourche project will be so stabilized as to permit its final acreage to be maintained at approximately 45,000 acres. [55]

In the matters of drainage, soils, alkalinity, and amount of water to be applied, in short, in the matters concerning irrigation as agriculture, the founders of the other original reclamation projects in the basin were similarly in the dark. Regarding the Huntley project along the Yellowstone, H. W. Mareau advised the Bureau during construction in 1906 that a quarter of the land was subject to danger from alkali. "Settlement on these lands in their present condition," he wrote, "will shortly be a source of failure." [56] The lands were nevertheless opened to settlement. In 1916 the U.S. Department of Agriculture began at a project experiment station to look for plants adapted to alkali soil. In 1917 the lands subject to Mareau's warning were suspended from settlement; the project manager reported that they were not capable of producing a profitable crop. These facts make it interesting to note that *in 1908* the Bureau had announced to prospective settlers: "The soil is exceedingly fertile and productive. A complete surface drainage system has been constructed throughout the Huntley Project to prevent waterlogging or the rise of alkali." [57]

"It takes three crops of settlers on a reclamation project," runs a saying common in the West for twenty-five years, "before the last crop will stick." [58] The writer has asked a few federal and state officials who have responsibilities in the execution of the federal reclamation program, as well as a few newspaper editors in the basin, whether they believe the saying. No one doubted its general truth,[59] though surprisingly enough, only one dean of a College of Agriculture could suggest facts by which to check it. Dug from the early project histories in the files of the Bureau of Reclamation, the facts offer corroboration. Up to 1923 at the Shoshone project, "there have been a large number of sales of homesteads by the original settlers. Very nearly all these persons have left the project." [60] After this initial turnover, the irrigated farmsteads developed at the cost of the initial settlers seem to show fewer than the average foreclosures and sales for taxes. They are more often sold voluntarily than are surrounding farms.[61] Compare this idea with the prevailing justification of federal irrigation projects as stabilizing agriculture and providing homes for initial settlement by deserving veterans, and you face the complexity of the psychological motivation which underlies the work of the Bureau of Reclamation. It is, of course, the paradox of the Homestead Act visited upon the last of its descendants in the line of public land policies. The original settler must have his unhindered chance to fail for the upbuilding of the West.

As early as 1924, when the agricultural depression began to hurt irrigators as well as wheat farmers, the problems of agricultural settlement of reclamation projects were publicly acknowledged. In that year Calvin Coolidge transmitted to Congress a proposal authorizing the Bureau of Reclamation to ease the farmer's difficult transition from rain farming to ditch farming.[62] A year later, the Secretary of the Interior expressed firm commitment to the idea. "The essential part of the Federal reclamation policy of the future is a program of land settlement and farm development." [63] Only when a program of farm settlement was demonstrated to the Bureau by the Department of Agriculture fifteen years later, as we shall see, were there actual accomplishments in this direction.

A program which was to be financially independent by the investment of proceeds from the sale of public lands and repayment by the users of water is subject to a financial accounting. Some of the Bureau of Reclamation projects in the Missouri basin are too recent to give us a fair indication of their capacity to pay out. But the nine original projects, all authorized before 1907, show clearly the extent to which traditional reclamation can pay for itself in this basin. As Table I shows, all these projects have been delivering water for thirty years or more, though not, of course, to the entire project acreage. In that period, the water users had paid back about one-third of the cost charged to irrigation—17.5 million out of 55.7 million dollars. That looks as though it might take a hundred years from the first delivery of water to the final reimbursement. And in fact no entire project had by 1947 averaged a return of more than 1 per cent of its investment per year from the time water first ran in its canals to 1947.[64]

TABLE I

Financial Experience to 1952 of the Nine Original
Bureau of Reclamation Projects in the Missouri Basin *

Project	Construction cost allocated to irrigation †	Repaid by water users	Written off by Congress
Belle-Fourche	$4,638,235	$1,343,227	$1,388,305
Buford-Trenton (old)	223,423	1,999	221,424
Huntley	1,552,159	874,546	62,050
Lower Yellowstone	3,633,219	1,756,166	392,345
Milk River	9,021,774	767,446	2,556,186 §
North Platte	17,377,923	9,534,829	——
Shoshone ‡	8,840,866	2,084,836	1,554,972
Sun River	10,059,013	1,155,003	89,651
Williston	409,095	——	409,095
Total, nine original Missouri basin projects	55,755,707	17,518,052	6,674,028

* U.S. Bureau of Reclamation, *Repayment Histories and Payout Schedules,* 1952.
† Exclusive of rehabilitation and betterment costs
‡ Exclusive of the new Heart Mountain Division
§ Increased by Comptroller's audit from the $1,735,969 provided in adjustment acts of 1926 and 1930

That does not mean that the water users, who contracted originally to pay back construction costs in ten years, are overdue in their payments. Congress permitted the contracts to be rewritten in 1920 and again in 1926, permitting repayment over twenty years and then over an indefinite period. Repayment has failed to go according to plan, moreover, because Congress legislated specific dispensations permitting payments to be postponed. The general moratorium on payments during the depression years 1932 through 1937 was inevitable economically; certainly it was inevitable politically. What amazes the careful reader of project histories is the number of the relief acts passed by Congress setting aside contract obligations and the willingness, even eagerness, of basin state representatives and senators to initiate relief. The pattern of congressional intervention has continued to the present day. An older example from a project history will serve to give the flavor of the relationship. "On April 11, 1922, the boards of directors of the two irrigation districts [of the Lower Yellowstone project] had a special meeting to consider a telegram from Senator Walsh, requesting the districts to advise regarding their needs in the way of relief from 1920 and 1921 charges." [65] The Lower Yellowstone irrigators, in fact, repaid $82 on their $1,243,429 obligation during the entire five years 1917 through 1921. Those were not all depression years on the farm; they were years when killings could be made dry-farming wheat.

Moratoria were not the only form of legislated relief from repayment. By 1952, Congress had finally written off 6.6 million dollars of the original investment in the nine Missouri basin projects. The reasons for the loss reflect no discredit on irrigators; as we have seen, they reflect the failure of original plans to deal realistically with problems of water supply, soil types, drainage difficulties, alkalinity, and construction costs.

One might conclude, in the face of these disappointments, that seven of the nine original projects are on their way to self-liquidation over a rather long period of years. The trouble is that already the payout period has outlasted some portions of the physical works installed. In 1947 the Bureau was compelled to launch an extensive repair program, over and above the maintenance work being paid for by the water users through their "operation and maintenance" contributions. For Missouri basin projects, this "rehabilitation and betterment" program had by 1952 been scheduled to cost over 10 million dollars. Part was added to the contractual obligations of water users, bringing that total well above the amount shown in Table I. Part had, again, to be written off. "Rehabilitation and betterment" takes care of depreciation physically evident to date. But there is no businesslike way of allowing, in the water users' obligations, for further capital depreciation before the construction costs are paid out.

We come to a startling conclusion. The nation's 55-million-dollar investment in the older basin reclamation projects has indeed been repaid to the amount of over 17 million dollars. Meanwhile, Congress has had to write off a loss of more than 6 million dollars from the original investment, and the Bureau of Reclamation has discovered 10 million dollars of accrued depreciation which was not provided for. In 1947, the Bureau entitled its summary of project finances *How Reclamation Pays*. But if the nation were to set up any kind of businesslike balance sheet for the original Missouri basin projects, it would have to show, against the 17-million-dollar return on its irrigation investment, 16 million dollars in actual deductions from the worth of that investment. That sort of business appraisal is not, of course, the only or even the appropriate way of evaluating irrigation. The Bureau's time-tested projects, together with the investment and toil of thousands of settlers on them, have produced many values for the nation. The point is that reclamation set out to be self-supporting in the West. In the Missouri basin it never was.

NEW MONEY, NEW CLIMATE

Failure of repayment is the essential reason why (except for a single project) reclamation reached a standstill in the basin between 1907 and 1933. As long as projects were financed from the Reclamation Fund, it was impossible to expand, for an insignificant amount was returned to the Fund by water users. Until 1945 the Bureau had spent 117 million dollars on construction in the basin and recouped 11 million dollars.[66] The authorization of Kendrick in 1933 from P.W.A. funds, though reimbursable according to reclamation law, marked a change toward a new basis of financing. In 1936 the President's Great Plains Committee reported that "most of the new large-scale projects are of doubtful feasibility, if that be measured in accordance with requirements of the national reclamation law, under which construction costs must be re-paid without interest in forty years." [67] In 1939 the Reclamation Project Act incorporated a new form of nonreimbursable subsidy to irrigation. Part of the project cost might be allocated by the Secretary of the Interior to flood control and navigation.[68] Power, meanwhile, from the time of the Kendrick project, has become for major projects and for the system as a whole a much more important source of repayment than irrigation.

By 1944, when present plans were laid, the Bureau had thus acquired potential solutions to its problem of repayment. Provided multiple-purpose projects could be located, the water user's impossible burden could be shared with other beneficiaries. But the prospect of expensive multiple-purpose dams made it all the more imperative for the Bureau to discover sources of capital outside the spent Reclamation Fund. The Bureau had, in short, to sharply reverse its forty-year strategy and appeal to Congress for appropriations. The wisest champions of federal reclamation could see that financial independence, which, as we have seen, never actually worked in the basin, would have to be abandoned as a strategy. Now the reclamation would stand or fall with votes in Congress. The answer was the National Reclamation Association. Its president testified:

The Association was formed in 1932. Those who participated did so at the original request of the late Dr. Elwood Mead, then head of the Bureau of Reclamation. At that time Bureau construction was dependent on accretions to the reclamation fund from the sale of public lands, oil royalties, and settler repayments. The fund was running out. The business depression was at its worst. Dr. Mead feared the extinction of the Bureau. I believe I do not exaggerate when I say that the Association, formed under those circumstances, saved the Bureau of Reclamation and the reclamation program.[69]

Almost at once a conflict arose between the Bureau and its "savior." For the latter began to reflect a concern for the interests of the water user at the expense of the power consumer who was to pay two-thirds of the bill under the new multiple-purpose planning. Secretary Ickes and more recently Commissioner of Reclamation Straus did not hesitate to identify the influence of private power companies in the positions taken by the Association hostile to cheap power. The battle is being fought out along this line today. But the popularity of cheap public power, already demonstrated in Colorado, Wyoming, Nebraska, and (notwithstanding the Montana Power Company) Montana, bears no relation to the tendency of reclamation lobbyists from the basin states to press for a larger share of the repayment burden to be carried by power customers. The National Reclamation Association remains essentially a single-purpose pressure group in an era of multiple-purpose projects.

About the time that the Bureau received its new national basis of support, it received another challenge to its previous concern with desert lands. It was challenged to enter the Great Plains, then the Dust Bowl, where the climate was dry enough in the 1930's, but would not be so every year. The experiments resulted from the findings of the National Resources Committee, the President's Great Plains Committee, and the Northern Great Plains Agricultural Advisory Council, all absorbed with the specific problems of the Plains rather than with the West in general.

Three laws of the resulting complex are important. One, the Water Facilities Act of 1937, empowered the Secretary of Agriculture to build and otherwise secure the construction of small dams, stock ponds, wells, and water-spreading facilities. A ceiling of $50,000 per structure avoided jurisdictional questions in relation to the Bureau of Reclamation. As we shall see, this act has borne good fruit. In 1939, the President was authorized to allocate an appropriation of 5 million dollars to such federal departments as he designated to construct irrigation projects on the Plains.[70]

The Wheeler-Case Act of 1939 went much further and supplied the detailed policy for projects the President authorized under the second act.[71] It brought the Department of Agriculture directly into the planning and settlement of projects on the Plains. The question of project feasibility was decided by the President upon recommendation of the Secretaries both of Agriculture and the Interior. Planning and to some extent the provision of going farmsteads were assumed as federal functions, as against "taking the water to the headgate" and there leaving the farmer to himself with his raw acres. There was no claim that the cost of small projects on the Plains could be wholly reimbursed by the irrigators. Subsidies in the form of W.P.A. and C.C.C. labor were authorized. When the war came, the labor of conscientious objectors was substituted.

Under these last two laws, the basin got five small projects: Buffalo Rapids (two divisions) on the Yellowstone in Montana, a new Buford-Trenton in North Dakota at the site of the abandoned project, Rapid Valley and Angostura in South Dakota at the foot of the Black Hills, and Mirage Flats along the Niobrara in Nebraska where Old Jules pioneered. Extensions were projected during the thirties to the existing Riverton and Shoshone units; the Colorado-Big Thompson diversion was authorized to supplement the water supply for existing nonfederal irrigation along the South Platte. But except for the ill-fated Kendrick scheme, these five Wheeler-Case projects offered the only *new* irrigation undertaken by the federal government in the basin during the whole of the Dust Bowl period.

All these projects have now begun to receive water. It is too early to appraise them,[72] but certainly they demonstrate a breadth of federal responsibility for irrigation novel to the homestead tradition. They undertook to make reclamation a going concern economically and to make it a practical transition for the new irrigator. They took cognizance of what former Commissioner Newell of the Bureau called "the human element" of settlement. The Bureau has not, as we shall see, disregarded the opportunities thus demonstrated. But the Wheeler-Case approach had two more tests to meet. Was it a model for irrigation even farther east, not in the semiarid, but in subhumid climates, where the Dust Bowl years showed dry farming to be vulnerable? Could the co-operation which was implicit in the laws, between the Secretary of the Interior and the Secretary of Agriculture, be permanently maintained? These were questions for the postwar years.

FEDERAL reclamation in the basin thus completed a cycle of policy. It turned back eastward for its new projects as for its financial support. Just as the homesteader was at one time in fact the automatic agent of national welfare, so the reclamation project could, as long as it paid for itself by civilizing the desert, be assumed to be for the national good. In the coming era, the era in which basin development is taking place, reclamation projects will no longer be taken for granted. They must justify themselves to the people who live on them: both dry farming and migration to prosperous cities can be assumed to be available alternatives. They must justify themselves to a nation with an agenda of many rival types of developmental public enterprise—roads and airports, soil conservation and rural electrification, for example—which were unknown in 1902. They must justify themselves in the river basin with its competing claims for water, but, more crucial still, with its demand for results in terms of cheap and abundant power and stabilization of agriculture. There is no question that federally built irrigation enterprises have an indispensable contribution to make on each score. Could the policies and agents for making it be discovered?

Unfortunately, they had not been found, or even looked for, when the Dust Bowl thrust upon public attention, national as well as regional, the need for adjusting occupance of the Plains to the limits of moisture. Not only solution, but even the preliminary trial and error outwaited the long drought. A succession of wet years after the war showed that in its fat years, as well as its lean, the Plains mocked tardy planning.

Chapter VII

THE WEDDING

THE MONTH Congress chose to charter the present Missouri basin develop-ment was the month of the Battle of the Bulge. Unfortunately, a democracy cannot wait to plan "an adequate reservoir of useful and worthy public works for the postwar construction program," as the Flood Control Act of Decem-ber 22, 1944, presumed to do, until the battle fronts no longer occupy the head-lines. Only a spectacular catastrophe at home could momentarily pre-empt national attention. Such a catastrophe the Missouri basin had provided in 1943 and 1944—not drought this time but floods—and headline writers noted that war production and transportation in the Midwest had been interrupted thereby.

PICK PLAN

The "Pick plan" was in its legal authority and its format a direct response to these floods. The first of them, caused, as usual, by rapidly melting snow in the Dakotas, struck the middle of the river late in March, 1943. Omaha was the center of the destruction. Congressmen from flooded districts at once introduced resolutions calling for a new flood-control survey. On May 13 it was authorized, not by a law or the order of an executive official, but accord-ing to a unique but long-standing congressional arrangement, by the mere resolution of the House Committee on Flood Control, making the assign-ment direct to the Board of Engineers.[1] Even as the committee met, a second crest fed by rains in Iowa and Missouri overflowed the lowest two hundred miles of the river. The Corps of Engineers had finished its rescue operations and was beginning to repair the damage of the May flood when a third flood came in June. From Kansas City down, the remaining levees, built over many years by towns and farmers' districts, sank into the waterlogged banks. Three record floods in one spring, even on the unruly Missouri, crowded some of the war news off page one.

Lewis A. Pick, then a Colonel of Engineers, had been in charge of the Missouri River Division for only a year; his primary wartime mission was to build airfields and arsenals. But in ninety days he dispatched to the Chief of Engineers in Washington a ten-page report which has from that time on been known as the Pick plan.

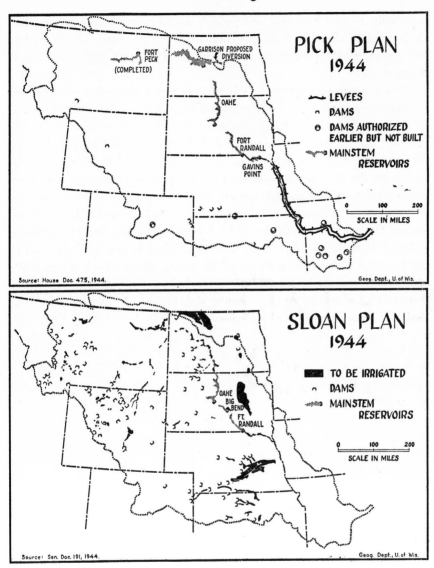

Figs. 8 and 9

It contained three groups of projects. The first, an obvious and direct response to the floods, was to build 1,500 miles of levees on both sides of the river from Sioux City to the mouth where no federal levees had been built before. In the narrow floodplain, not much land can be protected behind each mile of levee. The exhaustive "308 report" on which Colonel Pick rested his technical case had found that even the most attractive of these agricultural levee units required expenditures "which would be materially greater than the benefits." Colonel Pick did not compare costs with benefits in his report; two sentences on flood damage contain the only effort he made at economic justification.

The second group of projects included both new and previously authorized but unbuilt reservoirs on tributaries. Five of the seven new dams were upon the headwaters of the Republican, a tributary first of the Kaw and thus of the Missouri, and a chronic flood menace. But they were in the Plains, at the edge of potential irrigation country. Two more were high in Montana and Wyoming on the Yellowstone and the Big Horn. These were upstream from much existing irrigation, and they raised the specter of federal management of scarce water without the elaborate defenses of reclamation law and Bureau of Reclamation custom by which western water law had hitherto been secluded from the commerce power of the United States. Their relation to flood control ("along the main stem" the House Committee had specified), moreover, was unexplained, and not at all obvious.

The third group of projects at first sight appeared more relevant: five major dams on the Missouri itself between Fort Peck and Sioux City. This was a bold application of new knowledge about earth dams and machinery for building them. Garrison, largest of the five dams, was located on a foundation Colonel Pick's predecessors had rejected as unsafe.[2] But he attached enough importance to it to have a new board of consultants re-examining the site within a few days of the first 1943 flood, apparently before the Flood Control Committee authorized his survey, and he wanted it built to the largest feasible size. When his estimate of 17 million acre-feet capacity, derived from fifty-year-old maps, proved one-third too small, he argued that the 23 million acre-feet of which the site was actually capable had in fact been intended.

Now, counting the existing Fort Peck reservoir, Garrison, and the other new dams, Colonel Pick proposed 60 million acre-feet of reservoir space to hold back water above Sioux City. Why? The survey report did not say how much storage flood control would take, but of 74 million acre-feet behind present dams, the Corps has tentatively allocated one-fifth to flood control.[3] To take a specific example, Glenn Sloan later told congressmen, "The 1943 flood could have been regulated to a safe capacity of the river channel at Sioux City, Omaha, and Kansas City with only 2,000,000 acre-feet of water in storage." A pointed suggestion was made in the report: large quantities of water would be diverted eastward from the Missouri into Devils Lake and the James River in North and South Dakota where towns had gone dry during the 1930's. But only half the proposed storage was above the point of diversion. The report appealed to the idea (popularized respectively by Hoover Dam and T.V.A.) of multiple-purpose, basin-wide development to go far beyond its flood-control assignment. But it relied for justification entirely on the public sense of shock at the disruption caused by floods. Provided only that authority to operate all reservoirs built under the plan was firmly reserved to the Corps of Engineers, all problems of reservoir heights and uses, distribution of irrigation water by the Bureau of Reclamation, power capacity and sale, and additional tributary storage would be worked out later. It is unlikely that a division engineer ever proposed so much, so quickly, or so vaguely.

The Pick plan's vagueness began to seem more purposeful on February 16, 1944. On that day three things happened. The U.S. Director of the Budget, acting on Presidential order, returned the plan to the Secretary of War, pointing out that (1) it was in conflict with the Bureau of Reclamation's plan for upper basin development; (2) it neglected watershed treatment, which the Department of Agriculture could only guess might cost a third of a billion dollars; (3) it neglected part of the power potential of the river; (4) if it were rounded out in these respects it would cost upwards of a billion dollars, but even its own estimate of $481,600,000 lacked "detailed analyses of tangible benefits"; (5) it did not show how it was related to the nine-foot channel project already proposed in a separate report by the Corps; (6) it was not presently in accord with the program of the President.

Also on February 16, without waiting to know the outcome of Presidential co-ordination, the House Committee on Flood Control opened its hearing upon authorization of the plan it had asked for the previous May. "We will assume responsibility," the committee chairman assured the Colonel of Engineers who apparently hesitated to hand over the plan until the review required by the President had been completed. George Washington, who not only founded the Corps but presided at the Constitutional Convention, might not have been satisfied that a member of Congress *could* assume responsibility for violation of an executive order by an executive officer. But the Colonel, submitting the Pick plan to the committee, correctly registered his agency's accountability, in planning for the nation's rivers, not to the President or necessarily to the Congress, but to certain committees of House and Senate.

In the committee room on February 16 sat five governors of Missouri basin states. Since the previous August when Colonel Pick had toured their capitals expounding his plan (like the House committee, the basin public learned of the plan without benefit of co-ordination in the executive branch), three of the governors, from the scarce-water states of Wyoming, Montana, and

North Dakota, had become increasingly concerned lest authorization of the Pick plan commit to use downstream (below the great new mainstream reservoirs) water which might otherwise be used to develop new irrigation. They came, therefore, with the plausible request that the committee defer action on the Pick plan (after all, a plan for postwar construction) until the Bureau of Reclamation had proposed its own basin plan. This the Budget Director also urged, and he promised that the wait need only be until May 1.

What the governors were confounded to discover was that a separate committee of the House—Rivers and Harbors—had already taken up, reported favorably, and asked for floor debate on a separate bill to deepen the navigation channel to nine feet. "We accept this as a coincidence," Governor Moses of North Dakota told the congressmen diplomatically, and the governors went to repeat their plea before the Rivers and Harbors Committee. Then they learned how difficult the "coincidence" had made their case. Were they alarmed (before the Rivers and Harbors Committee) that for a deeper channel the Engineers would need more water? "They cannot get it any place else unless they have it at Fort Peck Dam, because that is the only place from which we are giving them water," a committee member assured them.[4] Were they (before the Flood Control Committee) concerned that the vast Pick plan storage would serve navigation at the expense of irrigation? Irrelevant, for the Pick plan is mainly a levee plan and in any case makes no commitments about the use of its storage: "Most of the remarks of the gentlemen ought to go before the Committee on Rivers and Harbors. . . ."[5]

A few months later it turned out that even a single committee had no intention of putting the two halves of the decision together. In the Senate both bills necessarily came before Senator Overton's Committee on Commerce. But they came separately, and when Congressman Case of South Dakota tried as a witness in the Pick plan hearing to consider the question of the use of stored water for irrigation or navigation, Senator Overton interrupted sharply: "Now, Mr. Congressman, we are considering a flood control bill. . . . All that is before this committee is flood control projects."[6] Meanwhile both the Pick plan and the nine-foot channel had been authorized by the House. The bill which authorized the latter carried an amendment disclaiming for navigation any water not already authorized. But the House knew that the Chief of Engineers had written, "There is no fixed amount of water authorized by statute for navigation purposes."[7] The reclamation plan had not even come before a committee for hearing.

What is remembered as the Pick-Sloan controversy, therefore, almost ended before the Sloan plan reached Congress on May 5, 1944. Up to that date, moreover, there was no way of showing that adoption of the Pick plan involved a decision as to water use. Not only was that due to the obscurantism of separate committees giving isolated consideration to separate bills on water storage and water use. It was also due to significant silence from the Corps of Engineers. As to the supply of Missouri River water upon which their designs were based, "I am not prepared to say what the flow is," testified Colonel Feringa for the Engineers.[8] Nor (although they had done so in 1933 and 1938) could they now say how much water a nine-foot channel would take. They could not, therefore, help Congress decide whether there was enough.

One other set of facts would at once have defined the Pick plan's connection with the navigation project: an allocation of its cost to the various purposes served. The Pick report had avoided the question simply by presenting no justification in terms of estimated benefits. When the Bureau of Reclamation commented that in a multiple-purpose plan the costs, part of which had to be paid for by users, ought to be allocated in advance of construction, the Chief of Engineers replied flatly, "I do not consider it practicable. . . ."[9]

SLOAN PLAN

The "Sloan plan,"[10] when it finally reached Congress in May, differed in many ways from the Pick plan, not least in its length (211 pages) and definiteness. It was the result of several years of reconnaissance by many Bureau of Reclamation planners, but the initiative was that of W. Glenn Sloan, then Assistant Director of the Bureau in Billings. Aimed first at drought, then flood, it called for reservoirs as far up in the headwaters as possible, wherever irrigable lands could be found below or power could be generated. Less of the reservoir capacity was to be on the mainstem, and Garrison Dam was rejected outright. About the same storage capacity as the Pick plan thus required ninety reservoirs. The stored water would irrigate 4.7 million acres of dry land, doubling the basin's existing irrigation. Half the addition would, however, be made by massive diversion from the mainstem in North and South Dakota, hundreds of miles east of any successful present irrigation. Nowhere else could this water be used; besides, this would bring water to the Dakota dust bowl, one of the two areas hardest hit by drought in the 1930's.

In this report, economic justification and repayment prospects were analyzed. Every structure was considered part of a single "project" account. Forty per cent of the cost of $1,257,645,700 was charged off to flood control and navigation (by calculations questioned by the Corps of Engineers); farmers would repay part of the irrigation costs; power users the remainder, in addition to power costs.

Finally, Glenn Sloan's report frankly declared that it would reduce water available at Sioux City for navigation "by somewhat less than half the original stream-flow." Whether this would supply a nine-foot channel he could not tell, but he suggested that Congress should allocate water between irrigation and navigation.[11]

The contest between Pick and Sloan plans, thus launched in May, was over on October 17. On that day an inter-agency committee, including Glenn Sloan and the new division engineer, General R. C. Crawford (Colonel Pick having meanwhile been assigned to Burma to build the Ledo Road), met in Omaha and arrived at a one-page agreement. In two days' work they had "reconciled" the Pick and Sloan reports. Those two reports, "as revised and coordinated" by the Omaha agreement, are now the legal charter of the Missouri River development. How deep did the reconciliation go?

Two subjects were agreed on: jurisdiction and works to be built. The Corps of Engineers would determine mainstem reservoir capacity and other flood-control and navigation storage; the Bureau would determine capacity for irrigation. As to structures, duplication was eliminated at three sites in the Republican River headwaters. The Bureau plan of twenty-seven reservoirs for the Yellowstone basin replaced the two reservoirs of the Corps of Engineers. Oahe, the Bureau's one high dam on the mainstem, was substituted for the low dam of the Corps. This accounted for the omission of a single Pick plan reservoir on the Missouri: its site would be under water. With these exceptions alone, reconciliation followed the formula: "all the engineering features of both plans were agreed upon."[12] Reconciliation meant chiefly that each agency became reconciled to the works of the other.

The Pick plan's huge Garrison Reservoir was now accepted by Mr. Sloan. Three weeks before he had testified, "It would increase the storage but all of the advantages that you would gain would be lost by evaporation."[13] There was no consolidated cost estimate or justification, though obviously the Sloan plan's favorable balance of benefits over cost had been disturbed by adoption of a much more expensive plan to accomplish the same results. Physical duplication remained: the Pick plan's diversion into the eastern Dakotas was still authorized, though apparently obviated by the Sloan plan's larger diversion above and below. In the area served by this diversion, as it turned out, both agencies proposed to build the same dam; its site being outside the natural Missouri drainage, General Crawford overlooked it. Of the question of adequacy of water supply for irrigation and navigation, finally, nothing was said.

The agencies have explained so facile a reconciliation of hitherto sharp disagreements on the ground that Congress had in the meantime given them a mandate as to priorities in water use. It is true that Senator O'Mahoney of Wyoming and Senator Milliken of Colorado had introduced a set of amendments to the flood control and the rivers and harbors bill protecting state interests in the "consumptive use" of water against navigation uses. The difficulty with this explanation is that Congress had recessed prior to the Omaha meeting without acting on the amendments. Senator Overton's Committee on Commerce had, in fact, whittled the meaning from them in the course of its hearings and redrafting of the bills. In New Orleans, later that summer, he had garnered the commendation of the National Rivers and Harbors Congress for this feat.

DECISION IN CHICAGO

On October 17, as the Commissioner of Reclamation more precisely put it, the agencies "understood the principle that Congress *was going* to lay down." [14] That the agencies should have been willing to found a compromise of their positions on the supposed future intent of Congress seems mysterious. It is not. For the actual language of the "principle" Congress laid down on December 22, 1944, was formulated in the Stevens Hotel in Chicago on September 7 and 8. The gathering that decided what Congress was going to do called itself innocuously the Water Conservation Conference; and it left to the annals of extracurricular bill-drafting a stenographic transcript. With two specific exceptions the conference resolutions, redrawing the O'Mahoney-Milliken amendments, are congressional policy for the Missouri basin development. What is more, they are the law of the land for any like developments elsewhere, being incorporated in the Flood Control Act of 1944, the Rivers and Harbors Act of 1945, and faithfully in all successor acts.

Settlement could be reached the moment irrigation interests had cemented an alliance which, for once in their half-century before Congress, permitted them directly to challenge the votes of the rivers and harbors bloc. The challenge came along the line in the nation's geography—and even to the participants it seemed the inevitable line—where the Mississippi drainage basin with its excess of water receives the scant runoff from its great dry-land tributaries.

Officers of the conference reflected the concert of forces: Attorney General Alban J. Parker of Vermont, chairman; Floyd O. Hagie, secretary-treasurer. Mr. Hagie was the skilled lobbyist who then directed the National Reclamation Association. States' rights in water provided the transcontinental bond. For six years Vermont had doughtily resisted an authorized Corps of Engineers plan to flood some of her valleys for the protection of Hartford and other alien cities downstream. The states along the Delaware River had by parallel acts of their legislatures (but not by compact) established "Incodel," an interstate agency for managing the river free of federal "dictation." Until 1940 and 1941, it was possible to hope that the Supreme Court might reserve the headwaters to the states. The New River and Denison Dam decisions demolished that hope after forty-one state attorneys general had pleaded for it in briefs submitted to the Court. Now it was certain that the United States could conrol tributaries in the interest of navigation on the mainstream below and for multiple purposes incidental thereto—even for power. The delegate from Vermont said at Chicago: "The discussion this morning properly so far has been directed principally to the problems of the arid and semi-arid states, and the problems of the Missouri River, but I think back of that . . . there is a still greater problem . . . whether we are going to maintain a republic in which the states have a voice in operations within their borders."

So it was agreed in the Stevens Hotel that the Corps and the Bureau alike, before they presented new plans to Congress, must submit them for comment to the states. It was agreed, upon the Missouri water question, that navigation should give way to irrigation and other "consumptive uses" present or future. But the water to which that priority applied was "water arising in States lying wholly or partly west of the ninety-eighth meridian." The product of the Stevens Hotel conference was the first general law of the United States relating the uses of water one to another. Into federal law it adopted the scarce-water principle preferring the most beneficial uses, and it extended that principle to water flowing from what Congress could only crudely define by a line of longitude as the arid and semiarid West.

To hold their alliance against the rivers and harbors bloc the reclamation states took up their rival's tactic, logrolling. A proposed change in the O'Mahoney-Milliken amendments required use *under reclamation laws* of irrigation water from multiple-purpose dams of the Corps of Engineers. For the rice plantations of the Texas coast and the rich irrigation districts of California's Central Valley this meant paying for water derived from flood-control dams. Worse, it meant that the benefited farms could be no larger than homestead size—160 or (for husband and wife) 320 acres. Texas and California were provided for forthwith by a proposed exemption from reclamation law of water "which supplements any existing locally operated irrigation system." This is the one resolution of the Water Conservation Conference which did not become law.

Finally the conference reached its most difficult decision. In cases where the delegations from the affected states opposed them, should rivers and harbors or flood-control plans be stricken from the authorization bills? It was on this most immediate issue that a compromise was made with rivers and harbors interests. Plans would be authorized with such specific exceptions to Corps of Engineers proposals as necessary. Spokesmen from states upstream on the Connecticut and Snake Rivers had their way. But on the Missouri no specific engineering solution had been found. "I have given up any hopes," said Judge Clifford Stone of Colorado, chairman of the drafting committee, "that in the short time before the bill comes up, that the agencies will voluntarily solve it." Decision of the conference was for authorization of the Pick and Sloan plans, to be co-ordinated by the two departments before a deadline set by Congress. And among other requirements of co-ordination, the departments would, according to the conference resolution, *have to agree upon an allocation of costs to the purposes served.*

This was the second conference decision not written into law. For after it had been made known to the agencies (Commissioner Bashore of the Bureau of Reclamation and his chief counsel were in their rooms at the Stevens during the session), and before it could be considered in Congress, the agencies had met and agreed upon a list of physical works, entirely avoiding the question of the allocation of costs. Yet so rigidly did the Stevens Hotel formula fix the language of Congress that the resultant Flood Control Act assumes a nonexistent cost allocation comprehensive of both the Pick and Sloan plans, "subject to the basin-wide findings and recommendations regarding the benefits, the allocations of costs and repayments by water users, made in said House and Senate documents. . . ." [15]

One other event took place between the meetings in Chicago and Omaha. President Roosevelt sent to Congress on September 21 a strongly worded recommendation for a Missouri Valley Authority.[16] When the existing agencies resolved their dispute and thus removed one of the principal justifications for integrated administration, President James Patton of the National Farmers Union promptly labeled it "a shameless, loveless shotgun wedding." Perhaps the President's M.V.A. proposal motivated hitherto reluctant partners. But the conditions of the marriage contract had already been written at the Stevens Hotel. And one of them, whereby Congress would, if it reconvened without finding an inter-agency agreement, require an allocation of costs to water users, may itself have provided something of a shotgun.

INDECISION IN THE BASIN

So far the Missouri basin itself has appeared merely as the battleground of opposing forces: agency programs and sectional blocs. That is almost, but not quite, accurate. For a time, early in the summer of 1944, it appeared possible for the public of the basin to discover its own interests for the whole great watershed. For the formation and expression of a consensus as to the best use of their water, citizens of the basin states had the rudiments of an organization. It was the Missouri River States Committee. This was the outgrowth, interestingly enough, of meetings sponsored in 1941 by the President's National Resources Planning Board to enlist all agencies, state and federal, in considering the best plans for the river basin. Each governor was a member along with two other representatives from his state. It was this committee that conducted hearings on the Pick plan and wrote the President in August, 1944, calling for a "coordinated plan," [17] not, it should be noted, a valley authority as he adroitly proposed in response.

In the critical month of March, 1944, the Missouri River States Committee appointed a subcommittee of state engineers to investigate the adequacy of water supply and the engineering soundness of the Pick plan and of the Sloan plan when it appeared. Public officials of the states could thus get some of the facts necessary to decide whether the Pick and Sloan plans would yield the best use of the Missouri's water. "Together," concluded the subcommittee, "their reports constitute a sound basis for the development of the Missouri River Basin." But as to whether there was water enough so that the two plan *could* be put together, they could only say after conference with engineers of the Corps and the Bureau, "Time will indicate more accurately the quantities of water required for the various uses in the basin."

Then the clash of the wider conflict short-circuited even this conscientious attempt at appraisal by a body responsible to the basin public. The Governor of Montana was indignant to hear, in a Senate committee room, the report of the subcommittee of state engineers, which the governors themselves had not yet reviewed and accepted, read into the record in support of the Pick plan. Governor M. Q. Sharpe of South Dakota had provided the copy.[18] Not only would the Pick plan build four dams in his state, but he happened to have chaired the resolutions committee of the Mississippi Valley Association a few months before when it took the position that "no infringement or depletion of the flow of the river that might interfere with its full development and use for navigation is intended." [19]

That the people of the Missouri basin had an agency to give impartial technical appraisal of the plans thus seemed possible—for a time. For a time, in 1944, it also seemed that they had a voice. On May 14, 1944, a ringing editorial appeared in the St. Louis *Post-Dispatch*. Copies of the appeal were sent to every editor in the basin.

This newspaper confesses an error of the past—a preoccupation with the interests of its own section to the exclusion of those of Montana, Kansas, Nebraska, and the Dakotas. All along the valley, from the mountains at 13,000 feet to the low plains of the river's mouth, men have given a similar loyalty to the interests of their sections.

Yet is this not our common problem? Will not all our interests be better served—
be multiplied—by working together toward a common solution? . . .

We urge the editors of the Missouri Valley to lift up their eyes, to make stout their
purpose. With unity we can conquer the one big problem that the one big river challenges us to solve.

The Lewistown, Montana, *Democrat-News* and the Bismarck, North Dakota,
Tribune responded editorially to the challenge. The *Tribune*'s editor, Kenneth W. Simons, visited the Tennessee Valley to learn the lessons which could
be applied with profit to the Missouri River basin. The Water Conservation Commission of his state, of which he was vice-chairman, circulated his
dispatches throughout North Dakota. But there it ended. Observing the
scene a year later, Joseph Kinsey Howard commented, "The *Post-Dispatch*
soon learned . . . that if men with the vision it sought did live in the valley,
few of them were publishing newspapers." [20]

Beyond the reach of daily contacts and personal observation, public opinion could not generate itself. It might have been evoked by the stimulus of
some scheme made practical by the formulation of its leaders or its experts.
But the Missouri River States Committee had been drawn into the camp of
one of the Congressional-sectional blocs. The executive branch of the government of the United States was afflicted with agency schizophrenia until the
time when it, too, registered the armistice arrived at by those blocs. The President and his personal agents in the Bureau of the Budget had offered, first
negative criticism of the specific public works proposed by the agencies, then a
radical, but wholly abstract, shift of administrative control. Only the Pick and
Sloan schemes had specific consequences for the towns in the Missouri basin.
The real public debate upon them in the Missouri basin could last only so
long as their avowed incongruity made them immediately unavailable. That
obstacle vanished on October 17, 1944. The basin populace was, if anything,
uncommonly well supplied with vision. What it lacked was a practical alternative.

The amazing thing is not that the valley authority proposal of the *Post-
Dispatch* and the National Farmers Union attracted no consensus of support
in the basin. M.V.A. had not, as its opponents never tired of charging, any
specific dams or power plants or reclamation projects to offer. The amazing
thing is that it received a hearing at all. The strength of the single newspaper's voice, even though it was sounded from St. Louis, just outside the basin,
and the heroic efforts by which the North Dakota Farmers Union, for instance, sent two hundred of its members by plane and bus to take a look at
the T.V.A. operations alone account for such public heed as was paid to an
abstract idea of administration in competition with a list of local public works.
The idea was not wholly abstract: it had been tried in the Tennessee Valley.

In the heat of the M.V.A. crusade its proponents were thus impelled more and more to hold up T.V.A. as a visible model and thus to lay themselves open to a double counterattack. Not only had nature provided a different set of water problems in the Missouri basin, but no great and now prosperous area of the United States, one-sixth of the nation, would model itself upon a valley one-thirteenth its size. "T.V.A. might be all right for sharecroppers and mountaineers," began the inevitable reaction.

The best that practical men in the basin could do, in the meantime, was to visit the national (or rather sectional) lobbies, hat in hand, to plead for the recognition of the special needs of the Missouri basin in the omnibus bills those lobbies controlled. This was the course of Mr. Simons himself during the summer of 1944. (His Pulitzer Prize editorials of six years before had been titled "Self Help in the Dust Bowl.") He had to concede even at the conference of states' rights proponents in Chicago that the Missouri River was disposed of as a pawn in a larger game: "A month ago some of us went to New Orleans and appeared before the Rivers and Harbors Congress and we got the treatment we expected to get, but frankly it is a matter of some pain to me that we come here among people who are our friends and they put in this change even worse than the Army engineers or the Rivers and Harbors Congress ever proposed to do." [21] The process was pretty accurately described by Senator Overton himself a year later. "There was an agreement entered into," he said, presiding over a subcommittee engaged in burying an M.V.A. bill, "between representatives of the arid and semiarid regions of the Missouri Valley and the members of the Commerce Committee." [22] It was the Commerce Committee (stronghold of the rivers and harbors bloc), not the Congress, and the representatives of reclamation interests in the basin, not the opinion of the whole basin, that decided.*

Nor did the President force the issue upon Congress for decision. He made it clear, on December 22, 1944, that he still wanted the works authorized for the Missouri basin in the Flood Control bill built by a Missouri Valley Authority. But he signed the bill, expressing merely the "distinct understanding" that the administrative question remained open.[23] Congress, it must be added, had given him grounds for such an interpretation of its action in pass-

---

* Since this chapter was written, Marian E. Ridgeway has published a book-length account of the participants and their strategies: *The Missouri Basin's Pick-Sloan Plan: A Case Study in Congressional Policy Determination* (Illinois Studies in the Social Sciences, Vol. 35; Urbana, 1955). That study focuses less sharply than my account on the regional orientation of interests, is less definite about what water was under contention, has M.V.A. nearer the center of the controversy. Even so, it contains testimony (new to me) supporting the decisiveness of the Chicago conference. That is the more telling because it was written without benefit of the transcript of that conference.

ing the bill. Senator Hill, acting majority leader, had declared in Senate debate: "So that as the bill now stands, as I understand it, there is nothing in it which would be prejudicial, or inimical, let me say, to the creation of a Missouri Valley Authority. As I understand, by the passage of the bill we would take the first step which the President recommended. The second step would be the creation of the Missouri Valley Authority." [24]

That was a very technical point. The political heart of the decision registered in the bill was that the Missouri basin would be developed within the balanced political power of the rivers and harbors and the reclamation blocs. When in the next Congress Senator Murray introduced the M.V.A. bill the President had advocated, both blocs received a direct challenge. Their answer was delivered by Senator Overton himself, presiding in turn over subcommittees of the Committee on Commerce (where the M.V.A. bill was rejected as a measure for navigation and flood control alone) and of the Committee on Irrigation and Reclamation (where the bill was found wanting as an irrigation measure alone). Senator Overton had profited from his experience of the previous summer with the dismemberment of comprehensive bills in single-purpose hearings. Needless to say, the reports of his subcommittees took the position that the question *who* would administer the approved physical works had already been disposed of by the Flood Control Act of 1944.[25] When in 1945 thirty-one "national land and water organizations" published a pamphlet attacking valley authorities, the coalition included the National Rivers and Harbors Congress, the Mississippi Valley Association, *and* the National Reclamation Association.[26] The 1944 Flood Control Act thus recorded at one stroke the marriage of the Pick plan with the Sloan plan, the *modus vivendi* of the nation's historic programs of abundant and scarce waters (and their sectional supporters), and the obviation of distinctive planning for the peculiar water situation of the Missouri basin.

THE CHANNEL CLEARS

In the following March, while the spotlight of public attention was focused on the abortive M.V.A. bill, authorization of the nine-foot channel for the Missouri River below Sioux City quietly passed as part of the regular Rivers and Harbors Act.[27] This left one minor riddle. Had the Pick plan, which on its face was designed for flood control and which had been championed by House and Senate committees on the vehement insistence that it had no connection with the deeper waterway scheme, been intended by the Corps of Engineers to supply water for this deeper channel?

Strangely enough, this question was answered by the officer of the Corps of Engineers who succeeded Colonel Pick. Addressing the Upper Mississippi

Valley Association at St. Louis on the day Congress received the statement of his agreement with the Bureau of Reclamation, General Crawford was quite as candid as the champions of reclamation had been in the Stevens Hotel conference in Chicago a few months before. "In bringing the two plans together," he told the navigation lobby, "it was only necessary for the Bureau to recognize the importance which we place upon cyclic storage in the interest of navigation." And he left no doubt concerning the meaning of cyclic storage. "Assuming the reservoirs to be full at the beginning of a 12 year drought cycle similar to that of 1930–1941, . . . making allowance for all depletions due to upstream irrigation, . . . it is believed that this is adequate for a 9-foot channel." [28]

That cleared up some history. By 1941 it was evident to those interested in navigation that even Fort Peck storage would not supply the channel every year. A barge-line operator who was a director of the Mississippi Valley Association made that point in the House hearings on the Pick plan; [29] the Corps of Engineers at last confirmed it in 1951.[30] But planning for a twelve-year drought meant planning for the political likelihood that irrigation would make increased claims on Missouri River water. As Fort Peck Reservoir slowly filled, for example, Montana congressmen asked more insistently why its water should be used to help barges over the Mississippi shallows below St. Louis. It was the purpose of the Pick plan to design storage for both uses, and on the assumption that each would give up some water if excessive drought required it, to defer a decision of priorities. The Sloan plan required such a decision because it proposed to leave to navigation a supply of water the Corps knew would be inadequate. "Reconciliation," as General Crawford candidly explained, involved increasing the storage to 83 million acre-feet above Sioux City (20 per cent more than in the Pick plan, 29 per cent more than in the Sloan plan), so that even with five million acres of new irrigation *having preference over navigation* there would probably be water for the nine-foot channel. Even the inconsistency of the Bureau of Reclamation's acceptance of Garrison Dam became logical in this light. It was the engineering underpinning of the O'Mahoney-Milliken amendments, for it would give navigation a supply of water beyond irrigation needs, and thus allay the fear that the voting power of rivers and harbors forces might some summer be roused to repeal the irrigation priority by the grounding of their barges in a diminished flow. Abundant-water interests could tolerate the amendments if (as General Crawford believed) they could have no practical effect. Reclamation interests could tolerate Garrison Reservoir once they knew it would not, in the guise of flood control, take irrigation water for navigation.[31]

The obvious question whether the United States could afford a 29 per cent increase in reservoir space beyond the Sloan plan, with no additional benefits, was, of course, avoided by the simple expedient of producing no comparison of proposed costs with the value of proposed benefits. General Crawford, speaking in the friendly atmosphere of the waterway convention, did not scruple to put a price tag on the advantages which the combination of the Pick plan for flood control and the Sloan plan for drought and flood control would convey *to river shipping*. "We have always felt that every acre-foot of water we could store during wet periods is worth at least $1.50 to navigation during the succeeding dry periods," he said. During the period of a twelve-year drought on which the plan was calculated, this would amount to 68 million acre-feet of stored water with a value of 102 million dollars.

It is interesting to recall that the Pick-Sloan plan was to many congressmen the alternative to a valley authority which they feared meant the relinquishing by Congress of initiative in planning and control over the uses to which tax-financed reservoirs would be put.

Chapter VIII

LEGITIMATE OFFSPRING

Some of you have about worn out that old chestnut about the "shameless, loveless, shot-gun wedding." I think it is about time that you recognized that there was a wedding and consequently the offspring, as I might refer to the subsequent works undertaken in the Basin, are legitimate children. It could be much worse, you know, from a moral standpoint if nothing else.

With this admonition to the half-dozen reporters present, Mr. W. Glenn Sloan made his final report to the Missouri Basin Inter-Agency Committee before his retirement. His opposite number, General Lewis A. Pick, had already left the Missouri River to become Chief of Engineers in Washington. Whether the match their programs had made was spontaneous (which Mr. James Patton doubted) is not now the important question. For its offspring —the works of navigation, flood control, and irrigation—are ten years old. During the last eight years they have been supported with appropriations of well over 100 million dollars per year. The question is whether the legitimate offspring of two programs which matured in contrasting climates, wet and dry, have proved to be adapted to the peculiar climate of the Missouri basin, which is both wet and dry according to the time and place. The question is whether the ten-year-olds show promise of growing to maturity and doing a man's work.

NAVIGATION

As to the nine-foot waterway authorized in 1945, legitimacy is quite apparent. It goes the way of the comprehensive navigation schemes of 1884, of 1912, and of 1927. Once more, as headway is being made in stabilizing the channel, private investment and new traffic create optimism. But what will the next flood do to the channel? Will national support continue for mainly local benefits?

Below Kansas City, the Corps had by 1951 been able to stabilize the channel. Though nine feet of depth had been established only four-fifths of the way to St. Louis, the training works were being destroyed no faster than they could be maintained and replaced. Then came the great flood of the

Kansas River in July, 1951. When it subsided, the Corps asked for 5 million dollars "to go in and repair our navigation structures that have been very badly mauled by this flood." [1] Now the Engineers can maintain the status quo—unless there is another bad flood down the Kansas.

The half of the 760-mile waterway which lies upstream from Kansas City presents a different story. In 1954 it was but 53 per cent completed, a good deal less than before the war.[2] Works already in were being held, for the most part, below Omaha. But in the 120-mile stretch from Omaha to the head of navigation at Sioux City, according to an officer of the Corps, "they are practically all gone." As a matter of fact, when World War II came, all but three and one-half miles of the Sioux City–Omaha channel had been "pinned down" with piling and revetment. Now for one hundred miles the river is out of control. It has resumed its old meandering from bluff to bluff, flanking and wrecking such defenses as stand in the way.

On the defensive, the Corps of Engineers deployed its inadequate resources to save works immediately threatened in a succession of crises. It has not proved to be an economical use of funds. In one year since the war, testified a former Kansas City district engineer, all he could do was to salvage the wrecks of incompleted navigation structures torn out by flood. "In 1948 I decided there was enough piles floating on the river to make a good business venture. I got two wartime sawmills, collected the piles and sawed up one million board feet of lumber which were used in the mattresses along the bank." [3]

Each year about 8 million dollars worth of work is done, but completion of the waterway gets farther away. In 1948, after the Pick-Sloan plan was going full blast, the Corps considered the entire nine-foot channel only 42 million dollars short of completion. It would be finished by 1953. In 1955, with 45 million dollars (in addition to maintenance costs) spent since 1948, completion was ten years and 104 million dollars away.[4] Inflation and poor estimating may be involved, but in addition the channel itself deteriorates. "Each year," a spokesman for the Corps confessed even before the 1951 and 1952 floods, "has seen an increase in the amount of wild river." The Corps will have to run a bit faster to stay in the same place.

For all this the Corps of Engineers has an explanation. Congress has not, since 1941, appropriated enough for the channel work. But two points need to be remembered in this connection. The appropriations of 1935–40, which alone in the whole history of the navigation project have sufficed to promise completion, were emergency relief appropriations. They cannot be credited to congressional understanding and support of the Missouri River waterway. Second, appropriations to the Corps of Engineers for the whole Missouri

River division have been running at a rate of 100 million dollars a year since 1947, far more than ever before. Too consistently to be by accident, the navigation channel has not proved an attractive phase of the entire basin development either to the U.S. Bureau of the Budget or to Congress. Why? The reason is that disinterested appraisers have never found evidence that the navigation project can save in transportation costs what the nation must invest to build and maintain it. Its economic worth, to say the least, has been a question mark.

In 1952–53 the Missouri Basin Survey Commission made the most careful independent evaluation of potential savings from navigation that has yet been made. The Commission under the chairmanship of James E. Lawrence, newspaper editor from Lincoln, was certainly not indifferent to the economic needs of the Missouri River basin. Staff economists of the Commission studied actual present movement of rail freight to and from the 109 counties and the five states which might benefit from navigation on the Missouri. They interviewed manufacturers, warehousemen, and other potential shippers to learn what traffic might develop in the future. To make their estimate exact, they then calculated, commodity by commodity, the savings which might accrue by the use of barge transport on a completed waterway in the year 1970. The annual traffic is estimated at 2,100,000 tons; the saving in shipping costs at $4,100,000. That was less than one-third of the estimated annual savings of $13,398,000 by which the Corps justified the navigation project. The Missouri Basin Survey Commission concluded, "The navigation benefits, however, are problematical. . . . It is therefore questionable if navigation should be continued as an objective of basin development." [5] This conclusion applied even to the practical question whether, assuming that the 200 million dollars already spent on the channel had been wasted, another 100 million should be added to complete the job.

Almost at the same time that the Survey Commission was making its estimate of savings from navigation, a House of Representatives subcommittee on appropriations headed by Representative Kerr of North Carolina looked into the way in which the Corps of Engineers reached its estimate. The subcommittee found, essentially, that the potential traffic predicted by the transportation economists working for the Board of Engineers for Rivers and Harbors in Washington had been raised from 4 to 5 million tons by the division engineer in Omaha, that the date of realization of this potential traffic was advanced from the year 2010 to 1980, and that the average yearly savings to be expected during the life of the waterway were thus raised from $4,900,000 to $13,398,000.[6] The subcommittee made no estimate of its own concerning future barge traffic or savings. But it discovered an estimate of the Engineers' own transportation economist which is not far from the estimate of the Missouri Basin Survey Commission. Both were about one-third the Corps' estimate. But the Corps not only sticks to the higher estimate of benefits; it has lately increased it, in figures submitted to a Hoover Commission Task Force, by another million dollars per year.[7]

As the estimated cost of the waterway climbed higher than even the Corps' own estimates of savings from barge transportation, the predictable happened. Blunt General Sam Sturgis, who followed General Pick as division engineer, began calling it a navigation *and channel stabilization* project. In 1950, 70 per cent of the benefits of the channel work were ascribed to bank protection and only 30 per cent to navigation.[8]

Bank protection is worth a close look. It is not achieved by building levees, though it is necessary before levees can be safely built. Bank protection means pinning down the meandering Missouri so that it will not eat away the cornfields on the outside of its bends. Over the years, the Corps calculates, that means saving 12 acres per mile of river every year, or 9,094 acres in the whole floodplain from Sioux City down. Of course, the actual riverbed never grows appreciably, whether the engineers are on the job or not. Acres lost on the outside of the bends are deposited as sandbars downstream, and like as not, on the other side of the river, in another state. But they may have been cleared, fenced, and cultivated cornfields when they caved in, and the river yields them back as willow-grown wilderness, only gradually raised to a safe level by the deposit of silt over the next forty years.

Within its floodplain, the wild Missouri is a constant menace to settled agriculture. But there is a considerable difference of opinion as to the savings obtainable by pinning it down. The Missouri Basin Survey Commission, which had on its staff some highly qualified agricultural economists, found that over the next fifty years, saving the 9,094 acres from bank erosion will be worth $106 an acre, which means saving $963,964 per year. But the Corps' estimate of annual savings is *twelve times* that much, $11,795,000. Incidentally, one of the reasons why the 1952 appropriations subcommittee in the House came to doubt the Corps' estimate is that the Engineers had in their estimates calculated at 1950 prices the crops they had saved since their navigation project began in 1912. They took credit for every bushel of corn at $1.30, instead of at its actual price, averaged over the forty years, of 70 cents.[9]

There is another aspect of riverbank erosion: the threat to railroad lines, bridges, and high-value property in Omaha, Kansas City, and other cities on the floodplain. The reason this is so difficult to appraise is, as we shall see, that much of this costly building has occupied the floodplain only *because* the Corps undertook to make it safe.

In any case, accepting the Corps' figure of 8 million dollars per year as the saving to these areas from pinning down the Missouri's channel and taking all the previous investment by the Corps as written off, the Missouri Basin Survey Commission concluded: "The benefits of the navigation and bank stabilization project probably are not sufficient from an economic viewpoint to justify completion of the project." [10]

In 1955, however, there was little chance that those who sought to weigh benefits against costs would be heard. For barge-line traffic on the Missouri, which almost vanished during the war and again in 1952, was booming. Operators of genuinely commercial barge lines (there were five sending tows as far as Omaha) told a Senate committee they expected 500,000 tons in the 1955 season. They had three years of unmistakable improvements in commercial traffic to back up that forecast (see Table II).

TABLE II

*Tons of Through Commercial
Traffic on the Missouri River* [11]

1952	59,285
1953	152,000
1954	287,000

Captain A. C. Ingersoll, Jr., President of Federal Barge Lines, now a private enterprise acquired from the government's liquidated Inland Waterways Corporation, said to the senators: "We are starting up the river tomorrow with our brand new 3,600 horsepower boat which was christened the day before yesterday, with a tow which would be the largest up the Missouri, 840 feet long and 150 feet wide." [12] Captain Ingersoll's high-powered towboat was named appropriately for the man who led the Mississippi Valley Association while the Pick-Sloan plan was negotiated—*Lachlan Macleay*. In Kansas City new coal- and cargo-unloading facilities were going up; Omaha and Nebraska City already had new terminals to unload barges of New Orleans molasses to be converted into cattle feed. General Potter of the Corps was confidently predicting that the Engineers' target of five million tons of freight on the waterway would be achieved in five, not twenty-five, years. Willingness of businessmen and municipalities to invest in towboats, barges, and terminals quieted the economic issue. The Missouri waterway must be worth its cost.

All this was, to anyone who could afford the luxury of the long view, reminiscent of 1912. Would the navigation boom last this time? On the asset side are improvements in the techniques both of river control and navigation. The Engineers know more about the river; they have much less left to do to anchor its shifting bed. The 1955 model towboats had enough power (in the case of the *Lachlan Macleay,* harnessed to four propellers) to bull through or even wash a channel through the less troublesome sandbars. Most valuable of all, Fort Peck, Garrison, and Fort Randall reservoirs upstream were letting out their enormous reserves of water at the end of summer to supply three-fourths of the minimum flow required to navigate the lower Missouri. The plan of the Mississippi Valley Association was bearing fruit. Industrial development has intensified along the waterway, too; more traffic is there to be tapped.

But the Missouri's peculiar liabilities as a waterway persisted. Its four-mile-an-hour current made for high fuel costs going upstream and risky speeds going down. Captain Ingersoll himself presented the perennial indictment of the Missouri.

Towboats navigating the Missouri are subject to excessive delays and damage from groundings in the shoals. For example, in 1954, Federal Barge Lines' towboats running on the Missouri, even with this light draft [six feet] grounded 76 times in 43 different places, and lost on this account 436 hours. The percentage of time towboats on the Missouri lost in groundings was 12 times as great as our fleet averaged on other waterways.[18]

Of course, Captain Ingersoll was urging that the Corps be given the money to deepen those 43 places. But in 1955-56, as before, that hope was frail. In the most stable stretch of river, below Kansas City, the Corps said it would still take ten years to pin down the channel at the going rate of appropriations —2 million dollars in 1955-56. Would floods wait ten years before tearing out the existing piling and revetments?

All these liabilities sound to the promoters of Missouri navigation like the initial criticisms of other waterways now successful—the Ohio, upper Mississippi, and Tennessee. It is a great temptation to assume that the Missouri will grow as a traffic artery as they have done—if it can only be completed. But there is a crucial difference. Those are all slack-water channels created by chains of locks and dams. That means no current, no shifting sandbars. And it means a very different economic situation, for a still-water channel does not present the Missouri's perennial problem of maintenance. For dredging the sandbars, patching revetments, replacing rotten piling, and other recurring duties of upkeep on the portions of the Missouri channel it had already built, in fact, the Corps needed 6 million dollars in 1955-56. On a river whose bed flows along with its water there is no end in sight for that outlay.

The trouble with the Missouri as a waterway, indeed, is precisely that it is a Plains river. It has a great floodway filled with silt; that makes it impractical to dam. But its huge shifting bed has a relatively low and unreliable flow of water; that makes it costly to navigate as an open river. From the nation's viewpoint navigation, if it develops to the full expectations of the Corps, will still not return to anyone what it costs to establish and maintain. From the viewpoint of the Missouri River towns and cities, navigation will ever be dependent on annual appropriations which cannot be justified on their economic merits and which are therefore insecure and usually inadequate.

The mainstem of the Missouri below Sioux City is one of the nation's most difficult waterways to put to economic use. But it is not as difficult as the present government program makes it seem. Rivers and harbors politics and the Corps of Engineers have imposed on the lower Missouri a governmental pattern that maximizes the physical difficulties.

No Local Contributions.—"Between 1923 and 1927, the local people and the Government made a real attempt to cope with the erosion problems of the river. . . . Direct contributions and actual work with pick and shovel for the protection of organized districts were forthcoming from the people affected." This bit of history was recalled a few years ago by an officer of the Corps.[14] But the Pick-Sloan plan called for no contribution at all toward construction costs of channel stabilization from the landowners who are directly benefited. It was a navigation plan, and navigation is traditionally nonreimbursable. The 9,000 acres of land saved every year from undermining by the wild river and the 188,000 acres of new farm land created by constricting the channel[15] go as federal gifts to the owners of the farms adjoining to landward. When these benefits were discovered a few years ago to comprise three-fourths of the total value of the channel improvement, and navigation only one-fourth, it was far too late for the Corps of Engineers to try to recoup the landowners' windfalls. It could scarcely do so, in any event, under the present discontinuous system of work, General Sam Sturgis once pointed out, "because if the Congress did not allow the Corps sufficient money to maintain the work that actually builds the land, the land might conceivably be lost to the river again." [16]

Quite naturally, a successor to General Sturgis was able to say, "This is probably the most popular work that we do in the valley . . . and values of land in the valley [floodplain] have increased from $75 up to $400 an acre." [17] But if this be wholly at the cost of United States taxpayers, why should those Missouri basin landowners whose farms are farther west, and whose benefits come by canals rather than dikes and revetments, bear all they can pay of the construction costs, and the complete maintenance costs, of the federal projects that help them? Here is a question the Pick-Sloan plan leaves unanswered but increasingly obvious. It is for the future. In the meantime, the old navigation-bank protection cycle repeats itself. Having neither

—*Corps of Engineers, U.S. Army*

Channel Stabilization. The fate of the Tobin brothers' barn, ten miles south of Decatur, Nebraska, explains the political demand to make spot repairs to the channel, instead of improving it permanently and continuously for navigation. A few weeks after this photograph was taken in April, 1954, the barn was gone. But one could still see upstream the remains of the pile dikes the Engineers had installed sixteen years before to protect this bend. The work was not finished and during the war could not be maintained.

Navigation. Not quite tamed by the Engineers, the lower Missouri began in 1955 to be subdued by specially designed towboats. Here is the most powerful of them, with four screws, each driven by a 900-horsepower diesel engine, pushing 10,000 tons of Pittsburgh pipe and steel plate upriver to Kansas City. Federal Barge Lines (now a private corporation) christened it the *Lachlan Macleay* after the long-time president of the Mississippi Valley Association. Radar and the fathometer take a good deal of the risk out of piloting. Releases from Fort Randall and Fort Peck assure plenty of water in the river. But where the channel stabilization works are incomplete or damaged (as along the far bank here) the master of the *Macleay* expects to run his barges upon sandbars. He then unties the tow, moves to its head, and washes away the sandbar with the current from the *Macleay's* propellers.

—*Federal Barge Lines, Inc.*

—U.S. Department of Agriculture

—U.S. Department of Agriculture

—Sol Studna, Kansas City

Council Bluffs, Nonpareil

Floods. Above: Kansas City, July 14, 1951. Looking across the central industrial district from the mouth of the Kaw.

Top left: Not all the Kaw's damage was to cities. The county agent of Douglas County lists losses on the Fred Grobe farm.

Center left: A flash flood on Medicine Creek, Nebraska, did this. Flash floods on most of the tributaries in the basin could still do the same.

Bottom left: Boards and sandbags on the levees saved Council Bluffs and Omaha in 1952. The big dams on the Missouri will save them from now on.

Big Dam. Through North and South Dakota the Missouri will soon be a chain of lakes, green, powerful, predictable. This is Fort Randall, first of them to be finished. In 1954 the spillway to the right had not yet spilled; the temporary earth plug is intact. From the free-standing concrete intake structure, twelve tunnels run beneath the dam. Eight of these feed hydroelectric turbines which can be located by the surge tanks above them. Four tunnels are being used here to release water for the lower river from the bottom of the reservoir.

—*D. E. Hutchinson, Soil Conservation Service*

—*Tony Pasquarella,* Saturday Evening Post

Little dam. The Soil Conservation Service built this dam on Jerry Kubic's farm as part of its pilot project in the Salt-Wahoo Creeks watershed. After a hard rain, water runs out for a week through the drain in the center, saving crops, fences, and culverts below. But it would take forty-three little dams in the small Salt Creek watershed to provide even partial flood protection for Lincoln, Nebraska. The little dams get less support than the big ones partly because they are less dramatic, partly because they must wait until farmers agree to install the terraces and grassed waterways that go with the dams. In the top picture farmers from a neighboring watershed are visiting the Salt Creek project to help them decide this question. It takes time.

Construction. Damming the Missouri presents big, sometimes novel tasks to the contractors. At Canyon Ferry, near the headwater, they slung a steel cableway across the gorge. From it the concrete buckets could be dropped swiftly to any part of the structure.

At Oahe in South Dakota the dam is 75 million cubic yards of rolled earth. Six concrete-lined tunnels carry floods safely around the dam. They could have been blasted out at about one foot per hour. The enterprising contractor, however, designed an electric auger to drill them at four to ten feet per hour. Here he is about to wheel his machine into action through the concrete tunnel entrance.

the local contributions which would permit and require permanent bank protection nor the single-minded concern to complete the navigation project
in systematic stages, the Corps has lost the initiative again to the Missouri
River.

Unfinished All the Way.—Twenty years ago, the Corps' most thorough survey of the Missouri River flatly urged the principle of concentrating the available funds on completing one intercity stretch of the waterway, beginning
from the mouth, before undertaking another. "In view of the amount of
work already accomplished in the section below St. Joseph . . . this work
should be fully completed . . . to determine whether a substantial amount
of commerce will move on the river thus improved, especially from Kansas
City to the mouth." [18] The Pick-Sloan plan ran counter to that advice by
stretching the authorized nine-foot channel up to Sioux City, while the existing waterway below Kansas City lay unfinished. But in 1949, the Corps
quietly shortened its lines more nearly to fit the volume of congressional appropriations, by stopping work on the upper 120 miles of the authorized channel—the section from Omaha to Sioux City. In order to achieve any permanent channel, it had to let that stretch "go wild" again.

The Missouri River and the people who live along it soon put the stead-
fastness of that decision to the test. In 1950 people of Decatur, Nebraska, and
Onawa, Iowa, began building a bridge across the river between their two
communities. The bridge was to provide the only highway crossing between
Sioux City and Blair (near Omaha) one hundred miles to the south. Moreover, the local sponsors discovered that they could build the main span
on dry land across a channel which the river had abandoned and to which
the Engineers planned to return it in the course of their channel improvement work. This method of construction promised to save $400,000. Any
bridge over a navigable waterway requires the approval of the Corps of
Engineers, and the Corps approved this scheme. By 1952, the two-million-
dollar bridge was erected, but the Missouri still flowed a quarter-mile away
through what was intended as the Iowa approach to the span. Three years
it stood that way, useless, while the Engineers held fast to their decision to
concentrate on the channel below Omaha. In 1955, the high and dry Decatur
bridge had become a notorious symbol of loose-jointed planning. The Corps
relaxed its priorities. In the 1955–56 appropriations it requested and got 5.8
million dollars to go back to work on the wild river between Omaha and
Sioux City. With that money, the Corps has turned the Missouri under the
bridge, where it belongs. It will take other years of work, and other appropriations, to make the rerouted channel permanent by extending the dikes
far upstream to solid anchorage against a bluff and by lining them with

stone. That money, concentrated on work in the most nearly complete stretch of the channel below Kansas City, would very nearly suffice to complete it. Above Omaha, it pays for urgently needed rescues of caving banks and the structures already built on them. It does not create a permanent navigable channel.

"This project," said General Sturgis of the Missouri waterway in 1950, "is in the same position as a 760-mile railroad or concrete highway all complete except for some of its bridges." [19] Five years later, ten years after the Corps went to work on the river highway as it is now authorized in the Pick-Sloan plan, General Sturgis' analogy remains entirely appropriate. And the Corps has given up the attempt to complete any usable stretch of it before scattering its forces along the rest. Anywhere but along the Missouri River, this would be considered a curious way to build a highway.

FLOOD CONTROL

What happened in the Kansas sky on the nights of July 10, 11, and 12 of 1951 could happen only on the grand concourse of the Plains. Out over the Pacific a "ridge" of high atmospheric pressure accumulated during the whole of June.[20] The Rockies barred its eastward route. As July came, the Pacific air began to pour around the ends of the barrier.

The southern lobe passed over Mexico to the Gulf, picked up what amounted to a foot-deep layer of water, and circled 600 miles northwest —as far as southern Kansas. Drought-shy farmers in Sherman County had paid the rainmakers $40,000 to water their wheat. The cloud-seeding planes never got off the ground.

The northern lobe of the Pacific airmass moved inland over Alaska on July 2. In seven days, it had advanced down the low-pressure trough east of the Rockies to the southern border of Kansas. Weathermen later drew a cross section of the cold front as a blunt wedge, 15,000 feet thick, with its heavy leading edge hugging the ground from St. Louis through the Oklahoma Panhandle. In the middle of Kansas it wedged under the mass of warm Gulf air and shouldered it suddenly three miles up. The atmospheric pincer movement was complete, the moist air chilled in the night sky, and the rains came.

There was nothing unusual about rain that summer. For six weeks, off and on, Kansas had received heavy rains—a year's normal supply by July 4. (Hays got an inch an hour for eleven hours on May 22.) Water lay in flat lagoons on the wheatfields when the storm began. The two strange things about the rain that started late Monday night, July 9, were that it covered the whole eastern two-thirds of the state and that it did not, as rains from collisions between warm and cold fronts are supposed to do, move on. Throughout Tuesday night a five-inch rain came down; on Wednesday night another four inches fell. Later on, the weatherman showed why. A second cold front had slid down close behind the first. It came a bit more from the east, from the Great Lakes. Thus it blocked the storm's exit in that direction and reinforced the wedge.

Kansas valleys are shallow, and their slope to the east is gentle. On July 10, streams were still bankful from previous rains. These were unfortunate facts for valleys that got 14 inches of rain in 72 hours. The water simply piled up faster than it could run east.[21] Ottawa, the county seat of Frankfort County near the Missouri border, has its business section along the Osage River, which the Kansans call the Marais des Cygnes. During Wednesday night the river rose 22 feet. Merchandise had to be abandoned in the stores. On Thursday morning a current 10 feet deep moved through Ottawa's main street.

The Pick plan had three reservoirs on the Osage. They would have reduced the crests on the lower Missouri and Mississippi, but they were all below Ottawa. Kansas and Missouri farmers, who would lose reservoir lands without getting any benefits, protested. Appropriations were blocked. The Corps worked out a new plan jointly with agricultural experts. It would have saved Ottawa. But that plan got congressional approval three years *after* the flood.

To the storm of July, 1951, can be credited one item of sheer good luck. Part of the water fell far enough south to run off into the Arkansas River. Part, including Ottawa's flood, fell in the watershed of the Osage and so traveled halfway to St. Louis before emptying into the Missouri River and swelling the bulk of the flood. That was not, of course, a piece of luck apparent to the people of Ottawa, Osawatomie, Council Grove, or Wichita. The river in which all the rest of the rain collected is labeled on the maps the Kansas, but it is called the Kaw. It begins its eastward course in the center of the state at Junction City, where the Smoky Hill joins the Republican River. The water which it thus collects in the northern half of the state of Kansas it delivers to the Missouri through Kansas City, only 150 miles away. On Wednesday night, July 11, both tributaries of the Kaw were in flood. The Smoky Hill poured through Salina 20,000 second feet of water. Abilene's business district was an island. The commander at Fort Riley, four miles from Junction City, moved 11,000 troops of the Tenth Division into pup tents on bluffs to the west. The Kaw occupied the barracks.

There were two new reservoirs up the Smoky Hill. The Bureau of Reclamation had dedicated Cedar Bluff Dam only a month before, designating it for flood control as well as irrigation. Farther downstream, Kanopolis Dam, a flood-control project started by the Corps of Engineers even before the Pick plan, was in operation. As long as the storm lasted, these dams held the Smoky Hill within banks—where it left their gates. They could not check the rain which fell below. At Salina, twenty-five miles downstream from Kanopolis, the division engineer estimated "that without the reservoirs the flood flow would have been twice as great." At Salina, 20,000 second feet covered approximately half the city with two to three feet of water.

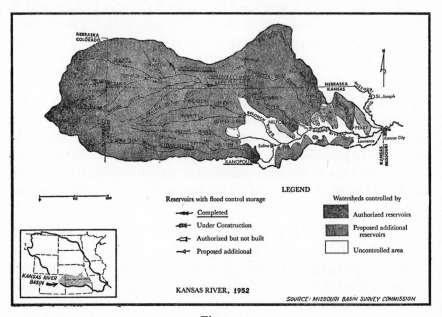

Fig. 10

There were three new reservoirs up the Republican: Bonny, Enders, and Medicine Creek—all built by the Bureau of Reclamation. They were too far up to catch this flood. Below them, the Army Engineers' Harlan County Dam was almost but not quite finished and only a few miles above Junction City, the Engineers had, a year earlier, recommended Milford Reservoir. It was an addition to the Pick-Sloan plan, and Congress had not acted on it.

The next city down the Kaw is Manhattan. It has the state college, an obstreperous newspaper editor who on July 1 was still insisting, "Only a Missouri Valley Authority could furnish the imagination, the many varied technical skills, and the will to do this kind of job," [22] and city fathers who also felt strongly about flood control. On Thursday the Kaw left its banks and ran straight north through Manhattan, just covering the parking meters. It reached five feet up the walls of the Wareham Hotel.

Thirteen years before, after the Kansas flood of 1935, Congress had authorized, along with Kanopolis and Harlan County, Tuttle Creek Dam twelve miles north of Manhattan. By storing the water of a tributary, the Blue River, it offers the last chance to take the peak of the crest off the Kaw before it reaches Topeka and Kansas City. The Army Engineers said that Kansas City was not safe without it. Six months before the July flood, the division engineer had been most emphatic. To defer this and the other flood-control reservoirs was "dangerous." "Not only Kansas City but also the tributary areas cannot be protected from storms like 1935 without reservoirs." [23] But Tuttle Creek Reservoir would cover 53,000 acres of land, most of it very good farm land. For thirteen years no money had been appropriated to start it, and in the year of the flood the Chief of Engineers had not asked for any.

APPROPRIATIONS COMMITTEE CHAIRMAN McKELLAR. You presented it to the Budget Bureau, did you?

GENERAL PICK. We did not, sir.

CHAIRMAN McKELLAR. What was the trouble?

GENERAL PICK. There is a disagreement among the local interests as to whether or not we should build the Tuttle Creek Project.[24]

On the morning the flood crested in Manhattan, the "local interests" brought their disagreement to a Senate appropriations subcommittee assembled to act on flood relief measures for Kansas. The former district engineer explained that Tuttle Creek was the only feasible site to get the requisite storage. He had spent three-quarters of a million dollars back in 1946 exploring every alternative, including combinations of small reservoirs. Organizations of farmers and townspeople in the valley of the Kaw and the cities along its banks pleaded for the reservoir. Mayor Z. R. Hook of Manhattan, official river observer and experienced advocate of flood control, was put on record for Tuttle Creek Dam. "I am sold on soil conservation for water-saving and soil-saving purposes. But this talk of stopping floods by small dams is all a lot of poppycock. Kansas was all grassland when the flood of 1844 came."

Mr. Richard Rogers, member of the city commission along with the mayor, disagreed. "Manhattan has always been against the dam," he said, though he confessed the flood had caused "a slight changeover." It was the farmers in the reservoir site who were still adamant. Their spokesman, J. A. Hawkinson of Bigelow, Kansas, was quoted thus by the

Topeka *Daily Capital:* "We have had this thing licked for 13 years. The Army Engineers have been praying for just this flood." The farmers who had lost their grain crops in the June cloudbursts wanted flood control, too. Mr. Hawkinson did not think it fair "to force 600 families off their land just because downstream people were foolish enough to build where they would be flooded out." The real purpose of the reservoir, he suspected, was "to flush out Kansas City's sewage."

It was the farmer's ancient defense of his homestead against those in the cities who would take it away. But the "local interests" thought their motives went beyond that. William Edwards, also from Bigelow, was apologetic because he could not say exactly how.

I do not know how I can explain to my colleagues from Kansas about the Tuttle Creek Dam Reservoir, or how I can explain to General Pick. . . . We aren't trying to hold our little selfish interests against the interests of the State. . . . I know we don't have the facts and figures and statistics that the Army engineers have. . . . I plead that we be given consideration to try, as has been done in other valleys, the Washita in Oklahoma, the Sioux project in Iowa, to put our project in the hands of the Department of Agriculture and out of the hands of the Army engineers.

That was it. The upstream farmers had nothing to propose that would have stopped the flood on the Kaw. "We simply ask for the chance to organize with the 13 counties in Nebraska, where the waters from the Blue originate, that we form a watershed district and put in . . . such retention dams on the small streams and save our upland soil. . . ." But they thought flood control meant control of the danger of the rain from the moment it hit the earth. That was a job for the experts who shared their objective. "The Army engineers," their editor had said in the Manhattan *Tribune-News*, "are among the last of the groups we would entrust with it." [25]

The Kaw divides Topeka and North Topeka. It had 5 feet of the unstored water of the Blue on top of it when it crested in Topeka at 37 feet. There had been warning. Twenty thousand people had evacuated their homes. There was room for some in the grounds of the statehouse, in churches, and in schools. The rest camped on the bluffs north of town. Two highway bridges over the Kaw in Topeka were washed out Thursday. The Santa Fe tried to ballast its railroad bridge with ten locomotives. On Friday bridge and locomotives collapsed into the Kaw. Drinking water was short, for with the waterworks flooded, the city began Friday drawing on the supply already in its reservoirs.

The North Topeka business district might have been behind a levee. But before the war, some property owners of that district brought suit to prevent the city's contributing land to the Corps of Engineers project authorized in 1936 for their side of town. In the aftermath of the 1951 flood, though, this was one thing they had no reason to regret. For the projected levee, like the levee the Corps actually built around the Topeka waterworks, could hold out only half the water that came down the Kaw on July 12.

Through Kansas City, Kansas, and beside Kansas City, Missouri, the Kaw carried the flood to the Missouri River. The bed of the Kaw is a nine-mile *S* through one of the nation's great railway freight transfer points, lined with factories and warehouses. The rain that had fallen, 8 inches deep on the average over 60,000 square miles of Kansas, poured in three days through that bottleneck. The Geological Survey calculated later that about midnight Friday it reached a volume of 510,000 cubic feet per second. Forty-eight years before, the Kaw had delivered to the bottleneck the greatest flood on record—260,000 second feet. One hundred seven years before, a larger flood is estimated, in the dim light of frontier history, to have reached 360,000 second feet.

The floodway which the river used in 1844 was one and one-quarter miles wide. In 1951 it had been narrowed to less than a quarter-mile (1,200 feet) by a continuous line of dikes 20 feet above the river's flood-stage. When the Kaw poured over the first of those dikes at midnight Thursday, it caught 800 residents by surprise. Many got out with no more than the clothes they wore. About 3:00 A.M. Friday the flood spilled over the Armourdale levee across the Kaw, and by 10:30 it overwhelmed the rich warehouse and industrial area in both Kansas Citys. For the whole of the nine miles through the *S,* the river took back its immemorial floodplain. The area flooded was no greater than in 1844 or 1903. But this time the area held rail yards, packing plants, stockyards, assembly plants, oil tank farms, and a financial district. Nine-tenths of the homes of the Kansas Citys were on high ground, but the people who lived near the packing plants lost their houses along with their jobs.

After the flood of 1903, the people of the two Kansas Citys resolved to protect themselves in the river bottoms they were beginning to occupy with industries and railroads. They formed local levee districts and raised dikes of varying heights. Kansas and Missouri laws hampered co-operation. The railroads had encroached on the floodplain with their embankments and built their bridges too low to pass the flood. But the two chambers of commerce finally set up a joint flood-control committee, and the engineers of all the railroads co-operated in the investigation of remedies. In 1934, the P.W.A.'s Mississippi Valley Committee found that "Greater Kansas City has the most serious flood problem in the Missouri Basin, if not in the United States; provision for its adequate protection constituted the most urgent water project of any kind in the Missouri Basin." [26] The committee found that Tuttle Creek and Milford Reservoirs were needed, as well as the local levees, to give this adequate protection.

The Corps of Engineers agreed. In 1943, after two more lesser floods, they proposed to Congress a plan for raising and strengthening the Kansas City levees combined with the previously authorized upstream reservoirs (Kanapolis, Harlan County, and Tuttle Creek) and cutting through a bend in the Missouri downstream to let floods drain off faster. As division engineer, Colonel Lewis A. Pick signed the report.[27] In 1944 it was adopted as part of the Pick-Sloan plan. By July, 1951, work was still going on, but *the levees which were overtopped on Friday the 13th were at the full height to which the Corps of Engineers had designed them.*

There are two reasons. The first is that the Engineers did not know how much water might come down the Kaw. Some candid officers have admitted the risk of designing to take care of past floods in the face of the limited records and wide variability of runoff from the Plains.[28] But the official project document submitted to Congress was quite positive. "As a result of extensive hydrological studies, it has been determined that the maximum probable discharge from the Kansas River is 370,000 second-feet (without reservoir control)." [29] Eight years later, in spite of some reservoir storage at Kanopolis (further aided slightly by the Bureau of Reclamation dams upstream), the Kaw brought 37 per cent more water through Kansas City.

The second reason is that, for the adequacy of their Kansas City levees, the Engineers had counted on upstream reservoirs that were not there. Colonel W. E. Potter, himself a former district engineer stationed in Kansas City, explained it to a congressional committee this way: "When the project was first designed, the flood walls would have had an elevation of some 30 feet. By making it reflect the reduction of flood heights made possible by upstream reservoirs in the Kansas Basin, principally Tuttle Creek and Milford, they were reduced to less than 20 feet." [30] That was a few weeks before the flood. Tuttle Creek had by then languished thirteen years without construction money, and because of "disagreement among the local interests" the Corps had not even asked for funds in the current appropriations. Milford, proposed only a year before, had not been authorized. "This project will hold the design flood," Colonel Potter assured the congressmen. But the "design flood" (the volume of water the Corps calculated the works would need to pass) was only 170,000 second feet. For eight years, seven of them under the Pick-Sloan plan, the Engineers had been working upon levees designed to hold back only the water that the nonexistent reservoirs might leave in the Kaw.

Flood control engineers bear no easy burden of decision. Since Tuttle Creek and later Milford balked, should they have left the Kansas Citys behind the old local defenses? Should they have built to the expensive heights necessary in the absence of upstream storage? When the flood overtopped the levees whose design he had approved, General Pick, who had flown to Kansas City for a firsthand inspection, accurately told reporters: "We have consistently pointed out that the Kansas City flood control measures would not be effective in event of a big flood unless supplemented by a system of tributary reservoirs." [31] The Corps thus doubtless did its engineering duty. Had it discharged its responsibility as a servant of a democracy?

There were three elements to the problem. There were the reservoirs, first, whose human costs fell 150 miles west of their major human values, and for the most part in another state. There were the levees, whose security was evident to the people behind them, but depended in fact upon the reservoirs far outside their vision. And there was a third element which might be overlooked. The floodplain on which the industries and stockyards and railroads built that made the Kansas Citys great was saved from the shifting bed of the Missouri and from the Kaw by the "navigation" works the Engineers installed.

Now, while the Engineers, as General Pick said, warned in their speeches of the need for reservoirs, they presented the three elements of the decision independently to Congress and to the people affected. And when only the floodplain works won approval, they spoke with pride of the visible benefits, as though these were secure. The year before the flood, the Corps of Engineers took the officials engaged in the basin projects, some governors, and reporters down the Missouri River on the *Sergeant Floyd* to see the improvements they had made in the channel. As the boat went by the magnificent industrial complex of the Kansas Citys, a spokesman for the Corps made this comment:

The booming industrial growth of our cities is being attracted to and concentrated on the level, accessible, and protected river-bottom land where good rail service is available. Examples are the Fairfax and North Kansas City areas of Greater Kansas City. They have shown such new growth at all times that even the residents of the Kansas City area are astonished. . . . It is not difficult to see that a great amount of money has been saved by stabilizing the river banks at this location so that the city could build or expand into the protected areas.[32]

Statistics bear out the claim. For when the Corps evaluated the property upon the floodplain in 1938 to justify its levee plan, the value came to 176 million dollars. When the Kaw reoccupied that same area in 1951, it flooded 500 million dollars worth of property. Part of the threefold increase was due to inflation. But part was due to more intensive occupation—new packing plants, a new automobile assembly plant, new oil storage tanks, the new homes of thousands of working families. "Does not an industry that locates in that particular area take a calculated risk when it goes in there . . . ?" inquired a congressman not long before the flood. "Yes, sir," replied a Colonel of the Corps, *"if they are actually aware of the flood problem."* [33] As the water subsided, leaving the muck, an Associated Press reporter interviewed flood refugees, many of whom had failed to evacuate their belongings even after the warning came. "They were so sure of the levees along the river," he reported, "big concrete flood walls and earthen dikes built to take more than the river had ever been known to give." [34]

THE CORPS OF ENGINEERS won what is probably the strategic battle against Kaw valley floods in 1955. Congress appropriated 7.5 million dollars for full-speed construction of Tuttle Creek Reservoir. The appropriation is noteworthy because it was achieved over the opposition of the Representative from the Tuttle Creek district, because it was not asked for in the President's budget, but most of all because it brought to life a flood-storage scheme which had been halted, even since 1951, by local resistance. Congress provided construction money in the aftermath of the flood, only to terminate work in 1953 with three-quarters of a mile of earth embankment in. Farmers in the Blue River valley were too bitterly opposed. This time Congress clearly decided that 500 farms in the Tuttle Creek Reservoir should be bought. There was no other way to prevent the flooding of 20,000 homes and farms, plus some of the nation's most valuable industry, in the next serious flood of the Kaw.

What accounted for the bold congressional decision? Opposition to the dam from the reservoir landowners was as determined as ever. But in 1954 and 1955, the Corps of Engineers for the first time clearly linked levee and floodwall plans to the reservoir plans on which they were physically dependent. In the 1954 flood-control hearings, Division Engineer General Potter testified so vehemently on the subject that he later apologized "for being so intense." "Sir, I cannot recommend more strongly than I am going to do now, that if the committee is not willing to authorize those reservoirs for construction, that you do not authorize the local protection projects; because they would be deathtraps for those people. They can't help but trust a levee that has been built." [35] The Engineers meant what General Potter said. They refused to ask for appropriations to build levees at Topeka and other Kansas River cities which would be affected by the lack of the proposed storage. They suspended work on the levees along the mainstem of the Missouri below the mouth of the Kaw. They even deferred navigation improvements there on the ground that floods from the Kaw could tear them out. These were inseparable projects hydrologically. When they were joined politically, Congress made a clear decision.

That is not to say that the danger of inadequate flood protection is ended for the Kaw valley. The Missouri Basin Survey Commission said, "When proposals for flood control based on the 1951 experience are considered, our investigations indicate that there are simply not enough upstream storage opportunities to prevent the remaining flood flow from overtopping the present levees in the Kansas Citys. . . . New general plans for flood protection of the Kansas Citys need to be worked out." [36]

Three highly competent consulting engineers, N. T. Veatch of Kansas City, Louis R. Howson of Chicago, and Abel Wolman of Johns Hopkins University, took a similar position. They opposed building Tuttle Creek and other proposed reservoirs on the ground that a widened and deepened floodway through the Kansas Citys would be needed even after the utmost possible reservoir construction. They advocated the floodway, instead.[37] The truth is that the Corps did not, in requesting funds for Tuttle Creek, present a complete plan for dealing safely with a Kansas River flood of 1951 magnitude.[38] General Potter asked for Tuttle Creek and two other reservoirs on tributaries of the Kaw—Perry and Milford. But after they are built, a flood like that of 1951 could still deliver 380,000 second feet of water to the Kansas City bottleneck, whose levees failed in 1951 when the flow reached 262,000 second feet. For the excess, he could only propose storage in seven small additional reservoirs. The Corps had selected their sites, but was not ready to propose them to Congress. General Potter roughly estimated the total plan to protect the Kansas valley at a cost of 323 million dollars. He held the plan economically feasible. Of course, whether it is politically feasible depends in part on whether any of the seven tentative reservoir locations create farmer opposition akin to that at Tuttle Creek.

Even as in 1943–44, the Missouri River division engineer took courage after a great disaster to challenge Congress to a bold decision. But whether all the features to which the federal government was thus committed are sound, whether they comprise the best combination of works, and whether the government can carry through to completion all the features on which the plan depends are unanswered questions. They are, as far as the Corps is concerned, unasked.

THE KANSAS CITYS and the towns higher on the Kaw are not the basin's only flood-control problems. Six million acres, all told, are vulnerable to the rivers. Most of this is natural floodplain land. Against the total hazard, the Corps has finished four storage reservoirs. Two are in the Kansas River basin—Kanopolis and Harlan County—one is Cherry Creek above Denver, the fourth is Fort Peck. Certain of the Bureau of Reclamation reservoirs hold additional flood capacity. The Engineers' great mainstem reservoirs, Garrison and Fort Randall, almost finished, can store floods. Oahe, between them on the Missouri, and Tuttle Creek are well under way. Work started in 1955 on two Osage River flood-control reservoirs in Kansas and Missouri.

But in addition to these major storage works, the Corps has built fourteen levees and floodwalls around individual cities (besides the Kansas Citys) ranging in size from Omaha to Forsyth, Montana. The average cost was a million dollars per city. That was only the beginning. In 1955, thirty-two new towns awaited construction of local protective works which Congress had already approved. Every year the Corps recommends, and Congress authorizes, more new projects than there are old ones finished.

The Pick-Sloan plan has achieved a lasting defense against high floods on one Missouri River front. That is in the stretch from Sioux City, just below the last mainstem reservoir, down to the mouth of the Kaw at Kansas City. There was an historic and personal vindication for the Corps and for Lewis A. Pick on that front in 1952. When a phenomenally thick and rapid snow-melt sent a record crest of floodwater down the river that spring, the levees at Omaha and Council Bluffs held. Since Garrison and Fort Randall dams were not closed until some months later, the Pick plan did not actually come into play. But General Pick flew to Omaha to direct 25,500 determined flood fighters. They raised the levees 4 feet with boards and sandbags and defended them like battle trenches. Sioux City and St. Joseph and almost all the farms in 800 miles of floodplain went under.[39] But the victory at Omaha was a true sign of the safety of the middle Missouri under the Pick plan.

But the Pick plan has, at least to an equal extent, increased the government's unfulfilled flood-protection commitments. It added the 156-million-dollar scheme to dike the floodplain farms below Sioux City. In ten years only 27 million dollars have been invested by Congress in that vast undertaking. And everywhere along the Missouri and its tributaries the Pick plan displaced local responsibility for building local protection. So the agenda of unbuilt but expected flood protection grows apace. And with the commitments grow buildings, houses, factories, utilities, roads in the potential flood paths. "I mean to control the water of the Missouri River," General Pick once said while he was division engineer. He took the first steps. It is a manifest destiny which succeeding Army Engineers might almost attain—if the United States supplied enough money.

Meanwhile, every comprehensive study of the nation's flood-prevention strategy has concluded that another approach is needed along with reservoirs and levees. Most of the Missouri basin's bad floods rise on the Plains. Reservoir sites are scarce there and very costly. The rains that can fall on the flat land are phenomenal, but they fall seldom. Between the floods, farmers and businessmen encroach on the lands subject to flowage. Zoning of these lands under state authority to exclude from them valuable, flood-vulnerable structures has become a standard recommendation, monotonously repeated in the reports of three national commissions.[40]

Even more remarkable is the consensus of five careful surveys within the past six years that directly benefited properties should help pay, through districts, municipalities, or states, for local flood-control work.[41] It is a kind of partnership that would encourage prudent assessment of the economic advantages of all the methods of flood prevention on the part of citizens along the rivers, rather than uncritical pressure for federal largesse. It would permit flood protection to be planned with some assurance that it will be built.

There is probably less chance of action on such proposals in 1957 than there was in 1940. The Pick plan has extended to the limitless drainages of the Plains the strategy of absolute control over the flow of rivers. There is no occasion, under that strategy, to control human occupancy or reckon its cost. It is an authentic strategy for the frontier.

RECLAMATION

In the decade since the Pick-Sloan plan was launched, the Bureau of Reclamation has been operating on a new scale. It is small compared to the plan's vast goals, big compared to the work of the previous forty-two years. From 1945 through 1955 the Bureau got 439 million dollars of appropriations against the 3.4-billion-dollar job (at present estimates) Congress authorized in 1944. The Bureau also got 186 million dollars to spend on its previously authorized basin works. The total, 625 million dollars, was a good deal more than five times what the Bureau spent in the basin from 1903 to 1945.

The principal result of the unprecedented investment is dams. Twenty-three of them have been finished in the decade. Most are of medium size; none compares with the Army's great earthen dams on the main river. But Boysen Dam on the Big Horn in central Wyoming stores 1.5 million acre-feet; brand-new Canyon Ferry, opposite Helena at the upper end of the Missouri, stores two million. Reclamation dams built in the last ten years hold 6.5 million acre-feet of water—almost double the contents of the twenty reservoirs the Bureau built in the preceding forty years.

What work is the stored water doing? Nine of the dams have hydroelectric facilities. Their combined capacity is 283,000 kilowatts. This is about the capacity of one of the Corps' mainstem dams, but the Bureau hydroelectric plants serve the western basin where the demand is keener. A third of the reservoir space the Bureau built since 1945 is kept for storing floods. There are very worthwhile recreation and city water-supply benefits, besides, from this water stored in dry country.

In its main job of irrigation, the Bureau can show large accomplishments since 1944. Including lands irrigated from other sources to which the Bureau furnished supplementary water, it is providing irrigation on 1,430,842 acres.[42] That is more than double the 656,519 acres watered wholly or partly from Bureau canals in 1944.[43] The increase deserves a closer look.

Semiarid Land.—Irrigating the Missouri basin is two jobs. One is traditional—subjecting the arid desert or the semiarid rangelands to cultivation. The other is the job the Bureau had only undertaken on a small scale and without much success up to 1944—stabilizing established agriculture upon the subhumid Plains.

It is in the first task that the Bureau has scored its successes since 1944. But the accomplishments come from the completion of earlier projects; the Pick-Sloan plan has added exactly 2,052 acres to the Bureau's 656,519 existing project acres in the semiarid states of Colorado, Wyoming, and Montana. As a matter of fact, Glenn Sloan's ultimate plan was not a revolutionary one for the dry western part of the basin. Some recent figures show that clearly. In the mountain valleys and at the foot of the mountains, the plan calls for eight out of ten farms to be irrigated; but seven in ten were irrigated already. On the semiarid Plains reaching into the western Dakotas, Nebraska, and Kansas, the plan ultimately would bring three farms out of ten under the ditch; two in ten were irrigated in 1944.[44]

By far the greatest achievement of the Bureau in the semiarid zone is the Colorado–Big Thompson project (Figure 11). It is no part of the Pick-Sloan plan, having been authorized seven years earlier.[45] Now it lacks only a few refinements to be finished. Vacationers at Rocky Mountain National Park see its three steel penstocks, 8 feet in diameter, leading water into the Estes Power Plant. That water has penetrated the 12,000-foot mountains of the Continental Divide via a 13-mile tunnel. Each year 250,000 acre-feet of Colorado River water, collected in Grand Lake and an intricate system of additional reservoirs on the western slope, are pumped up to the tunnel. From Estes Park, the water has 2,000 feet to fall before it reaches the water-hungry Colorado Piedmont. The drop yields 180,000 kilowatts of electricity. At the foot of Big Thompson Canyon, the imported water spreads north and south. Carter Lake and Horsetooth Reservoir store up the constant flow through the tunnel and power plants until the peak of the irrigation season. The beet fields, cherry orchards, and alfalfa farms of northeastern Colorado had virtually dried up the mountain streams: Cache La Poudre, the Big and Little Thompson, St. Vrain and Boulder Creeks, the South Platte River. Now they flow all summer.

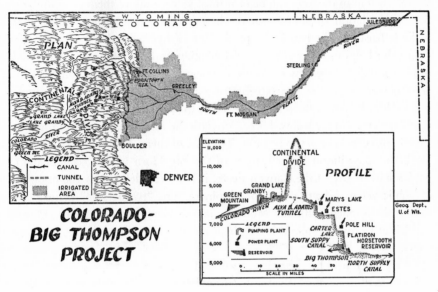

Fig. 11

In 1954, the worst drought of a decade put the unfinished project to the test. Little snow fell on the Front Range the winter before; there were no early rains. Natural streamflow was 40 per cent of normal. Farmers who planted outside the area insured by the Big Thompson diversion watched their seedlings wither. But to 400,000 acres (eventually it will serve 615,000), the new Bureau project brought 300,000 acre-feet of water—even more than the normal quota. The 1954 harvest in that area was worth 41 million dollars, very little less than normal. Without Colorado–Big Thompson water, the harvest would have dwindled to 19 million dollars.[46] The Northern Colorado Water Conservancy District, which takes in all the benefited land, farm and city, had no regrets that it had undertaken to repay all the cost not covered by power revenues. The Bureau has been criticized because the total project cost rose from 44 million dollars, the estimate upon which Congress authorized it in the depression year of 1937, to 159 million dollars in 1955.[47] But nobody doubts any longer that the project will accomplish its mission of safeguarding the thoroughly successful irrigation at the foot of the Rockies and supplying the water and power needed for the future growth of the cities in the triangle from Denver to Fort Collins to Sterling and Julesburg.

The Big Thompson project would have progressed unchanged if Glenn Sloan had never submitted his report. But that is not to say that the Pick-Sloan plan is without its effects upon the semiarid side of the basin. Two of the effects will in the long run be of utmost value. Both of them depend upon the accumulation of stored water wherever mountain valleys or canyons make it feasible. The first is the production of hydroelectricity, which has a dual role: helping repay the cost of irrigation and sustaining the associated urban growth. Three new dams are in operation now almost wholly to generate power—Kortes in the North Platte canyon between the old Seminole and Pathfinder dams, Boysen at the head of the Big Horn's upper canyon, and Canyon Ferry not far below Three Forks on the Missouri. But the big hydroelectric projects have yet to be built. The first of them, Yellowtail, which will block the magnificent lower canyon of the Big Horn with a 500-foot dam, got its start in 1955. Like Canyon Ferry, it had been delayed by the question of public versus private power development. The "partnership" principle is now to be applied, with the Montana Power Company and Pacific Power and Light Company submitting their proposals to distribute the 200,000 kilowatts.

Yellowtail illustrates the political value of large-scale storage and planning. It is proceeding because Wyoming (in which water is stored) and Montana (which receives part of the irrigation and power from it) agreed in 1951 upon the allocation of the waters of the Big Horn and all other Yellowstone tributaries that flow across the state line. It is hard for an outsider to appreciate the stubbornness of the problems thus solved. The Yellowstone compact was twenty-one years in the making: a settlement was actually ratified by the state legislatures in 1947 only to be vetoed by the governor of Wyoming upon complaint of a few irrigators along the Tongue River. As recently as 1952, the Wyoming legislature rejected the compact which had been worked out with South Dakota to divide the waters of the Cheyenne River.[48] But the large plans have brought a new perspective to bear. Enough "new" water has been made available by storing the hitherto wasted flood flows so that no state's supply has to be cut for the development of another. And the steady round of interstate meetings, the publicity given to basin-wide opportunities, has allowed state officials to take a much less parochial view than would otherwise have been possible. This, too, Wyoming illustrates. In 1951, some of her citizens objected to the Bureau's construction of Keyhole Dam. Its water would benefit the old Belle Fourche project across the line in South Dakota. Protests followed the familiar channels to the Wyoming congressional delegation in Washington. But they had their answer from the state engineer *of Wyoming,* Mr. L. C. Bishop, who was bold enough to write Senator O'Mahoney:

As I see it, these people have had their day in court (at a hearing in Moorcroft before me, prior to the allowance of the permit and two hearings before the Missouri Basin Inter-Agency Committee later) and I sincerely hope that you and the other Wyoming representatives will join me in fulfilling the obligation of the State of Wyoming to the end that the Keyhole Dam may be completed as planned under the permit issued at a minimum expense to the United States.[49]

But something else has happened to federal irrigation in the western basin during the last ten years which, if it is not isolated and corrected, will be disastrous. It is that neglect of the problems of soils and settlement which plagued the Bureau's original projects.

During 1950, qualified veterans of World War II drew lots for 104 new farms on the Riverton project in Wyoming. Riverton was, of course, an old project, but the Pick-Sloan authorization permitted its 42,000 acres to be increased to 100,000. There was a good deal of fanfare connected with this rebirth of the irrigated homestead. It turned out to be a rebirth of all the old troubles. Before the year was out, the veterans were complaining to their senators that the project was waterlogged. Water was seeping up in their fields. The Bureau sent out three of its seasoned engineers to investigate. Their report, which reached the Washington officials of the Bureau in the summer of 1951, has been made public.[50] "Many of the lands now settled and those proposed for future development and settlement," concluded the Bureau investigators, "are not suitable for irrigation farming or are not adequately protected against adverse drainage conditions associated with irrigation." In 1950 it was a bit late for the Bureau to be mistaken about soils and drainage. But technical mistakes were not the whole of the trouble at Riverton. "Prior to awarding these units," said the report concerning fifty-four farms opened as veteran homesteads the year before, "it was discovered that shallow soils over shale and high sodium conditions prevailed over much of the land." Their drainage troubles, in other words, were known in advance. But the veterans were invited to take up all but seven of the ill-fated farms. Having invested some thousands of dollars of their capital and two or three or four years of their lives trying to farm land predestined to failure, the veterans made their protests heard. Congress passed a special law permitting the Bureau to offer these settlers exchange homesteads on more promising irrigation projects; by 1955, seventy-eight of them had quit Riverton to resettle in the Columbia basin, in Idaho, Arizona, and California.[51]

Improper classification of land which turned sterile under cultivation was

a problem well known to the Bureau by 1916; it was the occasion for congressional write-offs in 1926; the Bureau hired a large staff of soils scientists
and agronomists to prevent it in 1946. One trouble at Riverton was that the
men who classified soils were inexperienced and lacked guidance. Expansion
had been too rapid. But such warnings about drainage as were given by the
soils classifiers were ignored, said the Riverton investigators, "because of in-
terference with the 'stepped up' program."

There is no evidence that Riverton is typical of the Bureau's newly irrigated acreage. Most of it can make successful farms. But there is evidence
that the expansive approach Pick-Sloan reflects, an approach which seeks the
ultimate development for all purposes of all the waters in the basin, in which
one agency is pitted against another for speed and magnitude of accomplishments, has had its pitfalls as well as its advantages for reclamation. Rein-
carnated in a "stepped up" Bureau, the zeal to settle the West can disregard
the subtleties of nature at a time when they have become calculable to modern
science.

Subhumid Land.—Glenn Sloan proposed to complete the watering of the
basin's semiarid states. But, as Figure 12 shows, his grand design was to
project federal irrigation into its subhumid part. Two-thirds of the 4.7 million
acres of new irrigation he proposed lie in this climate zone. Even so, he
could plan to irrigate only one subhumid farm in every six. But that would
mean a radical departure for the eastern Plains, where wheat and corn grew,
on forty-nine farms out of fifty, without irrigation.[52]

The greatest natural resource for irrigating the subhumid Plains is the
Missouri River. Unlike the weak rivers that rise upon the Plains themselves,
unlike the hard-working Platte, it still carries large quantities of unused water.
Diverting that water eastward in the Dakotas, where the land is flat and where
droughts come too seldom for farmers to adapt to them and so hurt the worse
when they come, was a vision more than fifty years old when Glenn Sloan
proposed it. John Wesley Powell broached the idea to Congress in 1890: "It
seems probable that the waters of the Missouri can be taken out at the great
bend . . . if we can get across or through the divide."[53]

Crossing the divide was an engineering possibility by 1944. Electric pumps
were available big enough to lift the river the necessary hundred feet. And
because the old glacial drainages to the east were 100 feet lower than the
bed of the Missouri, the water dropping down the eastern slope would generate enough electricity to run the pumps. From Oahe reservoir, not far
above Powell's "great bend," the 1944 plan called for a diversion to irrigate
three-quarters of a million acres in eastern South Dakota. But Glenn Sloan
also proposed a new point of diversion. He planned to take the whole low

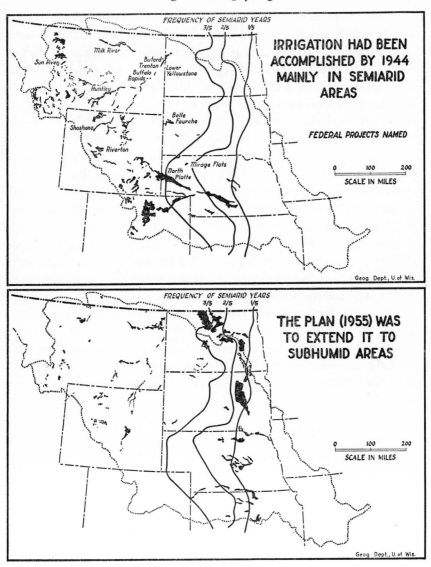

Fig. 12

flow of the Missouri out in Montana below Fort Peck. At the end of a 200-mile canal it would irrigate over a million acres in central North Dakota just short of the Canadian border. The excess flow would refill the shrinking Devils Lake and find its way eventually into the Red River of the North on the Minnesota border.

After ten years of searching investigation and ten million dollars worth of surveys, the plans to divert the Missouri onto the subhumid Plains seem as far from being realized as they were when the Bureau of Reclamation announced them in 1944. Not until 1957, in fact, could the Bureau say whether they can be justified economically. Again the physical problem is soils. Glenn Sloan did not have time for a study of them before he recommended the great irrigation schemes to Congress.

Unlike the majority of tracts which the Bureau has so far tried to irrigate, the million-acre sites in North and South Dakota were worked over by ice age glaciers. That left the ground low enough to permit the Missouri to be dropped over the divide, and attractively level on the surface. But the glaciers concealed here and there beneath the surface a mortal hazard for irrigated farming. Soils scientists, both in the Bureau and in the state colleges of agriculture, understand it now; it naturally escaped detection in the "windshield reconnaissance" of the irrigable areas prior to 1944. Some of the proposed tracts were once the beds of glacial lakes—Lake Souris at the Canadian border, Lake Dakota along the James River to the south. Beneath their waters settled the fine sand and loam which make for bumper crops—when water conditions are right. But among the minerals in which these soils are rich is the sodium, the bane of irrigation engineers. In solution, it breaks down the particles of soil into a compact and impermeable claypan. Soils scientists do not have to speculate about what happens to such soils under irrigation. In the almost imperceptible low spots of the former lake beds, even more where the subsoil has been deposited in horizontal layers by the direct action of the glaciers ("glacial till"), they find once-mellow loam converted by standing water into shallow, poorly drained soils. In spite of the most elaborate drainage ditches the Bureau could afford to dig, canal water would mean waterlogging here.[54]

Detailed soils surveys have gradually forced the Bureau to rule out large portions of the tracts marked irrigable on the 1944 maps. In North Dakota, the westernmost lands in the loop of the Souris River have been eliminated; in South Dakota, the glacial till soils around Redfield. In both states, the Bureau has had to look still farther east for replacement acreage. In the South Dakota tract this has meant that more of the irrigation water must be conveyed east across the James River. For the lands presently classed as irrigable in eastern North Dakota, the Bureau now proposes to divert water from Garrison Reservoir (as General Pick proposed ten years ago). Compare Figure 13, the present Garrison diversion plan, with Figure 9. Glenn Sloan's planned diversion dam much farther west in Montana has been abandoned, though only after the Bureau, in 1952, excavated its foundation.[55]

All that the Bureau can assert now is that with these changes it is *physically*

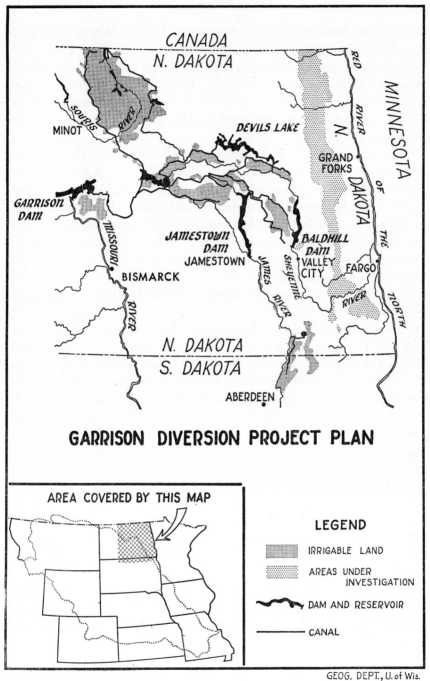

GARRISON DIVERSION PROJECT PLAN

AREA COVERED BY THIS MAP

LEGEND

IRRIGABLE LAND

AREAS UNDER
INVESTIGATION

DAM AND RESERVOIR

CANAL

GEOG. DEPT., U. of Wis.

Fig. 13

feasible to put Missouri water on the subhumid Plains. Whether it is economically feasible we will know only in 1957. Cost estimates of the two diversion projects have risen from 214 million dollars in 1944 to 672 million dollars in 1955. It would not be surprising if they should rise further, as the Bureau more precisely calculates the length of distributary channels required to reach scattered areas of suitable soil, and the expense of thorough drainage works.

The great imponderable is the willingness of farmers to use the canal systems once they are built and to pay for them. The Bureau has prudently established irrigation demonstration farms in both irrigable tracts, supplying the water by pumps. The farmers working them have achieved impressive returns from irrigation. But returns from wheat on "dry" farms have been impressive, too—in fifteen wet years. In 1948, for instance, the average farmer in Renville County, North Dakota (the heart of Glenn Sloan's proposed irrigated block), made a net income of $4,800. He owned $5,400 worth of tractors and tractor-drawn machinery.[56] Would he get down and work the ditches?

On this point there is not yet dependable evidence. True, the North Dakota legislature in 1955 created a conservancy district, somewhat like that which has contracted to repay the irrigation costs of the Colorado–Big Thompson project. But the North Dakota district blankets twenty-two counties in which the scattered irrigable tracts may be located. No decision has yet been made by county governments, much less by individual landowners, to assume repayment obligations. And the promotional enthusiasm which may be generated for such an enormous irrigation project bears no necessary relation to its lasting earning capacity. After the Bureau's soils classifiers had already rejected the western tract in Glenn Sloan's Missouri-Souris diversion plan in 1952 and thus rendered the headworks and canal as he planned them impractical, the "Missouri-Souris Projects Association" still pressed the Bureau and Congress to begin construction of the abortive diversion dam. Glenn Sloan, retired by that time from the Bureau, served as representative of the Association.

But the eastern Plains are still *sub*humid. Droughts will come again. If water is available in Bureau projects, will it not then be used enthusiastically? Once used in time of drought, will not irrigation prove itself to be a more prosperous and stable way to farm the Plains?

Two years ago there were only speculative answers; now we have some scraps of evidence. For in the central Great Plains, along the southern edge of the Missouri basin, the droughts have indeed come again. For four years continuing through 1956, dry-farmed crops failed in western Kansas, southern Nebraska, and eastern Colorado. The drainage of the Kansas River, which had just yielded the highest flood in a century, had an even lower rainfall, in 1952–53, than in the Dust Bowl year of 1936. Here was nature's test of the appropriateness of the Reclamation program to the climatic extreme for which it was designed.

In the upper Kansas River basin, the Pick-Sloan program had by 1952 installed six irrigation-flood control reservoirs. They were not all filled with water when the drought began, but the stored supply was ample. How much were they drawn upon for irrigation? In eastern Colorado just across the Kansas line, an area so dry that the topsoil blew off the wheatfields, Bonny reservoir had held water since 1951. Below the dam was an old irrigation canal, through which farmers gladly took a supplemental supply to 750 acres. In the much larger area which Bonny was designed to irrigate— 6,250 acres—no serious interest in irrigation developed. On the Smoky Hill, southernmost tributary of the Kansas River, the dry years failed to generate demand for the use of the water standing at Cedar Bluff and Kanopolis dams. These were planned to irrigate 52,500 acres. No district has been formed to contract for the use of water.

Along the Republican River, the northern tributary of the Kansas, Reclamation projects had more takers. The Bureau has two projects in growing use here—Frenchman-Cambridge in southern Nebraska and Bostwick straddling the Nebraska-Kansas line. Bostwick receives its water supply from the Army's Harlan County dam. These two projects supplied water to 8,850 acres in 1953 and to 17,463 acres in 1954. It was a valuable service in a drought-vulnerable area. These projects have been under construction for eight years; the first repayment contract was negotiated in 1947. Irrigation was not, even then, a novelty in this area in the sense that it will be in the central and eastern Dakotas. Before Pick-Sloan work commenced, in fact, 17,620 acres were under private irrigation within the Frenchman-Cambridge district. At the end of three dry years, the Bureau had been able to double the total acreage under the ditch. But water was stored capable of supplying 135,000 acres.

Causes appear, when one digs into the history of negotiations of the repayment contracts, quite sufficient to explain a certain degree of resistance on the part of the water users. The cost estimate of the Frenchman-Cambridge project has risen from 27 million to 70 million dollars since it was proposed to Congress and to potential irrigators in 1944. The cost of the Bostwick project has climbed from 8 million to 47 million dollars. The Bureau intends to saddle as much as possible of the cost on the expected electric power revenues of the Pick-Sloan plan. The subsidy of irrigation by the power program amounts to three-fourths of the cost of Bostwick and six-sevenths of the cost of Frenchman-Cambridge. Yet the small fraction left to be repaid by water users just about equals the value of supplying water to a farm as it shows up in the real estate market. The situation is presented in the Bureau's 1955 testimony before the House Appropriations Committee (see Table III).

TABLE III

Repayable Costs per Acre Ultimately Irrigated

	Frenchman-Cambridge	Bostwick
Federal investment per acre	$893	$654
Repayable from power revenue	768	484
Repayable by water users	125	170

As to the current market value of irrigation, the Bureau spokesman testified: "I would say the dryland value of the farms in this Bostwick Division in Nebraska and Kansas, depending upon the shape the farm is in, would run somewhere between $100 and $200 an acre. . . . Under irrigation my best guess at current land values would be that it would sell somewhere between $300 and $500 an acre."[57] "Which is less," commented a California congressman, "than the amount we are putting on this in cash." And the Bureau man added, "That is unquestionably true in most of the Missouri Basin units." That is a concern of the taxpayers. The proposition to the potential irrigator in the Bostwick area is to pay $170 for a Bureau water supply, plus his own development costs of leveling his land, digging field ditches, and converting his equipment and buildings to irrigated farming. He could buy a fully converted irrigated farm for $200 to $300 over the cost of his dry farm. The current Bureau proposition is advantageous but no bargain. But Bostwick farmers remember that their repayment obligations per acre under Bureau contracts have been renegotiated upward in the past. The Bureau has already opened negotiations to increase the repayment obligations of Frenchman-Cambridge irrigators to something like the Bostwick rate. In 1954, the directors of the local irrigation districts reported to visiting members of a Hoover Commission task force (men with experience of Reclamation) "that a majority of the water users are willing to renegotiate and submit to higher rates, but that they have not been able to secure from the Bureau assurance that the new agreements would be firm and final. Accordingly, they are "sitting on their hands," and in most cases making no payments, either on construction or operation and maintenance."[58]

There is another source of resistance, confined to the downstream end of the Bostwick project in Kansas. Farmers to be dispossessed by the construction of the small Lovewell reservoir caught the militant spirit of the Tuttle Creek reservoir landowners nearby, who stood off the Army Engineers for thirteen years. Their opposition has not stopped the building of Lovewell dam, but combined with economic objections of some owners of irrigable lands, it has resulted in the shelving of the easternmost unit of 12,000 acres from the Bureau's Bostwick project.[59]

There are areas in Kansas where Bureau irrigation plans have been met by a lively interest on the part of the farmers. This is the case of the Kirwin project south of Frenchman-Cambridge, where the Bureau got a signed repayment contract before completing the storage dam. But the fact remains that at the end of the years of drought, and ten years after the Pick-Sloan plan was started, the Bureau of Reclamation has not provided a single new acre of irrigation in the Missouri basin in the state of Kansas. Meanwhile in the single drought year of 1954, Kansas farmers installed their own wells and pumps to bring 60,000 new acres under irrigation.[60]

Taking the Missouri basin as a whole, Pick-Sloan projects vastly increased the acreage receiving a stable water supply, but they added only 27,697 new acres to the total irrigated area.[61] Irrigation has been extended onto the sub-humid Plains, but not by federal reclamation projects. The 1950 Census of Agriculture shows that in the five years 1944–49 Nebraska irrigation increased by one-third; irrigation in the Dakotas by one-half. This was all before any Pick-Sloan projects began to benefit those states. The Census shows 272,000 acres added to the irrigated area of these Plains states in the five years 1944–49.[62] (In the ten years 1944–54, the Bureau added less than one-tenth that acreage to its new projects under the Pick-Sloan plan.) The great expansion came by tapping ground water with electric pumps. Up and down the Platte Valley in Nebraska, and in the western Kansas River basin, there was a boom in well irrigation. Even in the heart of the proposed Missouri River diversion project in South Dakota, farmers showed a more immediate interest in tapping the artesian aquifers than in bringing in Bureau canals. In Montana, the state Water Conservation Board brought 6,400 acres of new land under the ditch in three small projects in 1954. Pick-Sloan projects so far have irrigated only one-third that much Montana land.

The evidence of ten years is in. The conclusion it warrants is a mixed one. The Bureau has succeeded in stabilizing irrigation where it was already established, as in the Colorado Piedmont. In this climate and part of this terrain federal reclamation is indigenous. Here the Pick-Sloan plan has facilitated the use of interstate rivers. It is providing new power installations, though whether it will market the power vigorously enough to make it an important paying partner for irrigation is another question. Even here, the promotional attitude it has engendered in some Bureau officials has permitted unnecessary mistakes in planning new projects.

On the new ground of the more humid eastern Plains the Bureau's great projects have yet to be built. But it would be tragic to invest in them, disregarding the clear lessons of a decade. The Bureau offers a single engineering approach—canals fed by multiple-purpose storage reservoirs. For subhumid portions of the basin, where ground water is abundant, wells alone or wells plus canals have proved practical and much more acceptable.

Economically speaking, the Pick-Sloan strategy was to support the giant works needed to deliver Missouri River water eastward in the Dakotas by writing off part of the reservoir cost to flood control and navigation, and by capturing the income from the large power production of the six ultimate mainriver dams. To this end, all Pick-Sloan irrigation projects are considered as a single pool of costs and revenues along with the Army dams. The Bureau has been unable to collect the costs of some of its much simpler original projects in the basin as fast as they wore out. It is quite clear that the new "basinwide account" makes even more nebulous than before the irrigator's sense of responsibility to pay back any particular share of project costs.

Politically, the Pick-Sloan approach proved to have advantages in the first few years which surprised the Bureau administrators. Having entered the business of flood control alongside the Corps, the Bureau found Congress on several occasions actually eager after bad floods to make appropriations for new dams. The Pick-Sloan authorization provided Congress with a list of 105 dams to choose from, all of which after sketchy reconnaissance had some sort of endorsement by the Bureau or the Corps. After 1947 floods killed thirteen people in the Republican River valley, for instance, Congress quickly passed a supplemental appropriation to start the Bureau building eight new dams.[63] All were for irrigation as well as flood control; all were on the Plains. There was one for each basin state in which the Bureau has legal authority to operate, plus one on the Colorado-Kansas border. Now, eight years later, two of the eight dams are serving their intended purposes of irrigation and flood control. Two more were built—Bonny and Cedar Bluff—and are providing highly localized flood protection but (except for the 750 acres under old channels below Bonny dam) no irrigation. The other four dams on which construction was to have begun in 1947–48 have never been built, though 5 million dollars have been spent on surveys. Two of these, Bixby in South Dakota and Cannonball in North Dakota, turned out to have no soil below them suitable for irrigation. The political alignment of reclamation with flood control brought early appropriations at the sacrifice of careful investigation, planning, and scheduling, and (as at Bonny and Cedar Bluff) at the sacrifice of advance commitments by the irrigators to pay their share.

The zeal with which a program "of, by and for the West" was extended across the basin's Plains is dwindling in Congress. Irrigation from this point on depends on general appropriations, not the Reclamation Fund; it offers not homesteads but a more intensive, stable, and costly agriculture. But this is an end toward which there are other means than irrigation, and there are other patterns of irrigation than the Bureau's. The Bureau has proved itself, in fact, severely handicapped in moving toward this goal. It is too narrow in its techniques, too rigid in its policies, too remote in its decisons. It cannot team up with the Department of Agriculture in the way that the Wheeler-Case experiment proved would work on the Plains without breaching its jurisdictional defenses. It cannot readily reappraise construction plans that now seem grandiose as long as it competes for public attention with the Army Corps of Engineers.

Subhumid agriculture needs stabilizing. In that task irrigation may, indeed, find a new frontier. So far the federal Bureau of Reclamation has not done much pioneering.

WATER AT THE GRASSROOTS

"THERE IS no greater change in a farmer's life," observed the former Dean of the North Dakota College of Agriculture, "than when he stops looking into the skies for rain, and begins to look down to the irrigation ditch." Dean H. L. Walster had watched a good many farmers in his Plains state attempt that change. Some have turned back. Inevitably the magnitude and difficulty of that change press the original Sloan plan, an engineering and reclamation plan, toward agricultural solutions. The decision of the farmer—what to do with his land—is stubbornly intruding upon the decision of the hydraulic engineer—where to divert the river. But across the lines of interdepartmental jurisdiction between Interior and Agriculture, that transformation is coming hard.

"The thousands of tons of mud and muck deposited by the flood," said William Edwards, a livestock farmer from the Kaw Valley, three months after the Kansas City disaster, "had surely been productive earth from some man's farm." [1] Hundreds of farmers, like him, are resolved that if such catastrophic damage to the cities below is to be prevented, the productive earth above shall be saved as well. The assertion of the Soil Conservation Service that the land suffers 75 per cent of all flood costs buttresses their determination. In the Missouri basin, the farmers have the votes. Reservoirs which put farms under water (this is not always a problem with dams in the Rockies or with the main Missouri River channel through the Dakotas) exclusively to hold floods back from downstream cities and farms, are not getting built. Or they wait for disasters to shock the entire nation. The Pick plan had no remedy for the upland farmer's floods. So the Department of Agriculture has drawn up a three-billion-dollar counterpart to it. Newspapers of the basin cities call it the Young plan, after Gladwin Young, who as a representative of the Secretary of Agriculture in the Missouri basin attempted to co-ordinate the Department's work with the river development. While the river is developed, the Young plan languishes in Congress. Yet even the Missouri River is but a minor force upon the vastness of the Plains. And in a basin where the livelihood of the people comes, more than in any other great American region, from growing or handling products of the soil, planning for water on the land, on the wheatfields, and at the grassroots is still a foundling. Whether or not there is a gleam of affection for it in the family of legitimate offspring, the terms of its successful adoption are yet to be worked out.

IRRIGATION IS FARMING

When the war ended, there were six Wheeler-Case irrigation projects authorized in the Missouri basin. A provision of the Wheeler-Case law permitting a nonreimbursable subsidy to the projects out of general appropriations expired six months after the end of hostilities—June 30, 1947.[2] This did not, of course, terminate the law's provisions for developing raw land into productive farmsteads before the settler was brought in. The provisions joining the U.S. Department of Agriculture in the farming aspects of federal irrigation, with the Bureau of Reclamation as water supplier, were still available. But the Department of the Interior has not chosen to apply these provisions to any postwar project. As a matter of fact, the adoption of the Pick-Sloan plan in 1944 effected the reauthorization of one of the existing Wheeler-Case projects (Angostura, just south of the Black Hills) as a conventional Reclamation project.

Few voices protested. An ineffectual resolution was adopted by the interagency committee considering basin plans in 1946. At the projects themselves, Department of Agriculture workers were bitterly disappointed. They saw in the Wheeler-Case approach an important step toward fitting federal irrigation to the Great Plains environment.

On behalf of the Department of the Interior, it must be said that the subsidy arrangement of the Wheeler-Case projects had become obsolete. Originally it included C.C.C. and relief labor; during the war, the labor of conscientious objectors. In the law, nonreimbursable federal costs were justified to resettle Dust Bowl farmers. To these forms of subsidy, the Pick-Sloan scheme was an alternative. Its "basinwide account" would compensate for Plains irrigation projects which, taken by themselves, could never be reimbursed. The Pick-Sloan plan did not solve the problem of bringing agricultural thinking to bear on what was essentially an agricultural problem.

Who Plans Irrigated Farming?

This problem the Department of the Interior set about to remedy as best it could. Aided by the Reclamation Project Act of 1939, which allowed it to support regional staffs without dependence on the income of the Reclamation Fund, it has tried since the war to enlarge its view from an engineering to a water-use perspective. By 1947, the Bureau of Reclamation had employed over two hundred agricultural technicians, ninety-eight of them from Department of Agriculture agencies.[3] The retirement of Eugene Debler and then Glenn Sloan from leadership in the Missouri basin regional offices of the Bureau further signaled the transition. The administrators who succeeded them leaned on a diversified staff, including agricultural men.

The enlargement of professional backgrounds among those engaged in surveying future projects has had varying results for the planning of irrigation since 1947. The Bureau abandoned those parts of the great Missouri diversion sites which were hazardous from the point of view of draining—the western portion of the Souris River loop in North Dakota and the glacial till soil along the James in South Dakota. Abandonment took place before construction, though after authorization and public announcements of plans, expensive both in the costs of surveys and in public hopes aroused and disappointed. Smaller irrigation schemes below some of the flood-control dams on the Plains were shelved at the same stage for similar reasons. Men inside the Bureau knew better than to irrigate these sites. After sometimes rather heated controversy, which in the case of the Souris and James River valley sites required the appointment of boards of outside consultants to restudy the projects, their warnings were heeded.

At other projects storage dams were built before problems of irrigated agriculture were faced. Sometimes it was due to congressional eagerness, as in the case of Cedar Bluff, Bonny, Shadehill, Dickinson—dams which were built for flood control and irrigation, but which promise very little actual irrigation. In the case of the large Lower Marias project in Montana, the dam is nearly finished. The Bureau proposed in 1955 to start a pilot irrigated farm to assess "serious water and drainage problems peculiar to the unit" before building the canals. But farmer interest did not justify even that expense.[4]

The Bureau had, by 1955, established sixteen "development farms" at the sites of future irrigation projects. All were in the central tier of states, where irrigation presents new problems: three in North Dakota, four in South Dakota, five in Nebraska, four in Kansas. Their purpose was partly promotional; Glenn Sloan conceived them primarily as demonstrations to surrounding farmers. But they were also experiments in the economics of irrigation and in the cropping systems adapted to it. In 1956, the Bureau planned to grant some $29,000 to the Department of Agriculture and the respective state colleges of agriculture to help conduct these experiments.[5]

In thus changing its emphases the Bureau of Reclamation encountered an inevitable obstacle. "There was a feeling," Congressman Rockwell of Colorado expressed it, "that here was a sudden desire to develop an agricultural department within the Reclamation Service." In the relatively sympathetic atmosphere of the House Committee on Public Lands, Congressman Rockwell in 1947 chaired what he called a "seminar" on the Reclamation-Agriculture jurisdictional problem which had come to a head in the Missouri basin.[6] The result was an impasse. Reclamation could not be allowed explicitly to "duplicate" the personnel of the Department of Agriculture. But Agriculture could not be allowed to share in determining the feasibility of a reclamation project because, as Wyoming Congressman Barrett told Mr. Charles F. Brannan, "you want to be certain the West doesn't compete too seriously with other sections. . . ."

Mr. Brannan, who was then Assistant Secretary of Agriculture, came to Washington from Denver. He had taken no small part in formulating and pressing for the Wheeler-Case legislation. Perhaps that was why he had the temerity to take his stand squarely athwart the tradition of the boomers of the West: "if there is going to be a subsidy . . . let us put it at the beginning, and let everybody know that it is to be put there." But Congressman Barrett, like his colleagues from the western states, intended to pursue "what is really a development program for the West" under the rugged slogan of "reimbursement by the settler." He had already discovered a Department of Agriculture employee saying in public that "the Government has been spending from $200 to $500 an acre for irrigation" in the West. (Sloan plan irrigation was even then priced at $300 an acre, according to the Reclamation Bureau.) "If that fellow wants to kill our reclamation program, he is going about it in a pretty good way."

The problem seemed to the Public Lands Committee to be a typical bureaucratic squabble. Chairman Rockwell suspected that it had been the stubborn personality of Secretary Ickes that had blocked solution. The Bureau of the Budget had already been trying to settle the question of jurisdiction through interdepartmental agreement. It is still trying. For the dispute extends to philosophies. So obvious did this become, even in the congressional committee, that an Oklahoma congressman finally asked Mr. Brannan to state "what the philosophy of the Department of Agriculture is." But philosophies, of course, are localized: in the country, in the departments, and in Congress. A California congressman got down to brass tacks:

Mr. Brannan, . . . taking the attitude that you are strictly a westerner, I am going to ask you a very pertinent question. Is it not true that Congress operates, you might say, on quite a sectional basis? . . . We also look on the personnel of the Agriculture Committee, and for years and years they have been strictly South and eastern controlled. Are we not, from the West, subjugating ourselves to a certain extent to the influences of the southern and eastern farmers . . . with their great preponderance on the committees and with their control of the Agriculture Department. . . .[7]

As for the Reclamation program, "it is," said Congressman Barrett, "our baby."

It is a measure of the good will of the bureaucrats concerned that they have extended across the rift in public purpose a modest list of co-operative agreements. These have been prompted, as might be supposed, not mainly in Washington, but in the basin itself. The Department of Agriculture tried in 1947–49 to defend its jurisdiction as conscientiously as the Interior Department rebuffed the Wheeler-Case approach. Colleges of agriculture, their Extension services especially, in the western states received encouragement from Washington not to accept contracts to do research or extension work for the Bureau of Reclamation until interdepartmental jurisdiction had been settled higher up. But the invitation to help plan the great agricultural changes which the Bureau of Reclamation had in store, and to do it with support from Reclamation appropriations, proved too attractive. By 1948 directors of the agricultural experiment stations in the Missouri basin states insisted on meeting in Washington with the Department of Agriculture research bureaus and the Bureau of Reclamation. In 1949, the Department sought and obtained a small appropriation to assist the experiment stations to perform soil surveys upon prospective reclamation sites and to do research in the economics of irrigation. An unprecedented series of studies has resulted, jointly supported, jointly conducted, and jointly used by the Department of Agriculture, the Bureau of Reclamation, and the colleges. We now have the beginnings of scientific knowledge about what water does to glacial soils. We know how much more time and money irrigation requires of the farmer, as well as how much more he gets out of it; how quickly irrigated homesteads have actually got into farm production; what irrigated crops can be marketed from proposed projects; how much water should be applied, and how much fertilizer; what crops do best.

Unfortunately, once the physical plans have been laid, the best foresight is not readily translated into wise decisions. Take the key objective of using irrigation to stabilize unirrigated farming on the Plains. It is one of the chief goals of the Sloan plan. For even under complete development, irrigation will directly reach but 5 per cent of the basin's farm acres.

In a semiarid grazing economy, using crude irrigation techniques, surrounding range land inevitably benefited from the irrigated oasis. Wyoming is the classic case. Only 5 per cent of its farm acreage is irrigated, but 57 per cent of all Wyoming farm units have some share of that irrigated land. Hence the unexampled stability of Wyoming's agriculture during the dry thirties.

It is not this small-scale irrigation on each individual farm that the Bureau of Reclamation plans farther east. Accordingly, the Bureau helped support

—*Harold Corsini,* Fortune

Montana wheat. The dark strips have been tilled fallow to store as much as possible of a twelve-inch rainfall for next year's crop. Water conservation brought near perfection creates this magnificent landscape. The Missouri River runs through the background bluffs. Water has some of its vital meanings for this basin apart from the river.

—B. C. McLean, Soil Conservation Service

On the Plains it is wind as well as water—too little or too much—that does the damage. The dark coating on top of the snowdrift in the Nebraska fence row is topsoil blown off the field of winter wheat behind it. The date is 1955, not 1935.

—N. T. Novitt, Bureau of Reclamation

On the Earl E. Colwell ranch near Mirage Flats, Nebraska, fifty of a thousand head of cattle died in the 1949 blizzard. In this basin control of the river leaves a lot of nature untamed.

a research project to find out what have been the stabilizing effects on the surrounding agriculture of five going Reclamation projects.[8] The findings are complex, but they demonstrate quite clearly that the hoped-for stabilizing influence does not automatically come into being with the introduction or even the continued operation of irrigated farms in the midst of a dry-crop or range economy. The Montana study showed that "the long, narrow irrigated areas are likely to have more range and dry cropland integration than are the large, compact irrigated areas where many farms are a substantial distance from range land or dry cropland." [9] Yet the present Reclamation plan for the sub-humid Plains is for million-acre tracts. Under the stimulus of the market alone, irrigation farmers may grow very little feed for the surrounding range livestock economy. The Milk River project was found to be relatively useful in this regard, but it could carry only one-tenth of the cattle in the county in case of drought. The North Platte project, well established and prosperous, provides a livestock market, but very little feed, to ranchers in the vicinity.[10] Irrigation farmers who themselves wish to integrate their operations with range livestock growing have found it difficult to acquire range near either project. Buford-Trenton, the North Dakota Wheeler-Case project, met this problem through co-operative ownership by the irrigators of 5,000–6,000 adjoining acres of range. Unless integration through such common ownership furnishes the key, stabilization may require "something resembling an ever-normal granary or ever-normal haystack. This organization should not only store large supplies of feed during the good years; it should make them available to stockmen at reasonable prices when drought increases demand." [11] This proposal is, of course, far removed from any conceivable function of the Bureau of Reclamation. Yet the benefits on which the Bureau counts may depend squarely on such agricultural adaptations.

There is, however, an even more immediate problem to solve on the way to interdepartmental co-operation. How are the Department of Agriculture's appropriations to be kept in step with the expanding needs of the Reclamation program. In pleading for $805,000 to step up the Agriculture program of assistance to irrigation during 1952–53, a Department spokesman used this illustration:

In December 1949 the president of Wyoming State College called a meeting of the Bureau of Reclamation, the Bureau of Agricultural Economics, the Soil Conservation Service, and our Bureau [Plant Industry, Soils and Agricultural Engineering] in which he stressed the urgency of the problem on the Riverton [Wyoming] project. The Bureau of Reclamation has provided a development farm. We participated in the selection of the area. However neither the Bureau of Plant Industry nor the Soil Conservation Service have had any funds to initiate the proposed research on this Riverton project. On the Riverton project . . . primarily because of salinity of the soil and drainage problems, approximately 15,000 acres have gone out of cultivation or have had production seriously impaired . . . . you have here 70,000 acres under irrigation with plans for doubling this area, but no research program is provided for.[12]

It was the war veterans given the privilege of homesteading unirrigable lands at Riverton who paid the real price for the lack of vigorous independent research into the agricultural feasibility of the extension.

Another illustration: The Farmers Home Administration (successor to the New Deal Farm Security Administration) is commonly the only source of credit available to the new irrigator. He already has a lien on his farm to repay the Bureau of Reclamation, but he needs a house, fences, farm buildings, and (by actual calculation on one project) $10,000 worth of stock and machinery. Yet the Farmers Home Administration can lend no more than $3,500 to each farmer. And its appropriations suffice to reach but one applicant in three who need credit unobtainable from private banks.[13]

The reaction of the House Appropriations Committee to these needs reflected, in its general tone, a current economy wave. But its specific form should give pause to advocates of voluntary inter-agency co-operation. Chairman Whitten of the Committee asked, ". . . should this committee let you get us in the position of providing funds by region . . . ?" The Agriculture witness pleaded his Department's need to perform these expanded services incidental to irrigation projects and brought along a Bureau of Reclamation witness to back up the plea. This did not impress a committee whose jurisdiction was strictly agriculture. Chairman Whitten could hardly, therefore, have realized the historical irony of his question, the exact reciprocal of that put by the chairman of the Public Lands Committee five years before. "Are you," he asked Secretary Brannan's emissary, "trying to set up a Reclamation Bureau within the Department of Agriculture?" [14]

Tri-County: Irrigation when It Does Not Rain

Halfway from Omaha to the Colorado border a broad band of irrigated farms stretches for 40 miles along the south bank of the Platte. It is the Tri-County Irrigation District (officially the Central Nebraska Public Power and Irrigation District).[15] East of the 100th meridian, this part of Nebraska averages 23 inches of rain; but in any year the Plains farmer here may actually get from 11 to 41 inches. That is not arid or even semiarid, but subhumid climate, wetter by 5 inches of rain than the great tract marked for Sloan-plan irrigation in South Dakota, 8 inches wetter than the Souris area. It is, so far, the farthest reach of large irrigation canals toward the humid edge of the Northern Plains. As such, it offers a providential experiment by which to test the feasibility of the Sloan projects for the subhumid zone. Tri-County irrigation has been under way for thirteen years. The first data are in from the experiment. They show that irrigation can work in the fickle climate of the eastern Plains. But it has worked under conditions which, in relation to the law and practice of federal reclamation, are heterodox.

One reason the Tri-County project has been free to conform to subhumid conditions is the very fact that it is not a federal project, though its capital came from the P.W.A. It was chartered under a 1933 Nebraska law, without connection to the U.S. Bureau of Reclamation. The District generates hydropower at the large Kingsley Dam farther west on the North Platte. It uses power revenues to help pay for building the irrigation system, just as the Sloan plan does on a larger scale. But to collect the cost allocated to irrigation it uses a novel contract far closer to the arrangement of the city customer with the municipal water utility than to the Bureau of Reclamation contract. Each farmer within the 168,000 acres of the project may sign up at the beginning of each year for a water supply to cover 40 acres or as much more as he wants. He gets the water at prescheduled times and pays a flat $2.50 per acre watered. On three years' notice, he may end all his obligations to buy water from the District. *The District has no lien against the farm* as a Bureau of Reclamation contract would require to assure repayment of project costs. The risk of the subhumid climate has not, in other words, been saddled upon the irrigated farm in order to stabilize the Great Plains economy. There was no need to mortgage the District farms to protect the invisible taxpayers of the United States. An organization of Great Plains farmers, sanctioned by the government of a Great Plains state, bears the risk. And even in a period of unprecedented wet weather, the risk has proved a good one.

Tri-County operates, secondly, as a gradual transition to a more reliable form of agriculture *for the group of farmers already there.* It was never intended as a way of peopling a desert tract. When the canals came through, farmers in the area simply applied water to the existing crop they had been growing at high risk—corn. They used less of their acreage for wheat, and since they had a quarter-section or more insured against drought, they could take the risk of dispensing with summer fallow in the wheat they did plant. The net increase in grain yield they fed to livestock, and the numbers of their animals increased twice as much as on the surrounding unirrigated farms. All this took more labor and returned more income. So gradually they sold off parts of their previously large farms. Irrigation thus provides a living for a gradually increasing number of farmers. Within the Tri-County District, farms averaged 10 per cent smaller in 1952 than in 1940; the dry farms outside had meantime become 10 per cent larger. Thus painlessly, the objective of a family-sized farm under irrigation is achieved. The results are not materially different from those which would have been achieved had the Bureau of Reclamation's 160-acre limit been imposed at the start. But the results have been attained without ultimatum. And every farmer knows there is no ceiling on the extent of the irrigation to which he can someday apply his managerial skill, should he excel at it.

The changeover to irrigation takes money and skill. Leveling a field for most efficient ditch irrigation, for instance, has cost Tri-County farmers $73 per acre. They have been able for the most part to bear this cost because they have been able to spread it over a period of years while they continued dry farming on part of the land. They have gradually acquired the ditching and other equipment and the livestock to handle larger irrigated fields. They have made the transition at their own pace, the young farmers faster than the old. Yet, oddly enough, within seven years from the delivery of the first water, 40 per cent of the entire project acreage was being irrigated. The Bureau of Reclamation's North Platte project, chosen as a conventional reclamation site in the much drier country on Nebraska's western border, has exactly the same portion of its original acreage in irrigation now twenty-five years after completion.

Irrigation, on the Tri-County project, is a way for farmers to make a larger income more reliably. It was not intended to serve the manifest destiny of the nation to settle the Plains with equal homesteads. In its own prosaic terms, it is working. Corn, which in the five years 1945–49 yielded 20 bushels to the acre dry-farmed, made 49.6 bushels in the *average* irrigated field. Alfalfa, otherwise unsuited to this part of the state, grew 4.4 tons to the acre. After paying his water cost, the typical farmer of a half-section, with 100 acres of it under irrigation, netted $1,389 in 1946. It was no bonanza, but it was $577 more than he would have earned without irrigation. Tri-County farmers still have a long way to go before they get the most out of irrigation. (By planting some sugar beets and using more water they could, according to the state agricultural experiment station, earn another $1,000 on the same half-section.) But they are on their way. This is the first generation of irrigators, not the third to come in after the first two have moved off bankrupt. They planned their own project. In a zone of climatic transition, they allow themselves time to learn to look to the ditch for rain. In a zone where artificial water will never reach more than one acre out of ten vulnerable to drought, they use it combined, on the same farm, with a larger dry acreage. Four out of five Tri-County farm operators prefer this practical form of integration. The Bureau of Reclamation has progresssed to the point of having one or two

"Development Farms" to demonstrate the advantages of irrigation in every prospective project area. In Tri-County, every farm became a development farm.

Experience on the Plains is a dear teacher. Out of the dry decade came the Wheeler-Case projects to demonstrate their workability on the western Plains and Tri-County, an unheralded state project, functioning successfully in the subhumid eastern Plains. The Bureau of Reclamation has yet to show that its traditional pattern fits either climate zone. Why should the state projects not go ahead to do the job?

The first obstacle is money. Fifty million dollars from the Public Works Administration got Tri-County and the related power projects under way. Irrigation on the Plains can no more dispense with a subsidy under local than under Bureau auspices. In 1952, interestingly enough, a Nebraska irrigation district still farther east than Tri-County proposed a solution to the subsidy problem.[16] This was the Nebraska Mid-State Reclamation District, organized under a new Nebraska law. Mid-State has a plan, prepared by Adolph F. Meyer, an outstanding Minnesota consulting engineer, to extend irrigation 100 miles farther east than Tri-County, on the opposite (north) bank of the Platte. The plan is a spectacular one. It calls for dams in twenty-three parallel ravines that now debouch flood waters perennially southward into the Platte valley. A canal interconnecting all these small reservoirs would lead water from the Platte to irrigate more than a quarter-million acres. In six small plants some 34,000 kilowatts of power capacity would be generated at drops in the canal. One of the most interesting features of the scheme is the plan to intersperse canal with pump irrigation. Pumps already serve a quarter-million acres in the area, and the use of ground water has a bright future. The pumps will pick up some of the irrigation water which would otherwise be lost to the subsoil. Moreover, they will ease the drainage problem.

For four years, property holders in the Mid-State District have paid a small tax levy to support the planning, and later part of the operating costs, of the project. This should, said J. K. McKinney, district secretary, demonstrate their serious commitment to irrigation through the wet years as well as the dry. Mr. McKinney thought construction of the project might cost 40 million dollars. Most of this could be financed by revenue bonds, reimbursed largely through the sale of power. But he asked the Missouri Basin Inter-Agency Committee why the Mid-State project should not, like the Bureau of Reclamation, charge off to flood control (and hence support by the federal treasury) the part of the multiple-purpose project allocable to that purpose. It was a fair question, still unanswered in 1955. Would conservation of the marginal waters of the Great Plains again prove too big a job for the local people who understood its needs and too unique a job for the national agencies, which could muster the money and the strength?

How to Get Irrigation Done

The Missouri basin desperately needs the security from drought to which irrigation is an indispensable contributor. It is not getting it under present Reclamation Act policies. They were designed to settle deserts, not to stabilize farming. The experience of this basin with irrigation suggests with amazing clarity what must be done, and what can be done to produce results.

1. Operation and reimbursement of irrigation farming enterprises which are publicly financed ought to be made the responsibility of state governments. Three reasons for this are inescapable. Businesslike repayment can never be expected while the homesteader or his district is dealing directly with Congress. All the sentiments of manifest destiny and the pioneering of the West stand in the way. It is the state, secondly, which can realistically assess the indirect commercial and social advantages which an irrigation project confers on communities around it. State law can recapture these benefits through taxation (Colorado and North Dakota already permit it through conservancy districts) and thus join the merchant to the farmer in repayment. Thirdly, the state agricultural program, with the experiment station and extension service, is the program best fitted, indeed indispensable, to predict the economic success of the project and assure the realization of the returns predicted. The United States should therefore enter contracts with the state in which each project is located for the repayment of the cost designated as repayable. The settlement and agricultural supervision, the legal organization of the district, and the adjustment of the payment responsibilities of individual farmers should be the direct concern of the state, of course with federal advice and assistance. All state governments in the Missouri basin are now amply competent to discharge this responsibility. Some are competent to go further. Nebraska, North Dakota, and Montana have demonstrated that they can plan and build successful irrigation projects. There is no reason why the United States should not facilitate their doing so, rather than assuming that its own aims can only be attained by building its own irrigation works.

2. The rewards of irrigation in the Missouri basin come only through its agricultural success. That should be its main emphasis in planning. Certainly, therefore, the Department of Agriculture should, as the President's Water Resources Policy Commission proposed, report upon the agricultural feasibility of irrigation projects before they are submitted to Congress for authorization. But that is not the fundamental problem. Money to support agricul-

tural investigation and planning must be committed in the same decision which launches other irrigation planning. All irrigation alternatives, whether by canal or pump, and by whomever financed, must be considered to promote agricultural stability on the Plains. Every irrigation farm must be considered a test and demonstration of the farming results. The whole gamut of agricultural programs—soil survey, selection of irrigators, extension, agronomic and economic research and experiment, credit, farm planning, soil conservation, Agricultural Conservation Program payments—can and should be geared to making a success of irrigation once it is jointly planned. The state government can focus on the project these services which are in any case largely co-operative state-federal services.

3. The United States can afford to give specific assistance to irrigation under these circumstances in return for specific conditions assuring federal benefits. The United States should maintain and contribute:

a) The data collecting, engineering, and other technical planning service. Conception of some of these services as reimbursable by the farmers under reclamation law cripples planning. Their availability to the states would permit the states to do much more of the planning of irrigation.

b) The cost of general public values created by flood control, stream sanitation, and other non-irrigation features of multiple-purpose projects. There is no reason why the Mid-State plan in Nebraska should not receive federal support for the flood-control benefits the United States finds will result from it, provided its control works will operate under federal flood-control directives.

c) Interest-free capital for financing irrigation projects.

d) Tax subsidy to the extent that the proposed project is found by the United States to reduce drought hazards which would otherwise create a potential charge upon the Treasury for drought relief.

But the conditions should be clearly imposed. Projects should meet the engineering standards of the United States. They should fit the basin-wide plan for river development. They should comprehend all the economical water-use purposes which the stream affords at the site. Cost allocation should be approved by the President and Congress. Maximum benefits to off-site farming should be designed into the project. This may mean small projects in preference to large ones or the inclusion of pump irrigation integrally with canal irrigation.

Unless changes are made in these three directions, it is very clear what will happen to irrigation in the basin. Wet years will balk both acceptance and repayment. Dry years will find projects incapable of sound expansion. The cumbersome and politically charged mechanisms of the reclamation program will continue to fall victim to the booster psychology alternating with the relief psychology. Pressure for reclamation projects will continue to be irresponsible. It will come from the chambers of commerce and the reclamation associations without regard to willingness to pay for the anticipated benefits. States will press for projects without regard to their conviction of their economic soundness. They will resist the use of water in other states without regard to their intent to use it within their borders.

Yet it is also clear that such basic changes in Reclamation Act provisions cannot be made for the country as a whole. Indeed, they ought not to be. It would be as reckless, for instance, to weaken the 160-acre limit in federal law for the huge irrigated plantations of California's Central Valley as it is frustrating and needless to apply it in Nebraska.[17] What is needed is precisely what the Pick-Sloan authorization claimed to provide: basin legislation.

FLOODS IN THE RIVER AND FLOODS ON THE LAND

Past the Nebraska capitol and into the city storm sewers of Lincoln flows a pleasant, if mildly sullied, stream called Salt Creek. Just before it empties into the Platte, it is joined by a creek of even more rustic name, the Wahoo. Their combined watersheds embrace practically all the area—fertile, almost level, and prosperous—of Lancaster and Saunders Counties, and the edges of four counties more. One three-hundredths of the surface of the Missouri River basin is in the Salt-Wahoo drainage. But with some special exceptions we will note, that barely visible fraction is the only part of the great basin in which there is now promise that flood control for the cities below will be linked with flood control on the land where the rain beats down.

On May 8, 1950, a flash flood of Salt Creek hurt Lincoln badly. Water entered 580 houses and 80 business buildings. Three of the city's bridges across the creek were broken. Outside the city the damage from both the Salt and the Wahoo, though less evident, was equally costly. Worst of all, the suddenness of the flood caught and drowned eight persons. During the next few weeks, every family in the drainage area was moved by the feeling that something ought to be done. But then there had been general indignation after the flood in 1947, in 1942, and even in 1908. Floods always galvanize the people who see them. This time the indignation was channeled into action, and the action still goes on.

The instrument of action was the Salt-Wahoo Watershed Association, a purely voluntary body with the avowed purpose of joining soil-saving with flood control in the stream channels. Though nominally all the watershed's 135,000 residents were members, the Association's charter was approved at a "mass meeting" of 425 people at the state fair grounds a few months after the flood. The group was more representative in its composition than its numbers. With influential city folk—Lincoln's mayor, several bankers, a newspaper editor—were teamed some of the solid farmers from the upper reaches of the creeks. Otto Liebers, leading dairy farmer of Lancaster County, was named co-chairman.

Results came at once. In July Nebraska Congressmen Curtis and Stefan asked the House Public Works Committee to authorize a flood-control survey by the Department of Agriculture. The committee complied forthwith. The Army Engineers had made their survey six years before, but it had languished for lack of local enthusiasm since its only proposed works left Lincoln and all the land above unprotected. Now the Engineers recalculated flood damages, and in October made public plans for four dams and long levees, including some storage above Lincoln. The reaction of the Watershed Association was forthright: "Under no circumstances will the Salt-Wahoo association or the people of the area be ready even to consider such proposals as the army engineers are making until the department of agriculture survey, embracing a combination of on-the-land soil and moisture conservation and small temporary reservoirs in the uppermost tributaries has been completed." [18] The Association did not stop with this public remonstrance. It "took the matter up both at the top—through Senator Wherry and General Pick—and at the local level—by inviting representatives of the army engineers to farm meetings it was holding throughout the area." [19] With the Corps' plan balked politically, joint planning became possible. By this time, Soil Conservation Service engineers had accumulated their own data as to flood damages and risks. Therefore, both agencies set out in 1951 to restudy the watershed's flood-control needs with collaboration at every step.

Now the Salt-Wahoo Watershed Association took on the job of keeping public interest alive while sound planning could be done. In June, 1951, it received considerable assistance from nature. A second flood struck Lincoln, this time from a cloudburst over tiny Antelope Creek. That reemphasized the need for flood protection as near the headwaters as possible. In ten days the Association called a public meeting in a Lincoln park still littered with debris from the high water. It appeared that the engineers of the Corps and the Soil Conservation Service had become a team in their planning mission. Serious problems remained before floods were stopped throughout the watershed. The metropolitan sanitary district, for example, had to be fitted into the control plan; a quarter-century before it had shortened Salt Creek from 66 to 31 miles without taking thought of the effects below. Nevertheless, there were strong reasons for optimism.

First was the leadership of the Association. Its instigator and co-chairman, along with Mr. Liebers, was Raymond A. McConnell, Jr., editor of the Lincoln *Journal*. Mr. McConnell's newspaper crusaded for the watershed approach to flood control with the imagination and zeal that once won it the Pulitzer Prize. The editor of a leading Republican newspaper in Nebraska, moreover, was able to get quick attention for the Association's proposals from the Nebraska delegation in Congress. By doing a great deal of traveling and public speaking, Mr. McConnell and his farm editor, Stanley Matske, and Mr. Liebers spread the idea of the small watershed association through much of Nebraska, Kansas, and Iowa. It is not easy to find champions of such verve and articulateness among the "grassroots" of every creek and river drainage.

The Salt-Wahoo approach was promising, secondly, because it was addressed to a very small watershed. The area did not reach outside the circulation radius of the Lincoln newspapers or the Lincoln retail trading area. It was in a single state and in only two Congressional districts. Once the urban-rural suspicion had been prudently allayed, its people had a visible common interest. If government programs for flood control, fragmented in Congress and the executive departments, could be put back together wholly by grassroots initiative, the best chance surely would be found in a drainage area so compact as this.

The joint flood-control survey was scheduled for submission to Congress on January 2, 1952. Congress never got it. Sometime between the flood of 1951 and the next January, to quote a congressman who looked into the situation, "the inter-agency honeymoon ended." [20] The Corps found it could not complete its resurvey until May, 1952. The Watershed Association insisted that some plan be included in the Department of Agriculture's supplementary report to Congress on the over-all agricultural program for the Missouri basin. So the agricultural flood-control plan was released first and independently of the downstream flood-control plan.[21]

The Missouri Basin Survey Commission analyzed both plans later in the year (Figure 14). As one might expect, it found that neither wholly met the needs of the entire watershed. Of the half-million dollars of annual flood damages which the surveys together assessed against the streams, $300,000 were for damages to farm lands about which the Corps of Engineers proposed to do nothing. On the other hand, the Department of Agriculture plan was focused on erosion and flooded bottom lands in the upper watershed. It could not give adequate protection to the city of Lincoln and areas below. The proposed works and benefits overlapped. Taken together, they claimed more flood-control benefits than there were flood damages.[22]

It seemed probable that approval of one plan might, in fact, rule out the other. General Sturgis of the Corps told Congress that construction by the Department of Agriculture of the little works to hold upstream floods might reduce damages from frequent lesser floods enough to remove the economic justification for building reservoirs and floodwalls big enough to save Lincoln from catastrophic floods.[23] But in 1952 the House Committee on Agriculture received the Soil Conservation Service plan; the Public Works Committee was left to receive the unreconciled plan of the Engineers. Here were two legislative committees, complained a member of one of them, "viewing the same problem from separate corners." [24]

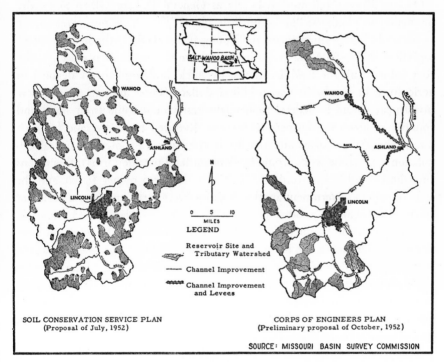

| SOIL CONSERVATION SERVICE PLAN | CORPS OF ENGINEERS PLAN |
| (Proposal of July, 1952) | (Preliminary proposal of October, 1952) |

SOURCE: MISSOURI BASIN SURVEY COMMISSION

Fig. 14. Two separate plans to control floods in the watershed of Salt and Wahoo Creeks.

THE YOUNG PLAN

Meanwhile, a third plan for the Missouri basin was introduced in Congress in 1949 on the scale of the Pick and Sloan plans. It was comprehensive for agriculture in exactly the sense that the earlier plans were comprehensive for the river: it proposed all the conservation measures deemed to be worth their cost—all the measures within the jurisdiction of the department that planned it. The popular name of the plan is that of Gladwin Young, then representative of the Department of Agriculture in the basin. But it was actually an institutional product compiled by men from many agencies of the Department: Forest Service, Soil Conservation Service, Bureau of Agricultural Economics, Production and Marketing Administration, Farmers Home Administration, Farm Credit Administration, Rural Electrification Administration, Agricultural Research Administration, Extension Service. These men had been used to planning for the agriculture of a state or the winter wheat belt or the corn region. But they could not let the dynamism of the valley development idea pass them by.

Once at it, they followed as boldly as General Pick or Glenn Sloan the injunction to planners: "Make no little plans! They have no power to stir men's souls." Over thirty years, the Young plan called for the investment of 8.5 billion dollars in Missouri basin agriculture.[25] By way of perspective, the 1945 value of all the land, buildings, livestock, and implements devoted to agriculture in the basin was 9 billion dollars. Three billions of the new investment would be federal money; the rest would come from states and counties or from the farmers themselves. Reduced to an average for each one of the 282,000 farms and ranches in the basin (a somewhat unreal calculation since some work would be done on land outside farms), this means that the United States would invest $5,000, the farm owner $9,000, and the state or county government another $750 for every farm unit over a period of thirty years. Taking another perspective, the Young plan would triple the rate at which the national government had hitherto spent money on agricultural programs in the basin—some 30 million dollars per year. It would add 3 billion dollars of federal outlay to the Department of the Interior's plan for 3.2 billion dollars, and the Corp of Engineers' plan for 2.7 billion dollars.

These, in summary form, are the results the Department of Agriculture proposed to show by combining this investment with the improvements installed by farmers and local governments.

The basin's 113 million acres of cropland (one-fourth of the nation's) would be put into sustained yield usage. That would raise farm output 30 per cent, Mr. Young calculated, as compared to 12 per cent resulting from Sloan-plan irrigation. It would also retard water and sediment flow. Two figures indicate the dimensions of the change. Of every 6 acres cultivated today, one would be taken from continuous corn or wheat and put to grass: 10 million acres to permanent sod, 10 million acres to rotation. The plow-up of the Dust Bowl during and since the war would thus be reversed. On the basin's range land, more extensive than its crop acres, half again as many cattle and sheep would be permanently sustained. Where in the last fifteen years 250,000 ponds to water stock have been created, 400,000 more would be installed. All this would cost the United States 1.2 billion dollars, the landowners three times that much.

To the 15,168 miles of shelterbelts President Roosevelt's plan got planted across the basin Plains, 245,000 miles would be added. Five million acres of forest land on the eastern and western edges of the basin would be planted in trees.

Water in the small watercourses on or below farms would be temporarily detained behind 14,000 to 16,000 small dams, totaling two-thirds the storage of Fort Randall reservoir. It would be detoured around gullies by 60,000 miles of ditches or dikes. Every watershed would be treated with something like the intensity of the Salt-Wahoo plan. It would cost the United States one billion dollars.

The 38,000 irrigated farms now in the basin will increase to 75,000 when the Sloan plan is fulfilled. The Department of Agriculture proposed to spend 200 million dollars to aid the transition by means of soil surveys, economic studies, credit and extension of information to new irrigators, farm planning, experimentation with irrigated crops.

As much more land in the basin needs drainage (5.8 million acres) as is irrigated now. The Young plan would rehabilitate half the present drainage systems; it would extend drains in the one and one-half million acres to be behind Corps of Engineers levees. Cost to the United States: 32 million dollars.

To support these action programs, the Department proposed to carry on relatively inexpensive but essential programs of research, extension of information to farmers, soil surveys, agricultural credit, special rural electrification studies. It is always very difficult for engineers and politicians to understand why, even to alter the farm practices of a quarter of a million highly individual farmers, such "frills" are required. An Iowa extension supervisor tried to explain it this way:

About twenty-some years ago . . . hybrid corn came to Iowa and other states, and in many places it was adopted overnight, yet . . . it took the Iowa farmer, with the extension service of Iowa State College spending a great deal of time working with the Iowa farmer . . . 18 years to decide whether he was going to take his seed corn out of this sack or out of that sack. That was the only change in operation he had to make. My point is that . . . a stepped-up program of agriculture in the Missouri Basin will require that a research and extension educational program be a very important part of it.[26]

Unlike its counterparts, the Young plan was contrived with the day-to-day participation of scientists and the state and county agricultural agents who knew firsthand the needs of the farmers who use the soil and water. In many respects it fitted those needs. It was an agricultural plan; agriculture yields a quarter of the basin's income directly, even more indirectly. The plan was aimed squarely at restoring permanent high yields, and thus hope, to the farm enterprises which are losing the more skilled and better trained of their youth. It bore some connection to the river in its proposals for retarding runoff of tributaries, making irrigation a farming success, and draining acres given flood protection. Thus it could have captured some of the perennial enthusiasm for the dramatic potential represented in a great stream system.

The Young plan would also have extended its improvements out upon the Plains, where man has searched seventy-five years for a permanent system of cultivation. "Today," said the Secretary of Agriculture, "we do not possess that system." It sought thus to do the indispensable thing: to tie the visible work in the river to the imperceptible work on the wheatfields and the ranges. It comprehended protection against drought as well as flood, and drought, though it be less frequent, holds the greater ultimate threat to the basin. It contemplated scientific testing of the relative economic advantages of alternative methods of farming. There was not much boom and bust in the Young plan. And it proposed to involve the ordered participation of state colleges and extension services, of county governments, and of special local districts in the general program. It recognized that most of the work of developing a river basin belongs to the people who farm it and live in it, but they need to know exactly what it is prudent to do, and they need the obstacles which are too big for them individually taken out of the way.

No one proposed to substitute the Young plan for the Pick and Sloan plans. Yet in its own field it came closer than either of its predecessors to meeting the difficult requirements that the history and geography of the Missouri basin pose for success. Its weaknesses lay in another direction.

THE POLITICS OF BASIN AGRICULTURE

On July 21, 1949, the Missouri Basin Inter-Agency Committee meeting in Helena, Montana, generally endorsed the Young plan and asked Congress to put it into effect. Those responsible for the Pick-Sloan plan acknowledged that it required rounding out on the agricultural side. Here was the acid test: could the existing departments and congressional committees, to which the development of the basin had been consigned in 1944, redefine the plan to fit the demonstrably unmet needs?

When the Young plan reached Congress two months later, it was already evident that the endorsements of the river development agencies were hedged. The letter of comment from the Chief of Engineers, who was now Lewis A.

Pick, neither approved nor disapproved the agricultural plan. The Secretary of the Interior wrote: "It is especially desirable that the Department of Agriculture accelerate its conservation activities in this basin, in view of the comprehensive land and water development program of the Corps of Engineers and the Bureau of Reclamation already authorized in the Missouri Valley." [27] But he took sharp exception to the participation of the Department of Agriculture in planning federal irrigation; it might result in "shifting the authority long vested in that Bureau [Reclamation] to the Department of Agriculture." Jurisdictional lines at this and other points came first.

A closer reading of the comments from these agencies reveals a more fundamental reservation. They did not accept the Agriculture thesis that the Young plan was needed in order to achieve the full benefits of the Pick-Sloan reservoirs, levees, and canals. General Pick chose his words with care: "In my opinion, your report presents an exhaustive analysis of the long-range *agricultural* problems in the Missouri River Basin . . . and needed measures to *complement* the coordinated plan for flood control, navigation, irrigation, hydroelectric power development, and related water uses now being prosecuted by the Corps of Engineers . . . and the Bureau of Reclamation." [28] And the Secretary of the Interior had favored adding the Young plan to the existing "comprehensive land and water development program." Congress perforce thinks in terms of tangible benefits. The Bureau and the Corps would be glad to have a new set of benefits bestowed on the basin by another department. They showed no sympathy for the notion that the agricultural plan was necessary to achieve and maintain the benefits they had already claimed for their own programs.

The Department of Agriculture, for its part, was unable to estimate just how much its proposed activities would further the irrigation and flood-control programs. It was one thing to assert the connection, another to measure it. The Young plan included an estimate, for instance, that the silting-up of reservoirs to be built under the authorized programs would eventually destroy 6 million dollars worth of storage capacity each year. In the case of small headwater reservoirs, the Young plan could prevent 60 per cent of this sedimentation. But without large-scale tests, no one could say how much of the silt could be kept from behind the major dams.

The flood-control situation on the Kansas River was another case in point. Would any less space be needed in the big reservoirs—Tuttle Creek, Milford, Perry—assuming the whole of the watersheds above had been subjected to the most intensive feasible treatment in terms of terraces, strip cropping, check dams, and grassed watercourses? There were no facts with which to answer, though there were hopes, and even myths, aplenty.

The Department of Agriculture's basic handicap in this connection was the inherent complexity and unpredictability of agricultural and forestry improvements as compared to engineering. Most of the Young plan's works were vegetative; plants do not respond to human effort as uniformly as does earth to the bulldozer. The Young plan's uncertainties arose, too, out of the Department of Agriculture's dependence for the installation of the planned measures upon their acceptance by farmers or forest owners not beholden to the Department. Pick and Sloan works could only be *used* by the actions of farmers and businessmen. Many Young plan works could only be *created* by them.

Of course, some of the uncertainties could be eliminated by tryouts on the scale of entire watersheds. In some cases such experiments would invade the jurisdiction of the Corps or Bureau. Even otherwise, they would take a long time and a lot of money. In the meantime, the Department of Agriculture could not present an over-all justification of the Young plan in terms of dollars of Pick-Sloan cost saved or dollars of Pick-Sloan benefits added.

Take the example of a single program of forest management designed to increase water yields from the lodgepole pine stands high on the slopes of the Rockies. Eight years ago, Dr. W. G. McGinnies and Mr. H. G. Wilm of the Rocky Mountain Forest Experiment Station at Fort Collins, Colorado, found out that the amount of water running down from this particular type of forest can be increased by *thinning* the timber stands. This is heresy to the emotional conservationist, and it has been accepted in the forestry profession not without controversy. But the reasons for the increased flow are simple. Snow which falls to the ground evaporates less than snow lodged on the boughs (and thus in contact with the wind on all sides), and it melts later in the summer, when water is of more value for irrigation. But how *much* more water the thinned forest yields is another question. The experimental plots sometimes delivered 30 per cent more. The Department of Agriculture's Forest Service has never had the money to test an entire watershed. Quite conceivably, such a trial might show that cutting lodgepole pine in the right way could take the place of one or more major storage reservoirs.

Now the Forest Service is trying to find out in another way. It is trying to interest commercial logging firms in cutting the timber to government specifications. Is there a market for the modest-sized logs? Perhaps, if pulp mills are attracted to the base of the Rockies. Can the timber be got out cheaply, without gouging the mountainsides with skidways which will start erosion? At the Denver regional office, foresters think they have discovered the solution to this problem—an aerial cableway developed for the exploitation of Swiss forests. They are trying to demonstrate its business worth to the loggers. Meanwhile, it has been eight years since a typical Young-plan treatment measure was discovered. Its worth to the basin's development is promising but unmeasured.

When it received the Young plan, then, Congress found itself in the position of a man who has let a contract for a house to two builders, only to be told by a third firm (after construction was well along) that for an additional outlay of 50 per cent the house can be made habitable and weather-proof. Congress was not apt to be impressed as long as the original contractors insisted that their job was comprehensive and the new firm offered no figures of savings from the original contract price or of values added to the structure.

From the very beginning, however, the Department of Agriculture had relied partly upon a justification of its plan in terms of agriculture alone, aside from enhancement of the river programs. Perhaps half the improvements contemplated in the Young plan concerned the use of soil, not water, or the use of water in ways that had no significance for the flow of streams. Range improvement, strip cropping (beyond the limited area which might be contributing silt to a reservoir), increase of soil fertility, shelterbelts, restoration of sod on potential dust bowls and most of the drainage works of the Young plan—these are measures worth while for their improvement of soil and farm income. But there is no reason in the measures themselves to justify accelerating them within the confines of a particular drainage basin.

Consider the practical political question facing the Young plan, regarded as agriculture and not as river-basin development. Why should federal spending for the sake of agriculture in the northern half of Kansas, which drains into the Missouri, be triple the amount spent in the southern half, which drains into the Arkansas? Why should the western third of Iowa, which drains into the Missouri, be similarly preferred to the eastern two-thirds? This is the sort of question a senator would demand be answered. True, a good many of the plan's proposals were tailored to the Great Plains—shelterbelts, range ponds, restoration of sod on the drier wheatfields. But the Plains cut across, they do not coincide with, the basin. Most of the Young plan's treatment of the Plains farms and ranches would fit the Oklahoma Panhandle, or portions of Texas, and be justified there as in Montana.

The difficulties of the Young plan were not technical. They were economic only in the sense that contributions to the Pick-Sloan development could not be measured. The Young plan inspired more confidence than its predecessors in terms of increasing production and income. But the plan did fail to deliver the Department of Agriculture from a political dilemma. If the Department, on the one hand, justified the plan as a missing link in the programs for harnessing the river, it ran afoul of the Bureau and the Corps—their administrative jurisdictions and their prior claims to deliver unaided the benefits of irrigation and flood control, as well as their other programs. If, on the other hand, the Department put the Young plan forward because of its direct worth to farmers and to the nation's soil, then why limit it to the Missouri basin? There may once have been a time when governors, congressmen, and department heads felt constrained to overlook the logic of that dilemma. That would have been in the years when advocates of the Missouri Valley Authority attacked the Pick-Sloan plan effectively for neglecting soil, watersheds, and agriculture. But by 1952 the need to join hands against M.V.A. had obviously passed.

Representative Jamie Whitten, chairman of the subcommittee which handles Department of Agriculture appropriations when the Democrats are in power, told the Department witnesses exactly what their political position was in 1952. The Bureau and the Corps, he said, "proceed immediately to bottle the water up through the dams. Then you have to get the funds for the other part of it as best you can." [29]

THE NATIONAL POLITICS OF WATERSHEDS

Within a year, it became plain how the Department of Agriculture could best get its funds. On February 25, 1953, editor McConnell led a band of twenty-five watershed enthusiasts from various parts of the country to the White House. Five months later, President Eisenhower sent a message to Congress commending the principle of local initiative and local financial contribution toward a nationwide program of small watershed improvement.[30] Simultaneously, the Department got an appropriation for its first new flood-control projects in ten years.[31] The amount was only 5 million dollars a year, but with it the Department could meet the demands of sixty local watersheds for flood-control structures. The projects, scattered among thirty-four states, engendered ample enthusiasm to support the President's request for permanent legislation. In August, 1954, Congress passed the Hope-Aiken law.[32]

This Watershed Protection and Flood Prevention Act is one of the turning points in the policy and political orientation of the nation's water resources activities. It creates a new program of flood control, potentially as large as that of the Corps of Engineers. It gives the Department of Agriculture a jurisdiction in the field of water engineering. The limits are carefully defined: watersheds must not be larger than 250,000 acres, dams not larger than 5,000 acre-feet. Watershed work has its own agency now, the Soil Conservation Service. It has its base of political support in a new National Watershed Congress teamed with the National Association of Soil Conservation Districts. The fundamental weakness Representative Whitten diagnosed may not be cured, but it certainly has been radically treated. The Department of Agriculture need no longer wait until the big dams have been built and then get whatever federal support may be left.

The most noteworthy departure from federal policy embodied in the Hope-Aiken law is that it puts responsibility for building the works of watershed improvement—the small dams and streambank protection works as well as the grassed waterways and farm terraces—on local units of government or private landowners. Demand for a watershed protection program is expected to originate with a soil conservation district or watershed association. Its application for federal help must be reviewed by the state government. In response to the application, the Soil Conservation Service will survey the watershed and, if protection measures are feasible economically, design them. The local district will build them. The Secretary of Agriculture has the power to make a federal grant to the district, but first he must get the comments of the Corps of Engineers and the Department of the Interior, and give Congress forty-five days in which to reject or modify the plan. Congressional approval is not required. The proportion of the cost to be paid by the federal government is for the Secretary to decide. The Department estimates it at half on the basis of the pilot watersheds; that means that the local district and landowners may provide the land treatment while federal money pays for the dams and stream channel work.

A number of safeguards have been designed into the Hope-Aiken law against the pattern of logrolling which has come to characterize the selection of rivers for improvement by the Corps of Engineers and sometimes by the Bureau of Reclamation. Yet dams of a capacity between 2,000 and 5,000 acre-feet must be authorized by resolution of the agriculture committees of the House and the Senate. The Secretary of Agriculture, who decides otherwise what projects will be built and with how much federal money, has few and vague standards indeed to determine which of these very localized projects are of national concern. The price which is paid for local initiative in this law is the minimizing of the priorities set by the larger river developments for watershed improvement work. To this extent, the act turns back from the faltering attempts the nation has made for twenty years to see river basins whole.

In the Missouri basin, meanwhile, the Department of Agriculture began to build watershed treatment works for which idle plans had been accumulating. Fourteen of the sixty small watersheds being improved throughout the country by means of the special appropriation of 1953 are in the Missouri basin, four each being in Kansas and Nebraska. After the Hope-Aiken law passed, the Soil Conservation Service received valid applications for assistance from basin watersheds at the rate of one a month. They were all very small—the largest only a quarter the area of the Salt Creek–Wahoo drainage. But in two years the Department had doubled the watershed acreage on which it was installing protective works.

THE INTERDEPENDENCE in planning the river programs—navigation, irrigation, hydroelectricity, and the control of major floods—is so obvious in the very physical disposal of the river's water that it thrusts itself upon narrow agencies and single-purpose plans. But none of these ways of using the water that is in the river has any obvious dependence on the use of water on the land before it reaches the river. The theories of hydrology suggest there must be relationships; so do the common-sense notions of the farmer. But only patient, costly experiments on entire watersheds will permit them to be measured and predicted. Common-sense notions, in the meantime, are the raw materials of single-purpose crusades.

The Pick and Sloan plans now have their counterpart on the headwaters. Federal work in the basin will be more diversified and better distributed as a result. The basin will be rid of hundreds of cancerous gullies, of scores of perennially flooded creek bottoms, of thousands of eroding acres. But the relation of these valuable improvements to river development is defined by a fence among department jurisdictions and a balance among politically organized interests. Both the fence and the balance are nationwide. Meanwhile nobody knows to what extent watershed improvement will check floods on Salt Creek or the Little Sioux or the Kaw, much less the Missouri. Nobody knows to what extent it will keep reservoirs or floodways clear of silt. More important, nobody knows what combinations of watershed and river works would most increase the usefulness of the basin's water to man. An independent agricultural flood-control program may even lessen the determination to find out.

The Young plan of five years before had called for intensifying all the federal agricultural programs which fit the land and the economy of the Missouri basin. Congress failed to accelerate, for a drainage basin, programs which had no connection, direct or indirect, with the flow of water. But the Young plan also provided for agricultural measures desperately needed to make full use of water flow and river developments: the stabilization of small watersheds, extended and more efficient irrigation, greater water yields from basin forests, drainage of bottom land behind the new flood-protection levees of the Corps. Of all these measures, the Department of Agriculture has now achieved adequate support only for the first. Other programs to which the Young plan gave deserved priority in connection with the river development remain neglected.

It was a great strength of the Young plan, too, that it drew upon the highly competent research staffs in the state colleges of agriculture to devise programs precisely suited to the basin and upon the rural extension service to communicate the programs to farmers. The watershed protection program now under way, though it involves some tillage practices on watershed lands, resorts in the main to a standardized set of engineering treatments—terraces, diversion drains, drop structures, detention reservoirs, gully plugs, bank protection works. They are easy for a federal organization to plan, easy to budget, easy for Congress to understand. Farmers in one watershed can learn them easily from those in another. They make a strong national program, but not necessarily what the basin of the Missouri River needs most from the Department of Agriculture.

The Department has won political backing corresponding to that of the Corps of Engineers and the Bureau of Reclamation by sponsoring a program corresponding to theirs. At bottom it is a technique. Among techniques there can be jurisdictional awards; there is no basis for a meeting of minds, for there is no common purpose. So it proved with Congress and the Missouri Basin Inter-Agency Committee when the new technique of watershed protection came to be authorized. In 1954 the Senate Committee on Agriculture and Forestry heard it advocated by Gladwin Young, who when he was a member of the Inter-Agency Committee five years before had given his name to a more comprehensive agricultural plan. But the senators also heard it attacked by another former member of the Inter-Agency Committee, General Sam Sturgis. Now, as Chief of Engineers, he had no objection to watershed measures *as agriculture*. But he would deny them even the name of "flood control." [33]

There was a certain irony in the way history repeated itself. Similarly, ten years before, Glenn Sloan had come before congressional committees to question the comprehensiveness of the Pick plan; Secretary of Agriculture Brannan had come before another committee seven years before to question the comprehensiveness of the Sloan plan. Similarly, Congress solved the controversy as to techniques by adopting all of them and giving each agency a part of the basin. The shotgun wedding had now become bigamous.

The national watershed program got its first impetus in the little watershed of Salt and Wahoo Creeks. There, too, it showed its first results. In 1953 the Soil Conservation Service began putting up the first of thirty-four flood-retarding dams on the headwaters of the creeks. It was Kubic Dam—20 feet high, capable of controlling the flow from a section of farm land. So far, the

Soil Conservation Service has only been authorized half of the works it proposed for the prevention of floods on Salt Creek. Even of the full plan, the Missouri Basin Survey Commission had concluded: "This would be a very inadequate solution for the flood problems of the lower reaches of the streams. Standards of construction and margins of safety are appropriate for the agricultural area for which it was designed, but would be undesirably low for structures whose failure could endanger a populous area as large as Lincoln." [34] The Upper Salt Creek has been joined in administration and politics to Barnitz and Sandstone Creeks of the Washita drainage in Oklahoma, to the East Fork of the Trinity in Texas, to the Pee Dee watershed in South Carolina. It stands severed in government thought and action from lower Salt Creek, where it runs through Lincoln, fifteen miles below the new dams. A flood like that of 1950, which provoked the watershed movement, would hurt Lincoln severely.

What nature joined man hath put asunder. Reunion is a creative enterprise which seems to begin at the grassroots. The assumptions which inspire the small watershed movement hold good in the Missouri basin. But the experience of the basin teaches a more homely truth. Reunion cannot reach federal programs and agencies, congressional decisions, or interest groups if it begins at the grassroots alone. It is a job for which the Constitution provided a President.

Chapter x

FRONTIER OF GOVERNMENT

THOSE CITIZENS of the Missouri basin who can identify the head of the basin development (it is usually estimated, though without data, that four citizens in five profess ignorance on the point),[1] name the Inter-Agency Committee. The Committee is a group of the seven field representatives of the federal departments importantly or incidentally engaged in the work authorized by the 1944 Flood Control Act, and the governors of the ten basin states. The federal agencies are the Corps of Engineers; the Federal Power Commission; and the Departments of the Interior; Agriculture; Commerce; Labor; and Health, Education and Welfare, whose Public Health Service deals with stream pollution. All federal members ordinarily attend, perhaps half the governors, and an audience of fifty to one hundred. The Committee meets ten times a year, visiting in turn the larger towns in the basin. After the first day's business, the meeting invariably includes an inspection of some nearby construction site, plus the manifestation of western hospitality by the chamber of commerce of the host city: an outdoor or indoor steak fry with speeches.

Despite its episodic and peripatetic nature, despite the formal equality it accords to vitally and casually interested members—to the Corps of Engineers and the Department of Labor, to Nebraska which is wholly within the basin and Minnesota which has five counties in it—the Committee is often thought of as an organ of *government*. The mistake used to be fostered by the argument that the Committee took the place of the T.V.A. board of directors. But it still persists. In 1955, for example, the officer in charge of the Corps' work on the Missouri told a House committee that the Corps considered itself bound by an Inter-Agency Committee decision concerning the operation of its reservoirs. The response was as follows:

Mr. Davis (Representative from Wisconsin). We come to the next question, then, as to why the Corps of Engineers . . . can delegate its responsibility for decisions of this kind to an agency not recognized under Federal law. . . . In other words, it would be no answer to the people or to Congress if something went haywire and the division engineer in Omaha came here and said "I didn't make this decision. It was made by this group of people."

We say, "What group of people? We never heard of them. Show us in the statutes where they get the authority to make this decision." [2]

Congressman Davis cleared up the reason why the sessions of the Missouri Basin Inter-Agency Committee are like nothing so much as unusually amicable meetings of a specialized agency of the United Nations.

The Committee has no legal status. Certainly it never was delegated any power to direct the basin program. For it was established by a mere interdepartmental committee in Washington to provide "a means through which the field representatives of the participating Federal agencies may . . . coordinate their activities among themselves and with those of the States." [3] In this function of self-"coordination" the Committee has achieved some success. Most noteworthy was the production, in 1951, of a *Report on Adequacy of Flows in the Missouri River* for navigation assuming that other uses had been developed. This was subcommittee work. So is the annual operating plan for the Corps' completed mainriver reservoirs, the subject of the interrogation just quoted. The Committee's expanding membership (eight in 1945, seventeen in 1955) and its public sessions make it likely that actual co-ordination will come outside its formal sessions. The essential limits of its powers appear in its annual programing of state and federal expenditures in the basin for the six years ahead. This is useful, but it is a compilation of independent estimates which the Committee lacks any way of reviewing. The thirty-year, three-billion-dollar Young plan was added after two discussions totaling less than two hours. In Washington, the Secretary of the Interior objected in writing to the key features of the plan which had won the unanimous endorsement of the Inter-Agency Committee.

In the beginning, the strength of the Inter-Agency Committee grew in a direction far afield from its stated purpose—communication with the public. It became a forum to which a local irrigation district, a group of citizens wanting flood protection, or farm owners about to be moved out of a reservoir site could bring their pleas. After 1950, these protests dwindled. [4]

An average session of the Committee is attended by seven reporters of press and radio and by about as many representatives of interest groups of one kind or another. Newspaper coverage of its sessions, while inadequate within the basin, nevertheless supplies most of the information the public gets about the progress of basin development. In two ways, the Committee has served as a public school: awakening within all states a sense of "one river, one problem"; and showing the technicians as well as the interest groups the interrelation of various uses of water. The misapprehension that the Committee is deciding what shall be done in the basin, interestingly enough, has furthered this educational work by catching the public eye.

But the Committee sometimes functions to resolve political forces as well as to form opinion, and to understand this it is necessary to appreciate the role of the governors. They formed their own basin organization, called the Missouri River States Committee, three years before the Inter-Agency Committee was launched. In 1944 they took the initiative in attempting to force reconciliation of the Pick and Sloan plans. Hence it is not strange that though they were officially invited to the Inter-Agency Committee in 1945 as fraternal delegates, they quickly made themselves *de facto* voting members. It would be minimizing their role to say that they are now on a par with the department representatives. For being political figures, they are quite free to broach political controversies which would be "hot potatoes" to the administrators of federal programs. This is what Governor Phil Donnelly of Missouri did in 1947 when he obtained a joint resurvey of the Osage River subbasin, and what Governor Val Peterson of Nebraska did in 1951 when he got a subcommittee study of the long-term additional power needs of the basin. Motives of political ambition ulterior to the basin development cannot, of course, be wholly absent from these sallies. But the fact remains that the more vigorous governors can win reconsideration, though not necessarily disposition, of inter-agency stalemates and get lesser gaps in the program filled. They have thus steadily increased their relative strength in the Committee. After all, in the slowly spreading atmosphere of basin consciousness, co-ordinated development of the basin *is* good politics for a governor.

The surprise has therefore been the growing conviction on the part of the governors that the Missouri Basin Inter-Agency Committee is an inadequate co-ordinator for the basin development. The leading critic through 1952 was Governor Val Peterson of Nebraska, also chairman of the governors' Missouri River States Committee. Unless the Inter-Agency Committee's responsibilities were broadened, he said, "we're going out of business." [5] Clearly, the governors feared that a valley authority might gain acceptance unless co-ordination was otherwise provided. But that was not their only motive. For even as the prospects of M.V.A. legislation declined, they pressed harder for an alternative. The Inter-Agency Committee had taught its political lesson of the interdependence of water plans in a drainage basin so well that its administrative impotence began to show.

NATIONAL REORGANIZATION

This inadequacy will be no surprise to those who have followed the reports of the Hoover Commission. Conflict, not co-ordination, its original study of federal administrative organization concluded, is built into the overlapping jurisdiction of the Corps of Engineers and the Bureau of Reclamation. "The result has been hasty planning, lack of sufficient basic data, duplicating cost of surveying and estimating, failure to consider the entire needs of the area, and the creation of strong opposing local pressures each seeking special benefits." [6] And the Agriculture-Interior stalemate upon irrigated agriculture and the Agriculture-Corps of Engineers hiatus as to flood control, though less obviously wasteful, may prove greater handicaps to basin development. Inter-Agency Committee co-ordination cannot remove these conflicts for two reasons. Washington departments disputing jurisdiction cannot permit field arrangements to jeopardize their national case. And the governors learn of disjointed planning only after conflict has become public and the sins condemned by the Hoover Commission have already been committed. These conflicts could be avoided only by administrative, not merely political, co-ordination.

The first Hoover Commission found a second defect even less amenable to remedy by a basin committee in the Corps of Engineers. This was its inappropriate use of domestic river improvement work to train two hundred military engineer officers. The merits of this criticism belong to a national, not a regional, study.[7] But it is perilous to disregard the connection of this administrative problem with the politics of reorganization.

Every domestic military expenditure offers powerful attractions to the member of Congress. Throughout the nineteenth-century era of limited government, there were virtually no other strictly national public works to be distributed. Besides, the uniformed services usually built incorruptibly. In half a century free of serious warfare, logrolling became the rule as well on the location of cantonments as on the improvement of rivers. In 1901, however, strictly military planning was sternly subjected to the integrated control of Elihu Root's General Staff. A decade later, Quartermaster General Ainsworth, who put his trust in the chairmen of the House and Senate committees on military affairs rather than in the Secretary of War, was sacked for insubordination. The river work of the Corps of Engineers alone escaped this bold integration; militarily, it was unimportant. Congress tightened its grip on the Engineers' civil functions as it lost its hold on the Army posts, and in 1902 formally recognized the Corps as the staff agency of the Rivers and Harbors Committee. Thus entrenched, the Corps and the Committee circumvented the civilian control of the Secretary of War and the President via the executive budget, two decades later, even as it had escaped the military General Staff. Administrative unity of water-resource developments in which the Corps plays a part can only be had at the price of challenging this hitherto impregnable line of responsibility to congressmen.

This challenge the earlier Hoover Commission boldly delivered. Its proposal was to transfer all the river and harbor work from the Corps of Engineers to a consolidated "Water Development and Use Service" in the Interior Department. The reaction was more than worthy of the challenge. That member of the Commission, Senator John L. McClellan of Arkansas, who was also chairman of the Senate committee which would sponsor its reorganization plans had another loyalty. He was simultaneously president of the Rivers and Harbors Congress. Senator McClellan led the Senate fight to deny the President reorganizing power over the Corps. Ex-President Hoover forthrightly assailed the double play. But the peak of public interest in the Commission's proposals nevertheless passed without the President's submitting, or Congress's considering, a transfer plan. The second Hoover Commission, reporting in 1955, let the sleeping dog lie.[8]

A "Water Development and Use Service" would have one advantage over the Corps of Engineers of which the Hoover Commission did not take sufficient notice. It would bring to the planning of navigation and flood control the vision and techniques of more than the single profession of civil engineering. There are some, though not enough, engineers in the Corps today who appreciate that channel deepening is but a means toward the end of economical transportation and that flood control involves the management of soil cover and building permits as well as dams and dikes. But they have no practical way to combine their efforts with those of the other technicians needed to complete the job. Fifteen years ago, the same criticism could be made of the Bureau of Reclamation. But since then the infusion of agronomists, economists, and soils men into the Bureau has broadened it from a profession to a purpose agency. Even if a similar proportion of non-engineers were taken into the civilian staff of the Corps, a corresponding broadening of purpose would be balked by the fact that the positions of command are used to train military engineers.

The proposal of the first Hoover Commission would not, it must be added, resolve the jurisdictional problem which now prevents federal irrigation from being administered as farming. It would not assure that the distinctive problems of the Missouri basin would receive distinctive attention in legislation and administration. But it would cut away the greatest single hindrance to improved management. Is it not, then, the first step in the solution of the governmental problem of developing Missouri basin water potentialities?

In order to answer that question, we need as much as we can get of historical perspective.

Inquiry into the condition of the Mississippi and its principal tributaries reveals very many instances of the utter waste caused by methods which have hitherto obtained for the so-called "improvement" of navigation. . . .

Such shortsighted, vacillating, and futile methods are accompanied by decreasing water-borne commerce and increasing traffic congestion on land, by increasing floods, and by the waste of public money. The remedy lies in abandoning the methods which have so signally failed and adopting new ones in keeping with the needs and demands of our people.

In a report on a measure introduced at the first session of the present Congress, the Secretary of War said: "The chief defect in the methods hitherto pursued lies in the absence of executive authority for originating comprehensive plans covering the country or natural divisions thereof." In this opinion I heartily concur. . . .

The military engineers have undoubtedly done efficient work in actual construction, but they are necessarily unsuited by their training and traditions to take the broad view, and to gather and transmit to the Congress the commercial and industrial information and forecasts upon which waterway improvement must always so largely rest. Furthermore, they have failed to grasp the great underlying fact that every stream is a unit from its source to its mouth, and that all its uses are interdependent. . . . A physician who disbelieved in vaccination would not be the right man to handle an epidemic of smallpox. . . .

So with the improvement of our rivers, it is no longer wise or safe to leave this great work in the hands of men who fail to grasp the essential relations between navigation and general development and to assimilate and use the central facts about our streams.

That robust indictment was not delivered to Congress by Herbert Hoover, Franklin Roosevelt, or Harry Truman. President Theodore Roosevelt hurled it in 1908 and accompanied the words with as dramatic a campaign for public attention as he used in any of his political battles. He took a bargeload of governors and reporters down the Mississippi with him to see for themselves and to be seen in the nation's newspapers. But he failed.

In three years it will be half a century since that first defeat of national reorganization of water resources administration. As a task force of the first Hoover Commission commented ruefully, reform "has proceeded at a geologic pace." [9] Once only during that period has the nation gathered its river programs under a single management—in the Tennessee Valley Authority. So the task force, but not the parent Hoover Commission, was driven to conclude that unless reorganization of departments in Washington was achieved valley authorities might be indicated. There has not, in the succeeding six years, been any acceleration of the geologic pace.

When for half a century the most glaring need for administrative improvement has met immovable political resistance, there is a persuasive argument for a change of the political issue from the nationwide to the basin scale. In the case of the Missouri basin, there are good intrinsic reasons as well. Methods of planning and estimating which are wasteful elsewhere in the nation become profligate for a river so thoroughly unknown. Navigation techniques which are economically questionable elsewhere fail physically on this obstreperous stream. Jurisdictional conflicts which cause duplication and friction generally, here bring flood control and irrigation to a stop, for water on the land overshadows water in the river channel. The Missouri basin will not find answers to all its water problems in the reorganization of Washington departments; it can expect the answer to none of them if it waits for that political miracle. From the first there have been lively movements in the basin seeking a solution by and for the region itself.

VALLEY AUTHORITY

After his *tour de force* in disposing of the M.V.A. bill by dismembering it among the Senate Commerce, Irrigation and Reclamation, and Agriculture Committees in 1945, Senator John Overton visited the Missouri basin, talking frankly about his achievement. "The first time we buried the valley authority bill," he said, referring to the authorization of Pick-Sloan reservoirs to be built by the existing departments, "it dug itself back out again. This time we buried it face down. The harder it scratches, the deeper it gets."

Senator Overton was accurate. Pick-Sloan now meant dams, reservoirs, transmission lines. M.V.A. posed a threat to the control of three powerful committees in each House, to two active construction agencies, and to many contractors. As the dirt and concrete moved, it became even clearer that the valley authority bill was a copy of T.V.A. with compromises. Its advocates had a magnificent vision and courage. But every year they became a more clearly marked minority because they did not start from where the basin program was. Recognition of the fact was signaled when President Truman, though still talking of M.V.A., in 1952 appointed a Missouri Basin Survey Commission to explore a more realistic and indigenous solution.[10]

Now, unexpectedly, as both supporters and opponents of integrated regional administration lose their preoccupation with the lesson of T.V.A., they actually begin to recapitulate its *legislative* history. The fine and brilliantly illuminated administrative record of T.V.A. has overshadowed the equally pioneering work in Congress before 1933. For from 1921, when the bill for completion of the government nitrate plant and dam at Muscle Shoals was referred to his Committee on Agriculture, until his eventual success in partnership with President Roosevelt twelve years later, George Norris was patiently and rigorously ascertaining the actual potentialities of the World War government nitrate plant at Muscle Shoals, and of the Tennessee River, which he came to see might be harnessed with it. Perhaps the greatest permanent contribution Senator Norris made to the T.V.A.'s success was a purely negative and preliminary one. He convinced the overoptimistic Senate of the hard fact that the surplus munitions plant could not turn out cheap nitrate fertilizers. It was a thankless legislative accomplishment, particularly in the Southeast itself, where the farmers desperately needed cheap fertilizer. But it kept T.V.A.'s fertilizer program out of a blind alley and freed it for its present fruitful experimentation with phosphates. The final form of the T.V.A. act emerged, as Senator Norris accurately records in his autobiography, "after long thought, study, and more than a decade of interminable conflict in Congress." [11]

COMPACT

By 1951 the momentum of the M.V.A. crusade had declined enough to permit some of the governors of the basin states to point out the weaknesses of the Pick-Sloan administrative machinery without inviting a remedy they approved far less. Moreover, the approaching completion of the large Army dams seemed to present new and difficult problems of co-ordination in the release of water.

As the federal government failed to strengthen its organization to deal with basin problems, initiative fell to the states. In January, 1952, the governors' Missouri River States Committee requested the nationwide Council of State Governments to prepare a draft of an interstate-federal compact dealing with the operation problems and the planning of future development. The Missouri River States Committee discussed the draft in Omaha the following December and with slight modifications approved it unanimously. The Draft Compact attracted increasing attention and support for the next two years. Bills authorizing the negotiation of such a compact were twice passed by the United States Senate, most recently in 1955, though they never reached a vote in the House.

The Council of State Governments published the proposed compact along with this explanation:

The suggested Missouri Basin Compact is an interstate compact among the signatory states, and between the states and the national government; by terms of the instrument the national government becomes an active party to the agreement. . . . The compact becomes effective when ratified by the seven "core" states of Kansas, Missouri, Montana, Nebraska, North Dakota, South Dakota, and Wyoming. The three other Basin states —Colorado, Iowa and Minnesota—are entitled to full participation if they ratify.

The compact creates a joint agency of the participating governments, the "Missouri Basin Commission." Its major purpose is to integrate and coordinate governmental activities—federal, state and local—relating to the conservation, development and utilization of the Basin's water, land and related resources. . . .

All participating governments are represented on the Commission. Each party state is entitled to one Commissioner, who has a single vote. The national government may be represented by from three to five Commissioners, as Congress shall determine. Collectively, the national Commissioners will have a vote equal to the total number of signatory states present at any meeting. . . . The compact provides that the votes of the national Commissioners must be cast as a unit unless Congress specifies otherwise. Except in the election of officers, no action by the Commission is effective or binding unless it receives at least three-quarters of the total vote cast.[12]

One reason for the attractiveness of the compact device was the prestige which it had acquired in the scarce-water states, in Colorado and Wyoming most of all, as a means of allocating water from interstate streams. Four such compacts had been executed, as we have seen, for western tributaries of the Missouri, three of them in the last ten years. Many people in the basin jumped to the conclusion that the Draft Compact involved an over-all allocation of Missouri basin water.

Somewhat on the same analogy, others suspected that negotiation and ratification of the compact would involve years of delay. And the Missouri Basin Survey Commission, which studied the draft, warned (with three dissents), "Certainly a Federal-State Compact would raise constitutional questions. . . ."[13] How could one Congress, approving the compact, bind future Congresses to it? This point the supporters of the Draft Compact conceded, thus disposing of the constitutional objection: federal consent to the compact could always be withdrawn. But so could any federal legislative arrangement for the basin be upset by a future Congress.[14]

A closer look at the Draft Compact made most of this argument seem academic. The compact, in fact, would allocate no rights, whether to water or to power, of deciding upon plans. For all its stress upon voting procedure in the proposed "Missouri Basin Commission," the powers of the Commission would extend merely "to review agency proposals." That power the state governments themselves had received ten years before in the Flood Control Act of 1944. As the consultants who drew up the draft compact say, "it is difficult to conceive of any order that the joint agency could give to any federal officer, other than an order to supply the agency with information in his possession."[15] But if the Draft Compact did not make that limitation evident, its reception in Congress did. The Senate passed the bill authorizing compact negotiations only after amending it to exclude from the scope of any resulting compact the power to co-ordinate federal programs as among themselves. But it was, of course, the lack of that power to co-ordinate federal programs that aroused the major dissatisfactions with the present Missouri Basin Inter-Agency Committee.

All this made it clearer that the states cannot gain any legal right to wield any of the federal constitutional powers. Search for such a right is romantic. The true authority of the states, not as governments but as bodies of citizens, in the exercise of federal powers lies in their representation in Congress. Twenty senators and some forty representatives will certainly have their way on matters of special concern to their states. Time and again, we have observed even a small fraction of that delegation block the authorization of great federal programs until modifications had been accepted. That is what happened to the Pick plan until the Sloan plan had been attached, to the Corps' plan for flood control in the Osage River subbasin, to the Bureau's Glendo Dam on the North Platte. Through the Nebraska delegation in Congress even the Salt-Wahoo Watershed Association balked the Corps of Engineers and the rivers and harbors legislative process.

Blocking unsatisfactory plans is one thing. Evolving a consensus upon a satisfactory set of policies and projects is quite another. The governors' Missouri River States Committee and the Missouri Basin Inter-Agency Committee served this purpose inadequately. The federal-state commission created in the Draft Compact probably would have served better. It would not have brought the states new power of decision: the power to review federal agency plans they already had; the power to block them politically they already employed whenever necessary. And it would not have created a new focus for public opinion regarding agency water plans; this the Inter-Agency Committee already provided. It would simply have consolidated these two functions in the same commission and thus have strengthened both. The only thing it could not have done is to develop new or modified plans broader than a single agency's jurisdiction, better suited to the Missouri basin than the existing nationwide programs.

The governors decided in 1955 that a compact was an arduous way to achieve so simple a gain. Meeting in Rapid City, South Dakota, they resolved on the motion of Dick Fabrick of Montana no longer to support an interstate compact to govern the development of water resources in the Missouri basin.[16]

CONDITIONS OF SURVIVAL

With this denouement of the interstate compact, popular discussion of reform of the Pick-Sloan machinery reached the lowest ebb since 1944. The Missouri basin development is not on the political, much less the congressional, agenda for early attention. But that does not mean that all is well.

In 1949 a task force of the first Hoover Commission concluded that the Pick-Sloan plan "is in no sense an integrated development plan for the basin."[17] The following year a study of the Missouri basin for the President's Water Resources Policy Commission raised a large number of specific questions about technical, economic, and managerial aspects of the basin development.[18] Both studies drew heavily upon the work of geographer Edward A. Ackerman. Governor Val Peterson of Nebraska and some of the agency heads in the basin objected bitterly to the criticisms (constructive as they were) contained in these studies on the ground that the authors had not carefully inspected the works in the basin nor taken testimony from basin residents.

Whatever the merits of that objection, it could certainly not be applied to the next and latest official study of the Missouri basin development. That was the 1953 report, *Missouri: Land and Water,* of the Missouri Basin Survey Commission. President Truman appointed eleven members to the Commission, including three senators and three representatives (two of them Republicans and four Democrats), two leaders of farmers' organizations, and the dean of the Wyoming School of Engineering. The chairman was Mr. James E. Lawrence, editor of the Lincoln, Nebraska, *Star.* Nine of the eleven members were residents of the basin. The Commission held seventeen hearings in every part of the basin, heard more than four hundred witnesses, and spent about sixty days in its sessions. It had a highly competent staff, headed by the civil engineer who designed the new locks for the Panama Canal, Paul J. Cannell, and one of the best-informed participants in the existing development, agricultural economist Harry A. Steele.

The Survey Commission's report stands as authoritative; indeed, it is the only professionally competent, on-the-spot survey of the development of the basin. It contained much basic information about the basin, much detailed analysis of Pick-Sloan programs. But its general conclusions were no less scathing than those which had gone before: "The Commission's findings affirm the contentions that there is lack of balance and lack of coordination in the present efforts. Upon this foundation the Commission has determined unanimously that the coordination and direction of the development of the basin's resource potential should be entrusted to a new agency created for that purpose." [19]

The Survey Commission's report dealt with the facts of 1952. The work in the basin grows and changes. Reorganization proposals must change, too. The time which is ripe for reorganization such as the Survey Commission proposed will present a new set of facts. The durable elements in the situation are the *potentialities:* the limits of nature and of attitudes and institutions. They are disclosed not by ten but by ninety years' experience of the American attempt to come to terms with the hydrologic peculiarities of the basin.

A Job Bigger than the River

In 1806 Lewis and Clark achieved a triumph of exploration out of the failure of their mission: to find "the most direct and practicable water route across this continent." In 1820 Major Stephen Long abandoned the steamboat that was to take him to the mouth of the Yellowstone and struck out overland from Council Bluffs. Ever since, the Missouri has denied fulfillment to frontier-sized demands. It is a mighty river—almost mighty enough. When the great reservoirs are full, the revetments in, the dredges working and the powerful tugs deployed, the river will carry barges—expensively. When the canals are dug and concreted, the headgates in and the fields leveled, river water will replace the inconstant rains—on one farm acre in twenty. If water is back of the turbines and all authorized generators are "on the line" by 1970, the basin will even then be getting from the river only two-fifths of the new power it will need.

There is not quite enough water, not quite enough fall, not quite enough reservoir storage at feasible cost. But that is not the only limit. For the Missouri River fails also to be quite as tractable as man expects. The flood that will come once in an *average century* can be held in dikes; not the one that will come once in five centuries. That once may be this year. And when we test the suitability for human use of all that vast plain which the reliable water of the river will never reach, we find at the end of all the techniques of dry farming, of stubble mulch, of summer fallow and of drought-resistant grain that same uncertainty. No more than the river will the skies deliver water quite predictably enough.

Enough, that is, for man as he sees himself occupying the basin: *the conqueror of nature*. For it is only his expectations that nature thwarts, the expectations that he imported from a more limitless frontier and that accumulated here because this frontier was his last. Nature is bountiful enough and predictable enough in the Missouri basin, if man will make his own demands a little more predictable. The need is not for preachment; Missouri basin people would never have been here if they had a penchant for subduing themselves upon suggestion. Nor is the need for technology alone. New devices for using the potentials of nature can just as well be misused. Barbed wire, windmills, Turkey wheat, forestation, cattle on the open range, railroads, canals, dust mulch, summer fallow, flood walls—each advance in technology failed when man overused it. The need is therefore to decide upon the rewarding limits of use in the very process of technological innovation, and to keep those limits clear and present.

How that can be done best is not for general prognostication; how it may

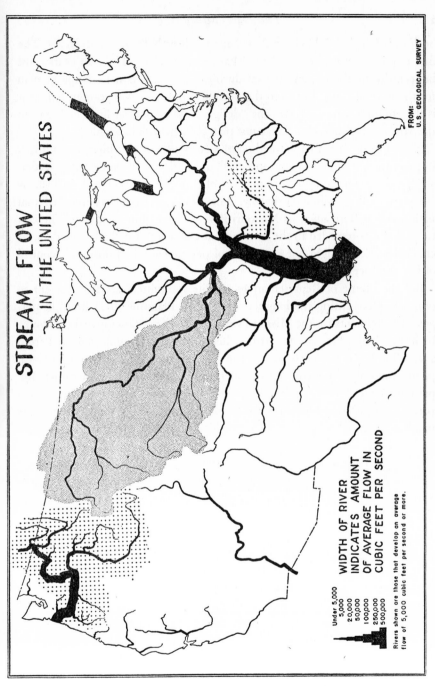

Fig. 15. The Missouri is a big river, but it does not carry enough water to dominate its basin. Compare the flow of the Columbia, or even of the Tennessee in a basin one-thirteenth as large.

be done better than it has been done emerges directly from past mistakes. The first requirement is a *steady* view of basin potentialities. The lean years must be seen during the fat, and the fat during the lean. It is not enough to plan for the normal rainfall or even the normal number of wet years in ten. Nor is the engineer who conceives the "design flood" as a real limit at home in the Missouri basin. Technicians must plan for what *can* happen.

Now, it is obvious that no method of securing the leadership for continuity in planning could be less appropriate than the device of posting that leadership in the basin for a maximum term of three years, shortened, in fact, by every overriding military exigency. The Corps of Engineers imposed that nationwide pattern upon its Missouri River officers quite routinely. The cost to the basin is recorded in the intermittent character of its hydraulic data, its channel works brought one step short of permanence, its priority for control of last summer's flood.

But the House of Representatives and its committees are still less apt to originate plans fitting the long-term potential. Planning great multiple-purpose developments for the Missouri's water must be a standing assignment or be improvised when disaster strikes. Being as far as possible removed from a standing body, Congress may retain the appearance of initiating physical plans—but only at the cost of surrendering real initiative to the weather. Impermanence can never quite be purged from elective government. But a particular legislature or chief executive or electorate can, if there is continuity in administration, be made aware of the long-term consequences of the choices they must make.

Excessive demands upon a limited environment call, secondly, for the exploitation of all control devices, the economic and the governmental as well as the physical. One of the surprises of the Survey Commission hearings was the wide demand for flood-control zoning. It is an old, rather obvious, wholly neglected way to fence human reliance on the river into an area from which all floods, not only design floods, can be fenced out. Engineering will, unaided, also fail to deliver cheap transport, abundant power, irrigated agriculture, conservation of topsoil. But the economic, legal, and biological complements to engineering will be less obvious than floodplain zoning. To these purposes must be assigned a team of whatever professions and whatever governmental techniques are required to yield the benefits. Present agencies vary from the Corps, which positively distrusts non-engineers, through the Bureau of Reclamation, which has rounded out its staff with agricultural scientists and technicians, to the Department of Agriculture with its wide-ranging economic and physical specialists—segregated rigidly from the hydraulic and electrical engineers in the other agencies.

It is hardly necessary to add that the controls upon the demands of the basin populace, if they work, are going to be largely self-controls. Federal restraints have regularly aborted. But self-restraints cannot commend themselves to reasonable men as long as the cost of uncontrolled expectations is invisibly shifted to the nation's taxpayers, or to some other group of water users. Why should Omaha vote for a municipal floodplain zoning ordinance, or the Huron, South Dakota, chamber of commerce question the economics of irrigating Jim River glacial soils? History demonstrates that the United States will underwrite the loss: by Corps of Engineers' dikes around the new floodplain subdivision; by enlarging the power customers' subsidy to irrigation. And over against these negative examples set the positive ones. Here restrained, and hence continuously profitable, exploitations of nature have been arranged by enterprisers collectively confronting the costs: in grazing districts, conservancy districts, drainage districts, soil conservation districts, watershed districts, rural electrification co-operatives. The least that the United States can do is to end artificial dislocations of costs from benefits. But it might also calculate the advantages of local institutions for self-control of water demands and make a place for them in its own larger programs.

A Defined Job

Once admit that the Missouri River will not cut the Gordian knot of resource misuse, and the program of basin development begins to grow to the very vastness of the Plains. On the river, Pick-Sloan's prospectus of 105 dams grew to 139 in eight years—twice as many as were built meanwhile. The Federal Power Commission considers damming the intensively used floodplain from Sioux City to Kansas City, and even to St. Louis. Pressures mount to exploit mineral resources, conserve fish and game, develop recreation as part of the program. The Inter-Agency Committee still has before Congress an agricultural development plan (the Young plan) as costly to the United States as either of the river plans. The Committee's program estimate thus totals 9 billion federal dollars. It is a little ironic that all the while it was under attack as too narrow in scope, the Committee was accumulating a set of plans as far beyond the capacity of the congressional purse as the claimed Pick-Sloan benefits were beyond the capacity of river engineering to deliver.

Only the stranger need be surprised. The image of the frontiersman conquering nature regularly dissolved in moods of disappointment into the vision of nature domesticated by federal works. Is not the destiny of the nation manifest in the full occupation of the frontier? So the development plan, as the basin presents it to Washington, booms. Grandiose schemes may, unfortunately, cost support for desperately needed ones. And no one can be sure what to do next. What the program needs is a test of relevancy.

It will not do to say, as President Roosevelt did in his message to Congress requesting the T.V.A. act: "It should be charged with the broadest duty of planning for the proper use, conservation and development of the natural resources of the Tennessee River drainage basin and its adjoining territory for the general social and economic welfare of the Nation. This Authority should also be clothed with the necessary power to carry those plans into effect." [20] The T.V.A. act did not actually give "responsibility to deal with resources as a unified whole," as Mr. David E. Lilienthal has sometimes tended to say.[21] And even so, in spite of skilled administration and unbureaucratic philosophy, the vagueness of its responsibilities for soil conservation has produced a jurisdictioral conflict with the Soil Conservation Service of the very type which now concerns the Missouri basin.

Nowhere in the nation does the drainage basin of a river form the planning area for conservation of *all* resources. Economic relations of cities and industries draw across the natural slopes of watersheds a thousand lines of contact and dependence. Each new oilfield, livestock breed, or road transport rate varies the working area of some economic process. The larger cities gather the greatest number of strands into the web; but theirs is a competing, dynamic, and functional, not a permanent and exclusive, regional influence.[22]

In the Missouri basin, the point applies more forcefully than elsewhere. Ponderosa and lodgepole pine, Montana and Dakota lignite, hard winter wheat, the beef business from range to feedlot to slaughterhouse—each opportunity to conserve or waste resources is part in, part beyond, part across the river drainage. Each resource-using business depends also on the others. But for the maximization of sound general investment the Federal Reserve districts radiating westward from Minneapolis and Kansas City and the Rocky Mountain Piedmont focusing in Denver are certainly areas more "natural" than the basin. The inherent truth recurs: in form this basin is (except at the Divide of the Rockies) a unit only to the surveyor; in history it is a corridor, in economics a tributary. It has no homogeneity in nature, and if its people see themselves as alike it is partly through the acceptance of a stereotype.

But one thing unites and at the same time distinguishes the basin: the flow of water. Water from the beet fields at Greeley, the sage-dotted range behind the Big Horns, the granite boulders under Long's Peak, the miles-long summer fallowed wheat furrows around Great Falls, the Badlands, the Sandhills, the windlaid loam of Iowa, the Bluestem farms of Kansas, the Ozarks and the corn bottoms—it is all inextricably one at Wolf Point twelve miles above

St. Louis. The vision that sees this basin as a unit can only be oriented toward water. The power to plan for the basin as a region must be power over water.

But precisely because the basin outranges its river, water plans will have to be directed toward ends that surpass river-use—toward cheaper transportation, sustained farm production, stability of economic opportunity, higher incomes. And the parallel development of other plans—plans for private investment, soil fertility, marketing, municipal amenities—will have to be enlisted to these same ends. In this basin, it now becomes crystal clear, "unified planning" of all natural resources, if it is more than a catchword, means frustrating the intelligent use of each.[23] But planning either water or land or investment without regard for the others equally stultifies itself. What the basin needs is not integration but relationship, not identity but articulation, not a plan but a variety of planning for known interdependencies. Since the unity of the basin is not organic but functional and since the function is water flow but not water flow for its own sake, the definition of the job must be in terms of a distinctive perspective and a way of giving effect to relationships among plans.

Water planning is the core; it justifies itself through linkage to other planning. To illustrate: flood and pollution control, water supply for cities and farms, navigation and hydropower generation must be seen and managed as one. They are river functions to which integration applies in fact. For none, it is true, will a Missouri River plan suffice; even flood control for this river has the added job of reducing Mississippi River crests. But the Missouri River dominates. Compare planning for land-use, forestation, cost and supply of electricity, industrialization, recreation, mineral use. Here the importance of water flow is not intrinsic but contrived, and it varies in degree from one program to the next. Some device is needed to keep the relationship to water planning continually under appraisal and to effect a due modification of these programs. The modification ought to be minor in the case of minerals, more significant in land-use, and important, though not determinative, in the case of electric power supply.

The *basin* program should certainly be defined to integrate the programs of flood and pollution control, navigation, irrigation, municipal water supply (in the wholesale sense), and hydropower generation. Because efficient hydropower calls for a high-tension transmission net over the central and upper basin, power distribution is also suited for integrated planning in this part of the basin. Figure 16 makes the point. But the water-planning process can only by a great and probably divisive strain assume responsibility for providing electric utility service for the state of Missouri. Still less can it determine best land use. It must have means continually to find out its interrelation with those questions and to influence without controlling them precisely in the degree of that interrelation.

The peculiar dilemma of the Missouri development in its present form is, in one sense, the dilemma of the superimposition of basin and Plains. On the Plains, the river alone is not enough. But once cut planning free of the streambed, and it spreads limitless in the undifferentiated terrain reaching from Canada to Mexico. It seems too little to get results and too big to get done. But the river as the *core* of a plan *linked to* the Northern Plains con-

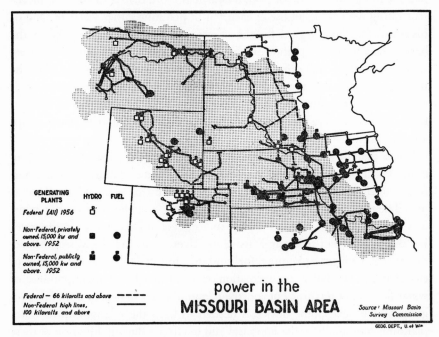

Fig. 16

verts dilemma into opportunity. Instability in the meaning of water is the characteristic of the Plains. The permanent works in the river, perennially functioning for flood control, power, irrigation, and the continuous minor uses, provide a stable base from which to project research and the accumulation of recommendations for the use of moisture on the land against the day when the need is felt in the rare but overwhelming crisis of drought. The men who plan the river need to know the Plains, and the men who plan for the Plains need to use the more predictable resources of the river. But the two are not one.

Community of Interest

By design the basin, which in nature is a region only for the flowage of water, may be made the region of broader adjustments of man to nature. The question is, by whose design? It was not, in 1944, the design of the basin populace, who knew little of their water resources, and who were in any case relieved of the challenge to make up their minds by a settlement creating a physical priority for irrigation, but building works for all uses at the same time. Nor was it the design of national opinion, or even the opinion of the whole Congress. It was the registration of a private and a bureaucratic settlement to which national attention could not be drawn, certainly not in wartime.

It is the nature of such settlements that they do not last. The clash of abundant-water and scarce-water forces is destined to recur in the basin. It will not be a contest for water—unless after complete fulfillment of the irrigation plan a drought like that of the thirties recurs. More likely, and sooner, it will be a controversy over the economic burden of the development. When drought returns to the Northern Plains, as it returned in 1952–55 to the Central Plains, and major irrigation works are found unbuilt because they are too costly, an embarrassing question will become public. Why should prospective irrigators on three million acres of the Plains be required to repay project costs (insofar as they cannot be added to electric rates) when the bottom land farmers along the Missouri River navigation project get their two million acres diked against the river at federal expense? It will be no accident if in the economics of reimbursement, as already in physical plans for water, East meets West in the Missouri basin. For here irrigation becomes most expensive in proportion to the power subsidy available, while the benefits of flood protection accrue most specifically to property owners along a narrow floodplain.

Nor will it be surprising if power customers, when they have exhausted the moderately cheap hydroelectricity now authorized and when their future needs can only be met by more expensive steam generation, ask why they should be charged rates to repay not only the cost of power, but two-thirds of the cost of irrigation as well. That triples the cost of construction which has to be paid back by users of electricity. According to a 1953 estimate, for instance, power customers will have to repay 2.9 billion dollars of costs. Without the irrigation burden, they would need to repay 874 million dollars.[24] The difference might be critical in attracting industry.

More likely still, the beneficiaries in the basin (irrigators, navigation inter-

ests, property owners behind levees, power customers) will find themselves
pitted against the federal taxpayers. Congress accepted watershed protection
without an accounting of its effect on the total federal investment. The Missouri Basin Survey Commission found a disagreement between Bureau and
Corps amounting to 500 million dollars as to the repayable portion of the
cost of mainriver dams.[25] The day of reckoning is not far off. Is navigation
worth its cost? Is bank protection a federal responsibility? Will irrigators
in fact make the payments due from them? Will the tremendous subsidy
of irrigation by power revenues in fact materialize, when it is due to com-
mence only forty-three years after the last generator has been installed, and
all power costs have themselves been repaid?

These are questions of distributive justice. They can be answered with
public consent only by constituencies feeling the impact of costs as well as
benefits. What the basin needs, therefore, is a careful classification of policy
decisions—national, state, and local—based upon their area of impact. This is
the practical, political question of federalism. The question of constitutional
powers became largely academic as soon as the Supreme Court vouchsafed
to Congress more legal scope that it is politically feasible to exercise, and the
states became dependent on the national purse for the full exercise of their
legal powers. In the basin, the proper classification has unusual significance.
Sober Republican governors and chambers of commerce are quite ready to
saddle navigation or irrigation projects of unexamined economic soundness
upon the Washington treasury. Is not the nation to make over the basin
in its own image? Congressmen, imbued with the same sentiment, are ready
here to apply logrolling to irrigation and even watershed treatment projects
for which they ordinarily ask strict prospects of repayment or demonstrable
benefits. The face it turns to Washington is least likely to be the basin's
own.

The amount and the rate of federal investment in the basin are the
vital question for the national public. There will always be the danger of
public disillusionment until that question is answered with all costs considered (not the river development minus the watershed protection it needs),
reimbursements put on a business basis, and benefits to the nation as a whole
identified. Because the basin is economically a tributary area, United States
taxes will have to supply a preponderant share of the public investment.
Moreover, early state and co-operative irrigation projects collapsed from inadequate capital and engineering; vigorous local levee districts all along the
lower Missouri succumbed to the superfloods of an uncontrolled and unmeasured river. But these are no more reasons for the United States to take
complete responsibility for the building of flood-control and irrigation works

than for public highways or soil conservation works, where, likewise, state finances and state expertise fell short. Residents of the basin need responsibility for proposing priorities among projects, for enforcing reimbursement policies, for gearing river works with the programs for power marketing, agricultural extension, and regulation of land use that will provide the actual human benefits. This sort of responsibility will develop a sense of community in the basin. It will knit together in the basin the lines of adjustment of interest to interest, of one city or irrigation district to another, which formerly led direct to House and Senate committee rooms. It is the way the basin will outgrow its frontier relationship to Washington.

A good deal of the literature on valley authorities assumes that decision-making by federal administrators at basin headquarters necessarily conveys this sort of self-determination. It may help by cutting lines of routine command from Washington and increasing accessibility to local advice and influence. In the case of the T.V.A., these were potent factors not only because of the inclination of its directors (other than its original chairman), but also because in mortal combat with the power trust it needed all that local influence. The prospect of influence so contingent will not attract the groups in the Missouri basin who now feel direct power over particular programs: irrigation, flood control, navigation, soil conservation.

But there is a more intrinsic reason why the basin needs not influence but a share in control. Only men clearly dependent for their power upon a consent of basin voters can lead in *self*-control; only the collective act of voting their satisfaction or dissatisfaction with basin policies can dramatize the common interest of basin citizens. "Virtual" representation enlisted the confidence of the small and relatively homogeneous Tennessee Valley. It will not suffice, in this great transition zone, to create *e pluribus unum*. The basin, not the nation or the state, must define the primary community interest. Yet, loose talk aside, no one has conceived a way to conduct elections or maintain direct representation for an area holding but one of the myriad political interests of its people: water use. To say no more, a political unit for spending but not taxing would be a travesty upon the principle of locating decisions in their area of impact. What the basin needs is a charter of representation through an appropriate combination of state and national elections.[26]

GOVERNMENT TO FIT

In 1953, the Missouri Basin Survey Commission proposed one such plan. Briefly, it called for a five-member Missouri Basin Commission appointed by the President from among basin state residents. They would serve full time. They would bring plans and programs into co-ordination by supervising, not replacing, existing federal agencies. Their chief means of co-ordination would be a consolidated basin budget, review of project and operating plans, control over surveys, and the allocation and accounting of costs. Any state might, in the first two years, elect not to have the Commission operate within its borders. Should such rejection come from any one of the five "mainstem states"—Montana, North Dakota, South Dakota, Nebraska, and Missouri—Congress would have to decide whether to go ahead with the Commission in the remaining states.[27]

Three members of the Survey Commission dissented. They preferred an interstate compact.[28] In any event, the Survey Commission had been appointed by President Truman without congressional sanction. It brought in its report in the first month of the Eisenhower administration. In the meantime, General Pick's dramatic defense of Omaha and Council Bluffs against the 1952 flood had brought the Pick-Sloan plan safely through a serious crisis of political support. The situation was as inauspicious as possible for action on the Survey Commission's report. No action has been taken.

Senator Hennings, who was vice-chairman of the Survey Commission, has nevertheless continued to try to find a way out of the impasse. In 1955 he introduced a bill that succeeded in harmonizing to an amazing degree the majority and dissenting positions of the Survey Commission. Plans approved by the proposed Missouri Basin Commission would, according to the Hennings bill, go to an interstate Compact Board for review and comment.[29] The bill comes to terms with the facts, both as to the results of present programs and the inclinations of basin citizens and groups.

The model presented below was designed in June, 1952. That was before the governors had proposed their compact, or the Survey Commission their federal Missouri Basin Commission. I have left it as it was, adding footnotes to compare it to subsequent proposals.

The law and organization to govern basin development will emerge from the political forces, the leading personalities, the droughts or floods, the prosperity or depression of the moment, rather than from a book. The remedy which is proposed here is intended primarily to make the diagnosis clear— the diagnosis of underlying, durable requirements and potentials already presented. To claim that such a proposal remains viable after three or four years is not much of a claim. In the century and a quarter that the United States has been dealing with the Missouri River and its basin, it has, after all, made a good many of the possible mistakes already. That makes a long-term diagnosis possible. Before accepting the need for a remedy, the United States will probably make a good many more mistakes. That makes a long-term diagnosis necessary.

A Federal-State Council

The governors of the Missouri basin states most nearly provide the type of representation the basin needs in policy decisions. They mobilize opinion in the area and are accountable to it. They are responsible for administrative programs encompassing all uses of water both in the river and on the land. Their advisory staffs are small, but the advice represents teamwork of the various professions and combines economic appraisal with engineering proposals. The President, since he lost the National Resources Planning Board, has not been as fortunate. These governors are, moreover, free of disqualifications. They are not corrupt; patronage does not elect them. They need not, as a group, pay homage to any "sacred cows"—not to private power, for Nebraska has none. Even states' rights to rivers will ordinarily attract the skepticism of the governor of Missouri. Neither political party will control them all; competition will be keen to see which party can best anticipate public reaction to basin programs.

There is one practical difficulty. The area of the ten basin states goes far beyond the drainage area. Minnesota is barely touched by the basin; only Nebraska is entirely within it. But this difficulty yields to an invention of the governors themselves, until 1952 used for their representation in the Missouri Basin Inter-Agency Committee. The ten may choose a smaller number (six has been satisfactory) to represent them.

The governors should be joined as authoritative critics of the basin policy, not by department field agents, but by the heads of the federal departments concerned. The change is warranted by the basic change in the duties of the Council as compared to the Inter-Agency Committee. It is not to co-ordinate by appeal to opinion. It is to decide basic policies and priorities, to criticize with authority. The reason for giving Washington departments *any* policy role is not merely to minimize change. It is to recognize that no agency concerned only with the basin could see the general implications of Missouri water use. Development of any region contributes to the general prosperity and protects its share of the nation's exhaustible resources. But in the Missouri basin the nation sees also its transcontinental transport routes, its grain supply, a good deal of its beef, and some of its finest out-of-state recreation. These are the matter-of-fact concerns beneath the sunset glow of the frontier image. Neither the usual valley authority proposal nor the present mode of administration recognizes the need to make basin water decisions in the light of contributions to such specific national interests. It would be possible to gain the criticism of governors and department heads separately, but that would be wasteful and needlessly divisive. Washington policy-makers need to learn what basin people want; state executives need to understand the nation's interests in their area.[30]

Proposal: The Secretaries, or adequately empowered Assistant Secretaries, of Agriculture, Interior, Commerce, and Health, Education and Welfare, the Chief of Army Engineers, and Chairman of the Federal Power Commission plus an equal number of governors selected by the governors of the ten basin states shall constitute the Missouri Basin Water Development Council. The Council shall meet at least twice a year to review work accomplished and to approve budget estimates to be proposed to the President and to the governors for federal and state expenditure respectively. Its decisions shall be subject to change only by Congress or the President as concerns federal works or state legislation as concerns state works. The Council shall decide the rules for operating the basin system of reservoirs, recommend new projects for construction, and propose changes in the law of basin development. The meetings of the Council shall be held publicly and in the Missouri basin.

A Federal Basin Water Conservator

So far, all proposals for reorganizing administration of the basin development head it with a board or commission. There are advantages: representativeness in policy-making and continuity are the obvious ones. Breaking the line of complete policy subordination to the President, so that basin viewpoints will have greater access, is a third. If these can be had otherwise (the first and third have been secured by the Council better than by a board), the single administrator commands an enormous superiority in dealing with the Missouri basin. He cannot duck responsibility for administrative integration of projects which are inevitably far-flung, diverse, attracted to different clienteles. He maximizes financial accountability. These are important considerations since he cannot begin with a clean slate but must work out relationships with older projects in the river and for water use on the land.

Most important, the single administrator can capture the imagination of basin people. Outsiders may be misled by the polemics against "basin czars" used in the fight against M.V.A. The heroic leader is so indigenous a part of frontier traditions that he will be imagined if he is not there. "Pick plan" was factually descriptive of one man's initiative; "Sloan plan" was less so. When the basin dubbed the Department of Agriculture's institutional product the "Young plan," the personifying habit was at work. Nobody in the basin raised an eyebrow when General Pick said, as *Life* magazine blazoned it, "I mean to control the water of the Missouri River." Already the Inter-Agency Committee has heard a proposal for installing a "watermaster" over the system of reservoirs. The difference between the "watermaster" and the "czar of a superstate" is legally that the former would not override state water rights, and politically that he would have the confidence of the governors— that he would be of the frontier tradition himself.

Proposal: From a panel of candidates nominated by the ten governors of basin states, the President shall appoint a Basin Water Conservator. His term shall be nine years. He may be removed by the President, but not for reason of political party affiliation. Upon the request of five governors, the Basin Development Council shall hold a hearing and make a recommendation to the President as to his removal. The Conservator shall establish headquarters in the basin, appoint the necessary staff, and be provided the necessary supplies, money, and equipment to carry out his duties.

These shall be:

to build or delegate responsibility for building all future federal works for controlling the Missouri River and its tributaries and for distributing the resulting water and power;

to operate these works, and such other works of this kind as may be turned over to him by the President;

to dispose of the products of plants he operates, and to collect payments for them, according to the basin law;

to propose to the Missouri Basin Water Development Council from time to time plans for the full use of basin water resources, indicating the relation of all necessary costs to all benefits, and the allocation of costs to the various benefits;

to present, as part of all such plans, proposals for federal and state action to capture all economic benefits to be derived from related improvements of water on the land, or other related resource conservation, these proposals to be, insofar as possible, the work of existing state and federal agencies; to carry on research, small-scale demonstrations, and evaluations of government programs necessary to arrive at recommendations to Congress, the President, and the states for full, sustained yield of basin resources;

to be accountable for spending from and receiving money into the Basin Account, to report annually the accomplishment of these duties to the Council, to propose to the Council a program of spending for the coming year, and six years ahead.

A Basin Water-Development Account

The financial unity of all projects and uses of water in the development can be managed, and dramatized, only by keeping a single set of books. But this reform, urged by the Hoover Commission and the President's Water Resources Policy Commission, has proved subject to an abuse which the latter Commission warned against. A single total, showing benefits greater than all costs, may hide the issues of distributive justice: Is one program unjustifiably subsidized? Are economically sound projects carrying the excessive costs of others without good noneconomic reason? The account should show not only the basin balance but how it will be affected by each proposed additional feature.

The account has an added purpose in the Missouri basin. It will keep present in the thinking of basin political leaders the threat to economic justification of the entire development of failure to repay costs contracted for by water users. It will put agreed reimbursements more on a business, less on a political, basis.

Proposal: All appropriations authorized by the basin law shall be paid into a Basin Account, and all expenditures therefrom debited to it. Receipts from project beneficiaries shall be credited to the Account and paid into the U.S. Treasury at the end of the year. All dams, transmission lines, power stations, canals, headquarters, and other permanent property shall be shown at their present worth as assets in the Account, and their annual depreciation debited to operating expenses. Annual costs and capital values shall be distributed to navigation, flood control, irrigation, power, water supply, stream sanitation, and other water programs, and receipts separately credited. At the end of the year the Conservator shall report to the Council the relation of actual receipts and payments for each use to that estimated upon authorization. The Account shall be public and shall be audited at the end of the year by the Comptroller General.

A Basin Budget

Budgeting is the administrative tool to meet four basin needs. It can unify consideration in the basin and in Congress of the various programs for water use: irrigation, power, flood control, and navigation. The key here is to require consideration of appropriations by a single subcommittee of House and Senate, based on a single proposal to the President and Congress.[31]

Budget review procedure can put responsibility on the Council, hence on the Conservator, to select the best justifiable combination of projects under the scrutiny of basin opinion, and technical appraisal of costs and results. It can then keep responsibility on the President and Congress to reduce or increase the total annual investment as the nation's revenues, business cycle, and priority of broad programs may require.[32]

Giving the Conservator what amounts to a single checkbook from which he may transfer funds (of course, upon estimates submitted beforehand to budget review) to other federal agencies and states permits his working out the precise degree of interconnection which the programs of those agencies and governments ought to have with the basin program. Within the single Department of the Interior at present, that budgetary device accurately synchronizes the work of the Bureaus of Public Lands and Indian Affairs, the Park Service and Fish and Wildlife Service, and the Geological Survey with the construction work of the Bureau of Reclamation.

Continuity of aim can survive the emergencies of drought and flood if annual selections of projects and construction tempos are made from a long-term budget of projects classified according to their degree of economic justification.

Proposal: Estimates for inclusion in the budget of the United States shall be submitted by the Conservator to a public hearing and review by the Council in the basin. The Council shall revise or approve the estimates and transmit them to the President together with the Conservator's proposal. The estimates shall include a group of projects costing not more than the tentative basin total proposed by the President, plus such additional project estimates, arranged in order of priority, as the Conservator and Council shall find to be economically sound and fit for immediate undertaking in the interest of the United States and the basin. Appropriations to the basin budget shall be made in a single bill; they shall be made to the Conservator, subject to the policy directives and supervision of the Council and the President.

Upon agreement with the Conservator, any state government may submit its own budget for basin development to review by the Council, whose proposal shall then be transmitted to the governor of the state.

The annual estimate shall include expenditures during the coming year, and for the next six years upon projects undertaken. It shall contain also the current ultimate plan for expenditure for each purpose and for all authorized projects. Current costs shall be compared with current estimates of long-term benefits for each project and purpose.

Research and Recommendation

Enough attention is finally being paid to the need of hydraulic data, topographic maps, and soil surveys (at least where irrigation projects are investigated). As to knowledge of the economic results and effects on governmental and social institutions of basin projects, the basin is a dark continent. Research is needed to answer three questions.

What will be the full costs and values of proposed projects? This is the missing information in present cost-benefit appraisals. Levees are decided on without knowledge of how much it will cost to unwater the land behind them. Irrigation is considered in ignorance of the farmer's capital investment required to reach the estimated crop yield. Fortunately, a profession of economic appraisers of the needed type developed in the former regional staff of the Bureau of Agricultural Economics and among the economists and sociologists in state agricultural colleges. The Bureau of Reclamation supports and uses their surveys modestly; the Corps neglects their facilities even in investigating agricultural levees; even within the Department of Agriculture, the Soil Conservation Service wastes their skills. Their approach, if amplified to include industrial and urban as well as rural effects, could quietly supplant the boomer approach to planning. It would, however, have to be brought in from the fringes of the planning process.

How can the aims of basin development be attained by programs outside the powers of the Conservator to act directly? Some of the most intriguing and crucial mysteries of basin planning remain totally unexplored. Is artificial precipitation of rain from clouds physically feasible and more economical than irrigation to supplement natural moisture upon the Plains? Would the stabilized and increased traffic emerging from the economic development of the basin, or the actual costs of operation, justify freight rate decreases to accomplish the goals now sought from a questionable navigation project? What are the most successful solutions yet tried for the problems of *extensive* living on the Plains in terms of the provision of highways, schools, local government, marketing, professional services?

What are the costs and effects of biological changes as influences upon water flow? Larger and better-timed snowmelt from thinned lodgepole pine forests, saving of water from devegetating canal banks, flood-control value of soil cover and soil-absorption power, effect of range vegetation on runoff—research knowledge on these subjects might warrant important modifications of the programs for water control.

Proposal: The Conservator shall arrange for the conduct of research necessary to appraise water-control projects, to evaluate alternative programs for attaining their ends, to explore possible changes in the basin development program. He shall contract for the conduct of such research with existing scientific agencies of the United States or the states, and with universities or private institutions insofar as they are qualified and willing to undertake it; to this end he may extend appropriate financial assistance from the basin appropriation. Guided by the findings of such research, the Conservator shall make, and the Council shall transmit to the President, Congress, or state governments such proposals for modification of existing basin laws, or the programs of existing agencies of government, as will best attain the purposes of basin development.

Existing Agencies

General conservative considerations, plus the specialized abilities of the staffs that have been put together, argue for minimum displacement of existing river construction agencies by the Conservator. On the other hand, the jurisdictional stalemates and rivalry, the poor estimating and narrow-professioned planning of the Corps, the poor repayment record of the Bureau argue for administrative reorganization. There is an overwhelming political problem in requiring the use of existing agencies for building river works. Congressional decision-making would remain bogged in the rivers and harbors and reclamation lobbies, beyond the ken of basin public or national attention. It is mainly in the orientation and the policy leadership of the Corps and the Bureau that change is desirable; the more the Conservator is empowered to displace them, the less he is likely to have to.

Other Department of the Interior bureaus, the Department of Agriculture, and other federal agencies, by contrast, need not be replaced or consolidated. They need to be supported in new program emphases by use of grants from the basin appropriation. The Council will greatly stimulate and facilitate this co-operative relation.

It is to the state governments that important shifts of program administration may be made. Some states are quite able to plan and construct smaller projects of the basin plan. All can take responsibility for settlement, farm planning and extension, and repayment of irrigation projects. States could take advantage of many presently wasted opportunities inherent in maintenance of construction camps, access roads, recreation facilities, and the conduct of research and program evaluation. They ought to do the relocating of families from reservoir areas. Flood-control zoning, integration of irrigation into the surrounding range or dry farming economy, pollution control, power distribution—these phases of the program must largely be carried out by the states.

Proposal: The Conservator shall plan and construct works in the river and works to distribute water and power from it. He may make use of the present staffs engaged in such work in the Corps of Engineers or the Bureau of Reclamation by transfer or by inter-agency agreement. In no other case shall he employ administrative staff to carry out his duties where existing state or federal agencies are able and willing to do the work. He shall contract with states and their subdivisions to carry out all parts of the basin development program which fall within their power and competence.

Existing Projects

Every federal river-use project in the basin which is not incorporated in the Basin Account and the control of the Conservator and Council detracts from the community of interest of basin citizens and the confidence of the nation in the economic soundness of the development. On the other hand, existing contracts for payment for irrigation and power cannot and should not be altered, except with the consent of the users. Waste of money under authorizations and managements now replaced (such as Kendrick irrigation or lower Missouri navigation) ought not be saddled on present users or on the economic standing of the present Account.

Proposal: All projects begun or completed under authority of the Flood Control Act of 1944 or subsequent law shall be controlled by the Council and Conservator and entered on the Basin Account at their actual cost. Earlier federal water-control projects in the basin may be so transferred at the discretion of the President upon recommendation of the Council, but only at their present value for purposes of the basin law. Repayments by users now under contract may be renegotiated, but increased only by agreement.

Basin Law

Changes so fundamental not only presuppose relegislation of the basin development; they would precipitate political controversy keen enough to call up the subject for public debate and decision. The basin would have to reach a consensus upon what it wants from its water. National opinion would have to decide the adequacy of present machinery and define the value of basin development to the nation. All elements of these decisions would not have to be determined at once. None is apt to be determined without searching investigation of the cost and efficacy of the present work.

Proposal: Congress should declare the ends to be pursued in Missouri basin development, delegate to an appropriate agent the more limited powers for controlling and using water toward these ends and for investigating and proposing changes in such programs, establish a basin account and budgeting procedure, and define the relation of new to existing projects and agencies. Such legislation should create policies for the repayment of costs by identifiable beneficiaries, modifying existing federal law as necessary. It should not include a list of works ultimately to be built, but should fix administrative responsibility for maintaining current a long-range plan and should decide upon the authorization of specific projects at the time it is proposed to build them. Legislation should be for this basin individually.

WHENCE CHANGE?

Champions of administrative reorganization and of consistency in public policy vastly overrate the public attractiveness of change. Changes of both kinds find powerful interests vested not only in the familiar "bureaucracy" but in political and legislative arrangements which embody the hard-won victories of pressure groups, business concerns, blocs of congressmen, sectional alignments. Against this inertia, two kinds of counter-force have prevailed. An executive who is in fact at the head of an agency may reorganize it. If he symbolizes the accomplishments of the agency to the public, his concerted appeal may prevail over the "grasshopper bites" (to use Herbert Hoover's stigmatization of the Corps of Engineers lobby) of the hundreds of thousands of individuals who have some clear personal stake in the status quo. The President almost never qualifies in this sense; the Secretary of the Interior, of Agriculture, and of the Army ordinarily does not with reference to a well-rooted bureau in his department.

Or political enthusiasm may be aroused for reorganization *as a way of reaping new benefits* from government. The American people have not the time to decide, even under the appeal of a propaganda crusade, who in government ought to do what. They are interested in getting major problems solved. That is why even the most enlightened public campaign for "streamlining" government per se is pressed toward the substantive, and illusory, claim of tax reduction in its bid for citizen support. The Hoover Commission tended toward, and its propaganda support wholeheartedly adopted, this latter course. The result, in the case of the Missouri basin program, was to alienate opinion in the basin (which wanted floods stopped and drought made harmless, not dollars saved) more than it attracted support outside.

The Missouri basin is filling with reservoirs and floodwalls. Almost every town has a contractor who has worked on a project of the Bureau or the Corps. Thousands of employees of these agencies, with deserved personal reputations for honest professional accomplishment, stand for the river-control program in the minds of basin citizens. Reorganization at this late stage is not only immensely difficult but even improbable. If it is to be achieved, it will come not upon its merits alone but from one or both of two initiatives. Those closely identified with the good (even if wasteful) works in the basin may themselves press for it. Or unsatisfied demand for some great substantive benefit on the part of the people may discover reorganization as the necessary means.

The Chief of Engineers, the Commissioner of the Bureau of Reclamation, and the Secretary of Agriculture could win any change they wished in the organization, and even considerable change in the law, of basin development. But they would have to agree. And they are working on different nationwide (or, in the case of the Bureau, western) tasks on behalf of different groups of the people's representatives.

There is one other group of executives closely identified with the basin work—the governors. They have already won a much larger role, by virtue of the interdepartmental, interprofessional view they have taken and their direct contact with the affected groups of people, than the federal officials contemplated. But the governors are relatively satisfied now that water will not be taken contrary to scarce-water law, which was so distinctively a state interest. They are not guardians of the federal tax dollar. They have no responsibility for repayment. A fair assumption of costs and power to select projects by municipalities and districts they can contribute greatly toward, but they are unlikely to initiate it. The governors, in short, might be challenged to take greater responsibilities. They will scarcely create them.

Likewise in terms of program, the Hope-Aiken act closed the last major gap that was obvious. There is no longer, year in, year out, a strongly felt need for a public benefit which the existing agencies do not seem to supply. The representatives of the nation in Congress see the nationwide programs extended full force to the basin: navigation, flood control on river and land, irrigation, hydroelectricity. The farmers and city dwellers in the basin know that they are getting generous federal improvements. Development *seems* comprehensive. The basin seems destined to pay the price of another Kansas City flood, another drought throughout the Northern Plains, to learn that it is not.

THE STORY of men entering a new environment has its familiar chapters; the Missouri basin is peculiar only in detail. Pioneering assumes (perhaps exchanging an old myth for the new) that the new land will yield to old ways. Experience teaches better but prompts heroic efforts, too, to make the new land like the old. Only painful failures present the question whether old expectations, conveyed in old institutions, may not themselves need change to fit the ineluctable novelty in nature.

The unconventional ways of water in the Missouri basin had driven out pioneers before. But it was the drought of the thirties and the floods of the forties that called for the supreme effort to make it behave conventionally. Giant reservoirs were the key technique, interlinked and multiple-purpose. Now the reservoirs are being dedicated. Perhaps it is inopportune to ask whether they will deliver the goods. Will the power be cheap enough and ample enough? Will the works that cut flood crests also cut flood risks? Will even a regulated river actually carry barges and irrigate farms? Will men make the most of water—on the Plains it is much of the water—which never runs down to the river?

Finally, may not the institutions for using water have to be replanned to the extent to which water cannot be? There is one special reason why this question remains inopportune. Fifty years ago the nation drastically revised the institutions of settlement. As the frontier closed in the Missouri basin, the prairie homestead gave way to the irrigated homestead. The nation had its plan for scarce as well as for abundant water. It is a subtle point that where the same water takes on different meanings as it flows from mountain to plain to bottom land, and from decade to decade, neither plan precisely fits.

History may again produce, of course, some prophet who is both humane and a geopolitician. He might, like John Wesley Powell, cleave so relentlessly to the emerging facts as to distinguish even for the last frontier the destiny that was manifest from the destiny that was possible. He might, as George Norris stubbornly did, block transitory solutions until the true potentialities of the basin at last are reached for decision. Norris succeeded only for the Tennessee; for the Plains, even Powell failed.

Each new drought or flood of catastrophic proportions will bring a new time of decision. Solutions will be heard then; they will have to be worked out earlier. That is the unglamorous opportunity—suited less, perhaps, for a Powell or a Norris than for a miscellaneous company of governors, editors, faculties of agricultural colleges, leaders of farmers' organizations and water conservation districts. It is to rediscover the Missouri, not as an extension of the Mississippi, or the San Joaquin, or the Tennessee, but in its own vast complexity. Even from the science of the second half of the century, the hydrology of the basin will still hold some secrets. Even the leaders closest to its farms and cities will not find out exactly what its people need with water. That is why the Missouri basin, seen no longer through the images of other climates—all wet or all dry—will appear again as a frontier.

NOTES

1 A century ago a pioneer American climatologist observed that the Mississippi itself could not be said to drain a "valley."—Lorin Blodget, *Climatology of the United States* (Philadelphia, 1857).

2 E. P. Rothrock, *The Surface of a Portion of the James Basin in South Dakota* (State Geological Survey, Report of Investigations No. 54; University of South Dakota, Vermillion, 1946). Maps showing two stages of development of the Rocky Mountains are printed on pages 9 and 15 of Frederic E. Clements and Ralph W. Chaney, *Environment and Life in the Great Plains* (Carnegie Institution of Washington, Supplementary Publications No. 24; Washington, 1936).

3 In his preface to Federal Writers' Project, *Kansas: A Guide to the Sunflower State* (New York, 1939), p. 1.

4 The classic account of this process, and still the best, was by Willard D. Johnson, "The High Plains and Their Utilization," in U.S. Geological Survey, *Annual Report, 1899–1900*, Vol. XXI, Part IV, pp. 612 ff.

5 Bruno C. Petsch, *Geology of the Missouri Valley in South Dakota* (State Geological Survey, Report of Investigations No. 43; University of South Dakota, Vermillion, 1946), p. 7; E. P. Rothrock, *A Geology of South Dakota* (State Geological Survey, Bulletin No. 13; Vermillion, 1943), p. 41.

6 The Missouri's glacial detour may prove temporary, in part. It has invited the presently planned diversion of irrigation water amounting to the entire summer flow of the river eastward over low divides and down into the considerably lower Souris basin (which drains into Hudson Bay) and into the valley of the James River. These were its original outlets, which, like the Grand Coulee of the Columbia, engineers find it useful to restore.

7 C. W. Thornthwaite, "An Approach Toward a Rational Classification of Climate," 38 *Geographical Review,* pp. 55–94 (January, 1948). The concept is further refined, with new maps covering the Missouri basin, in C. W. Thornthwaite and J. R. Mather, "The Water Balance," *Publications in Climatology* (Drexel Institute of Technology, Laboratory of Climatology; Centerton, New Jersey, 1955), Vol. VIII. Hydrologists, relating stream flow to precipitation by postulating a "limiting annual water loss," have approached this concept of water balance.—Roy E. Oltman and Hubert J. Tracy, *Trends in Climate and Precipitation-Runoff Relation in the Missouri Basin* (U.S. Geological Survey Circular 98; Washington, 1951).

8 Data obtained from U.S. Geological Survey, *Surface Water Supply of the*

United States (Water Supply Paper 1036; Washington, 1947), Part VI. See also U.S. Army Chief of Engineers, *Missouri River,* 73d Congress, 2d Session, House Doc. No. 238 (1935).

9 Excellent maps of the underground water supply may be found in Geological Survey, *Annual Report,* 1899–1900, Vol. XXI, Part IV, p. 565, and plate facing p. 575.

10 Willard D. Johnson, "The High Plains and Their Utilization," and a continuation in U.S. Geological Survey, *Annual Report,* 1900–1901, Vol. XXII, Part IV, pp. 631–69; C. Warren Thornthwaite, "The Great Plains," in Carter Goodrich, ed., *Migration and Economic Opportunity* (Philadelphia, 1936); Clements and Chaney, *Environment and Life in the Great Plains;* Walter P. Webb, *The Great Plains* ([Boston], 1936); President's Great Plains Committee, *The Future of the Great Plains* (Washington, 1936). From this last we take our definition of the Plains.

11 The political and watershed boundaries coincide fairly well along the Canadian border, though a Missouri tributary, the Milk River, drains a bit of Canada. But only the artifices of civilization separate the Canadian plains of Saskatchewan from what Americans call the Northern Plains.

12 Raphael Zon, "Climate and the Nation's Forests," *Climate and Man, Yearbook of Agriculture* (Washington, 1941), p. 493.

13 Ivan Ray Tannehill, *Drought: Its Causes and Effects* (Princeton, 1947), pp. 215–16.

14 C. Warren Thornthwaite, "Climate and Settlement in the Great Plains," *Climate and Man, Yearbook of Agriculture* (Washington, 1941), p. 179.

15 J. B. Kincer, "Precipitation and Humidity," in O. E. Baker, ed., *Atlas of American Agriculture* (Washington, 1935; article first published 1922).

16 Thornthwaite, "The Great Plains," p. 221. The best recent discussion of possible causes of such variations is U.S. Forest Service, *The Possibilities of Shelterbelt Planting in the Plains Region* (Washington, 1935).

17 Lawrence Svobida, *An Empire of Dust* (Caldwell, Idaho, 1940).

18 It was authorized through House Doc. No. 308, 69th Congress, 1st Session, in 1928.

19 73d Congress, 2d Session, House Doc. No. 238 (1935).

20 In its Water Supply Paper 1146, *Surface Water Supply of the United States* (1949), Part VI. The most reliable physical records of the river are found in this series.

21 Tannehill, *Drought,* p. 110.

22 Richard Joel Russell, "Climatic Change Through the Ages," *Climate and Man, Yearbook of Agriculture* (Washington, 1941), p. 74. Oltman and Tracy, *Trends in Climate,* show a general downward trend in precipitation over the whole period of instrumental records, but most pronounced and consistent in the Plains part of the basin. It may have ended after the 1930's.

23 Clements and Chaney, *Environment and Life in the Great Plains.*

24 The imaginative dean of the North Dakota College of Agriculture published part of Mr. Will's work, a professional forestry journal carried Mr. Weakly's study, and the Denver papers gave some notice to Mr. Potts. The Plains Conference for Archeology has, in the last ten years, provided a forum for scholarly

review of dendrochronology. But the climatologists, ecologists, soils scientists, and geologists need to be brought into the exploration. The public needs to know what they find. George F. Will, *Tree Ring Studies in North Dakota* (North Dakota Agricultural Experiment Station Bulletin 338; Fargo, 1946); Harry E. Weakly, "A Tree-Ring Record of Precipitation in Western Nebraska," 41 *Journal of Forestry*, pp. 816–19 (1943).

25 John Woodward, "Origin of the Prairies of Illinois," 77 *Botanical Gazette*, pp. 241–65 (1924). The best explanation I know of is that of John R. Borchert, "The Climate of the Central North American Grassland," 40 *Annals of the Association of American Geographers*, pp. 1–39 (1950).

26 H. L. Shantz, "The Natural Vegetation of the Great Plains," 12 *Annals of the Association of American Geographers*, pp. 81–107 (1923).

27 "Soils of the United States," *Atlas of American Agriculture*, 1935, Part III, p. 14. Marbut's soil classification may be found in "Soils of the Great Plains," 13 *Annals of the Association of American Geographers*, pp. 41–66 (1923).

28 U.S. Geological Survey, *Quality of Surface Waters of the United States* (Water Supply Paper 1102, 1947), p. 236.

29 F. W. Albertson, "Man's Disorder of Nature's Design in the Great Plains," *Annual Report of the Smithsonian Institution*, 1940, pp. 363–72.

30 Weakly, "A Tree-Ring Record of Precipitation in Western Nebraska," p. 819.

31 His evidence is in three articles: "Dust Storms," 14 *Kansas Historical Quarterly*, pp. 129–44, 265–96, 391–413 (1947).

32 "The West Against Itself," 194 *Harper's Magazine*, p. 4 (1947).

33 W. G. Sloan, "The Silt Problem in the Missouri River Basin," Missouri Basin Inter-Agency Committee, *Minutes*, June 29, 1950.

34 "Man, the State of Nature, and Climax: As Illustrated by Some Problems of the North American Grassland," 74 *The Scientific Monthly*, p. 31 (1952).

CHAPTER II

1 *Prehistory and the Missouri Valley Development Program* (Smithsonian Miscellaneous Collections, No. 2; Washington, 1948), p. 10.

2 *North American Indians of the Plains* (New York, 1934). Wissler's concept of aboriginal human ecology in this area is developed in his *The Relation of Nature to Man in Aboriginal America* (New York and London, 1926).

3 Society for American Archaeology, "Radio Carbon Dating," 17 *American Antiquity*, p. 21 (1951).

4 Plains Conference for Archeology, *Proceedings of the Fifth Plains Conference* (University of Nebraska, Lincoln, 1949), pp. 111–14.

5 James C. Malin in *Grassland Historical Studies: Natural Resources Utilization in a Background of Science and Technology* (Lawrence, Kansas, 1950), Vol. I, *Geology and Geography*, develops in rich detail the significance of the Missouri bend, with the first two decades of Kansas City as the focus.

6 *Democracy in America* (Phillips Bradley ed., New York, 1945), Vol. I, p. 398.

7 The classic account is Hiram Martin Chittenden, *The American Fur Trade in the Far West* (3 vols., New York, 1902). Bernard DeVoto has put it in enduring literary form in *Across the Wide Missouri* (Boston, 1947).

8   Message to Congress, January 18, 1803. To Bernard DeVoto, whose study is definitive as to scholarship and geopolitical perspective, the dispatch of Lewis and Clark "was an act of imperial policy."—*The Course of Empire* (Boston, 1952), p. 411; see also pp. 404–22, 608, 626–27.

9   The Mullan Road, which provided the first wagon route from the Missouri to the Columbia headwaters, was not completed until 1862.

10 Reuben G. Thwaites, *Early Western Travels, 1748–1846* (Cleveland, 1904–7), Vol. XXVIII, p. 10.

11 The text of this and other expressions of the continental mind, missionary department, are published in Chittenden, *American Fur Trade,* Vol. III, p. 125.

12 Here I follow Robert R. Russel, *Improvement of Communication with the Pacific Coast as an Issue in American Politics, 1783–1864* (Cedar Rapids, Iowa, 1948). From a viewpoint like Russel's, James C. Malin studies the railroad and slavery struggles inside Missouri.—*The Nebraska Question, 1852–1854* (Lawrence, Kansas, 1953).

13 Federal Writers' Project, *Nebraska: A Guide to the Cornhusker State* (New York, 1939), p. 224. A more derisive account of Nebraska's speculative pioneers was delivered by one of them who later became a great conservationist, J. Sterling Morton. It is printed in Addison Sheldon, *Land Systems and Land Policies in Nebraska* (Lincoln, 1936), pp. 36–40.

14 *The Great Plains,* p. 153. Chittenden made the same general point in 1902.—*American Fur Trade,* Vol. II, p. 745.

15 Before publication of Webb's book, research toward answers to these questions was pioneered by Ralph C. Morris, "The Notion of a Great American Desert East of the Rockies," 13 *Mississippi Valley Historical Review,* pp. 190–200 (1926).

16 *American Fur Trade,* Vol. I, p. xi.

17 Charles O. Paullin, *Atlas of the Historical Geography of the United States* (published jointly by the Carnegie Institution and the American Geographical Society; Washington, 1932), is indispensable here as at other points in this and the following chapters.

18 Published in Milo M. Quaife, ed., *The Journals of Captain Meriwether Lewis and Sergeant John Ordway,* 22 *Wisconsin Historical Society Publications,* p. 219 (1916).

19 Stephen H. Hart and Archer B. Hulbert, *Zebulon Pike's Arkansaw Journal* (Denver, 1932), p. xxxv.

20 Elliot Coues, *The Expeditions of Zebulon Montgomery Pike* (new ed., New York, 1895), Vol. II, p. 523. No more does Pike's map, published in the Coues volume, suggest a desert. The inscription across the western basin on his "Chart of the Internal Part of Louisiana" reads: "The River Kansas takes Its Source in these Plains."

21 Edmund W. Gilbert, *The Exploration of Western America, 1800–1850* (Cambridge, England, 1933), pp. 158–59.

22 "A General Description of the Country Traversed by the Exploring Expedition," Report to John C. Calhoun, Secretary of War, Jan. 20, 1821, in R. G. Thwaites, *Early Western Travels,* Vol. XVII, pp. 147–48.

23 Thwaites, *Early Western Travels,* Vol. XVI, p. 120.

24 "Country Drained by the Mississippi: Western Section," in Edwin James, *Account of an Expedition from Pittsburgh to the Rocky Mountains, 1819–1820* (Philadelphia, 1822).

25 Aside from those cited by Webb, these two bore the inscription "Desert": Chapin's Map, 1839, reproduced in Paullin, *Atlas of the United States,* and W. M. Thayer, *Marvels of the New West* (Norwich, Conn., 1888), p. 220. On the other hand, these ten maps used some other designation or none at all: Pike, in Hart and Hulbert, *Pike's Arkansaw Journal* ("Plains"); John Carey, "North America," 1806, reproduced in Gilbert, *The Exploration of Western America,* Fig. 1 (no legend); John H. Robinson, M.D., *Map of Mexico, Louisiana, and the Missouri Territory* (Philadelphia, 1819) ("prairies"); Matthew Carey, "A New and Accurate Map of North America," *Carey's General Atlas* (Philadelphia, 1814) ("Great Savannas"); U.S. Corps of Topographical Engineers, *Map of the U.S. and Their Territories* (Washington, 1850) (no designation); *A New Map of the Great West,* published by Miller, Orton and Mulligan (New York, 1856) (no designation); Bradbury map cited below ("sand plains" confined to a small area east of Santa Fe); Arrowsmith Map, 1814 (no designation); Alexander von Humboldt Map, 1811 ("Savannes qui s'étendent à l'Est de la Sierra Verde"); Robert Greenhow Map, 1840 (no designation). The last three are reproduced by Paullin.

26 *Report of the Exploring Expedition to the Rocky Mountains in the Year 1842* (Washington, 1845). Much the same description gained wide currency through Washington Irving's popular account of the fur-trading explorations of Captain Bonneville in 1832–35.—*The Rocky Mountains, or Scenes, Incidents and Adventures in the Far West* (Philadelphia, 1837), Vol. I, p. 54.

27 *Thirty Years' View* (New York, 1854–56), p. 456.

28 Coues, *Expeditions of Pike,* Vol. II, pp. 524–25.

29 Thwaites, *Early Western Travels,* Vol. XVII, p. 128.

30 *Travels in the Interior of America,* in *ibid.,* Vol. V, p. 267.

31 Paullin, *Atlas of the United States,* Plate 30.

32 *Across the Wide Missouri.*

33 *Virgin Land* (Cambridge, 1950).

34 *The Poetical Works of Henry Wadsworth Longfellow* (Riverside Press ed., Boston, 1886), Vol. II, p. 10.

35 Report to John C. Calhoun, Thwaites, *Early Western Travels,* Vol. XVII, p. 148.

36 James D. Richardson, *A Compilation of the Messages and Papers of the Presidents, 1789–1897* (Washington, 1896), Vol. III, p. 387.

37 The first quotation is from a letter of Jefferson to Horatio Gates, July 11, 1803. The longer quotation is from his letter to John C. Breckenridge, August 12, 1803. These appear, with the draft amendments, in Paul Leicester Ford, *The Works of Thomas Jefferson* (12 vol. ed., New York and London, 1904–15), Vol. X, pp. 4–7, 14.

38 Message of December 7, 1824.

39 U.S. *Executive Documents,* Vol. I, pp. 22–23 (1835–36). Act of June 30,

1834, "to regulate trade and intercourse with the Indian Tribes," 4 Stat. 729–735.

40 Smith, *Virgin Land*, pp. 177 ff.

41 *American Fur Trade*, Vol. I, p. ix.

42 "There being really no reliable line or meridian which can be named as the boundary of our mythical American desert," wrote the most enthusiastic of the Nebraska boosters in 1881, "I do not hesitate to say that it will never *be found.*"—Charles Dana Wilber, *The Great Valleys and Prairies of Nebraska and the Northwest* (3rd ed., Omaha, 1881), p. 143.

43 *Climatology of the United States* (Philadelphia, 1857), p. 481. This constancy he thought to be more characteristic of the West than of the East (p. 164).

44 John M. Holloway, *History of Kansas* (Lafayette, Ind., 1868), pp. 560–61.

45 *Ibid.*, p. 566.

46 John Bell Sanborn, "Some Political Aspects of Homestead Legislation," 6 *American Historical Review*, pp. 19–37 (1900).

47 Abraham Lincoln, Second Annual Message to Congress.—Richardson, *Messages and Papers of the Presidents*, Vol. VI, pp. 133–34.

CHAPTER III

1 "The Significance of the Frontier in American History," *Annual Report of the American Historical Association* (1893), p. 206.

2 Of the many accounts of this episode, only one contains the evidence of an interview with General Dodge (before he wrote his autobiography) as well as of contemporary newspaper accounts: F. I. Herriot, "Iowa and the First Nomination of Abraham Lincoln," 12 *Annals of Iowa*, pp. 452 ff. (3d Series, 1909).

3 The story is told in Horace E. Deemer, "The Part of Iowa Men in the Organization of Nebraska," 9 *Annals of Iowa*, p. 181 (3d Series, 1909). There is a marker in the city at the point.

4 Grenville M. Dodge, "Surveying the M. and M.," 18 *Palimpsest*, p. 311 (1937). This is the most reliable written statement by Dodge, though later than the interview just cited.

5 Carl Sandburg, *Abraham Lincoln: The Prairie Years* (New York, 1926), Vol. II, p. 200.

6 *The Great Plains* ([Boston], 1936), pp. 227–28.

7 Ernest S. Osgood, *The Day of the Cattleman* (Minneapolis, 1929), p. 189.

8 New Haven, 1943, pp. 295–300. Osgood's book is still the best over-all account of the range cattle industry. Louis Pelzer, *The Cattlemen's Frontier* (Glendale, Calif., 1936), develops the problem of organization within the industry to control overexpansion and disease. Fred A. Shannon, *The Farmer's Last Frontier* (New York and Toronto, 1945), contains in Chap. X an argument, in answer to Webb, that the industry was from the beginning maladjusted in its marketing and financing.

9 U.S. Commissioner of the General Land Office, *Report*, 1862, p. 96.

10 12 Stat. 489 (1862).

11   Smith, *Virgin Land,* pp. 33–34.

12   Executive message of March 9, and order of March 7, 1864.

13   Grenville M. Dodge, *How We Built the Union Pacific Railway* (Washington, 1911), p. 21.

14   *Ibid.,* p. 72.

15   James B. Hedges, "The Colonization Work of the Northern Pacific Railroad," 13 *Mississippi Valley Historical Review,* pp. 311–42 (1926). Richard C. Overton, *Burlington West* (Cambridge, 1941), reveals the explanatory power of a study of railroad decisions for the history of settlement. Paul Wallace Gates, *Fifty Million Acres: Conflicts over Kansas Land Policy, 1854–1890* (Ithaca, 1954), though more concerned with chicanery in the railroads' acquisition of Indian lands, gives in Chaps. VII and VIII a picture of land promotion methods. In Kansas settler resistance developed early.

16   *Burlington West,* p. 434.

17   Hedges, "The Colonization Work of the Northern Pacific Railroad," p. 341.

18   *Burlington West,* p. 372.

19   For the Mennonite episode, see Ernest Correll, "President Grant and the Mennonite Immigration from Russia," 9 *Mennonite Quarterly Review,* pp. 144–52 (1935).

20   John P. Johansen, *Immigrant Settlements and Social Organization in South Dakota* (South Dakota Agricultural Experiment Station Bulletin 313; Brookings, 1937).

21   Raphael Pumpelly, *My Reminiscences* (New York, 1918), Vol. II, pp. 625, 645.

22   J. R. Buchanan, "The Great Railroad Migration into Northern Nebraska," 15 *Proceedings and Collections of the Nebraska Historical Society* (Lincoln, 1907), p. 33.

23   "The Great Middle Region of the United States, and Its Limited Space of Arable Land . . . ," 120 *North American Review,* pp. 20–21 (1875).

24   For a sample from Jay Cooke, see Henry V. Poor, *Manual of the Railroads of the United States, 1872–73* (New York, 1872), p. xxii; for the compulsion of even a responsible railroad president to think of "Belts," see Adams' famous letter of December 18, 1882, to the Boston *Advertiser,* quoted in Henry Kirke White, *History of the Union Pacific Railway* (Chicago, 1895), p. 62.

25   *The Rise of the City, 1878–1898* (New York, 1933).

26   *The Farmer's Last Frontier,* pp. 307–8.

27   Isaiah Bowman, *The Pioneer Fringe* (New York, 1931), p. 138.

28   A. E. McClymonds, "Soil Conservation and Good Land Use in the Northern Great Plains Region," 64 *Soil Science,* p. 332 (1947).

29   Henry N. Copp, *The American Settler's Guide* (Washington, 1880), p. 12.

30   12 Stat. 413 (June 2, 1862).

31   17 Stat. 605 (1873).

32   U.S. Commissioner of the General Land Office, *Report,* 1868, pp. 173–74, 197.

33   *Report,* 1882, pp. 12–13.

34   Thomas Donaldson, *The Public Domain* (Washington, 1884), pp. 541–42.

35   17 Stat. 605 (1873), as amended by 18 Stat. 21 (1874), 19 Stat. 54 (1876), and 20 Stat. 114 (1878). For the arguments, see 4 *Congressional Record,* p. 3085 (1876), and 7 *Congressional Record,* pp. 1853–56 (1878).

36 U.S. Commissioner of the General Land Office, *Report,* 1885, pp. 51–53.

37 Sheldon, *Land Systems and Land Policies in Nebraska* (Lincoln, 1936), p. 120.

38 26 Stat. 1095; 27 Stat. 593.

39 U.S. Forest Service, Lake States Experiment Station, *Possibilities of Shelterbelt Planting in the Plains Region* (1935), pp. 39–40.

40 Quoted by Benjamin H. Hibbard, *A History of the Public Land Policies* (New York, 1924), p. 419.

41 Sheldon, *Land Systems in Nebraska,* pp. 64–69.

42 To appreciate the prescience of this concept, note that it was based on weather records ending ten to twenty years before the readings which the Weather Bureau now considers thoroughly reliable.

43 *First Annual Report of the United States Geological Survey of the Territories, Embracing Nebraska* (Washington, 1867). For the account of this rivalry I am indebted to Henry Nash Smith, "Clarence King, John Wesley Powell, and the Establishment of the United States Geological Survey," 34 *Mississippi Valley Historical Review,* pp. 37–58 (1947).

44 James C. Malin, *Winter Wheat* (Lawrence, Kansas, 1944), pp. 107–8.

45 Nebraska State Board of Agriculture, *Report, 1876 to 1879* (Lincoln), pp. 108–13.

46 20 Stat. 394 (1879).

47 8 *Congressional Record,* pp. 1202, 1211, Appendix 217 (1879). The point is developed fully in Smith, "King, Powell, and the Geological Survey," and in Chap. XIX of his *Virgin Land.*

48 William B. Stockman, *Periodic Variation of Rainfall in the Arid Region* (U.S. Department of Agriculture, Weather Bureau Bulletin N, 1905), p. 9; and John G. Hoyt, *Drought of 1936* (U.S. Geological Survey Water Supply Paper 820, 1938), p. 24.

49 Reprinted in the *Reclamation Era,* September, 1936, p. 201. Wallace Stegner calls attention to an equally provocative, and more specific, speech by Powell to the Montana convention four days later.—*Beyond the Hundredth Meridian* (Boston, 1954), p. 315.

50 It is not easy to establish which these counties are. The definition used here is those drained in major part by the Missouri. To get the list, tabulation based on this definition and supplied by the Department of Commerce had to be freed of gross errors by adding Yuma County, Colorado, Laclede and Lawrence Counties, Missouri, and five Minnesota counties; and by excluding Allamakee County, Iowa. In other published totals, differences of over a million people depend on the inclusion of St. Louis County and the separate city of St. Louis. The county alone is here included; it has some drainage into the Missouri. The city has none, though it takes its water from the Missouri and empties it into the Mississippi.

51 Testimony of the Director, Bureau of the Census, in 79th Congress, 1st Session, Senate Committee on Irrigation and Reclamation, *To Establish a Missouri Valley Authority,* p. 109 (1945).

52 Carter Goodrich, ed., *Migration and Economic Opportunity* (Philadelphia, 1936), p. 245.

53 For Montana in the 1920's, data are in Works Progress Administration, *The*

People of the Drought States (Series V, No. 2, 1937), p. 11. For the period of the 1930's, Montana is covered in Carl F. Kraenzel, *Farm Population Mobility in Selected Montana Communities* (Montana Agricultural Experiment Station Bulletin 371; Bozeman, 1939); Kansas, in Carroll D. Clark and Roy L. Roberts, *People of Kansas* (Topeka, 1936), p. 89.

54 George W. Hill, "Rural Migration and Farm Abandonment" (Federal Relief Administration; Washington, 1935 [mimeographed]).

55 E. A. Willson, H. C. Hoffsommer, and Alva H. Benton, *Rural Changes in Western North Dakota* (North Dakota Agricultural Experiment Station Bulletin 214; Fargo, 1928); W. F. Kumlein, Robert L. McNamara, and Zetta E. Bankert, *Rural Population Mobility in South Dakota* (South Dakota Agricultural Experiment Station Bulletin 315; Brookings, 1938), p. 36—the test of stability (same residence) is more exacting in this study; Kraenzel, *Farm Population Mobility in Montana;* Malin, *Winter Wheat,* pp. 131 ff.—an abstract of Malin's original article, "The Turnover of Farm Population in Kansas," 4 *Kansas Historical Quarterly,* pp. 339–72 (November, 1935).

CHAPTER IV

1 Ben Jensen, 81st Congress, 1st Session, House Committee on Appropriations, *Hearings, Interior Department Appropriations Bill for 1950,* Part II, p. 370 (1949).

2 193 *Harper's Magazine,* pp. 481–91 (1946), and 194 *Harper's Magazine,* pp. 1–13 (1947).

3 Arthur F. Bentley, "The Condition of the Western Farmer as Illustrated by the Economic History of a Nebraska Township," 11 *Johns Hopkins University Studies in Historical and Political Science,* p. 290 (1893).

4 Isaiah Bowman, *The Pioneer Fringe* (New York, 1931), p. 122.

5 Quoted from the Goodland *News,* March 24, 1892, in the account by Martha B. Caldwell, "Some Kansas Rain Makers," 7 *Kansas Historical Quarterly,* p. 312 (1938).

6 In a revealing and robust pamphlet, *If and When It Rains* (Denver, 1938), p. 60.

7 In his preface to Federal Writers' Project, *Kansas: A Guide to the Sunflower State* (New York, 1939), p. 2.

8 *If the Prospect Pleases: The West the Guidebooks Never Mention* (Norman, Oklahoma, 1945), p. 43.

9 *Old Jules* (Boston, 1935), pp. 406–7.

10 *Winter Wheat* (Lawrence, Kansas, 1944), p. 33.

11 The only full, thought not independent, account is Harold V. Knight, *Grass Roots: The Story of the North Dakota Farmers Union* (Jamestown, 1947). Data on grain marketing are in U.S. Farm Credit Administration, *Cooperative Grain Marketing in the United States* (Circular C-122; Washington, 1941); on other cooperatives, in National Council of Farmer Cooperatives, *Bluebook* (Washington, 1948).

12 *The Great Plains* ([Boston], 1936), p. 509.

13 8 *Congressional Record,* pp. 1563–64 (1879).

14   On this point see Wendell Berge, *Economic Freedom for the West* (Lincoln, 1946), p. 53; A. G. Mezerik, *The Revolt of the South and West* (New York, 1946), p. 167; George R. Leighton, *Five Cities* (New York and London, 1939), p. 175.

15   Max Coffey, "A Great Job Born of Necessity," in a special section of the *World-Herald,* February, 1949.

16   *The Changing West* (New York, 1939), pp. 74–76.

17 · *Main Currents in American Thought* (New York, 1927–30), Vol. III, p. 392. For a current tracing of the origin of this note, though without geographic reference, see Henry Nash Smith, *Virgin Land.*

18   The accepted histories are Solon J. Buck, *The Granger Movement* (Cambridge, 1913); John D. Hicks, *The Populist Revolt* (Minneapolis, 1931); Paul R. Fossum, "The Agrarian Movement in North Dakota," 43 *Johns Hopkins Studies in Historical and Political Science,* pp. 9–183 (1925); Theodore Saloutos and John D. Hicks, *Agricultural Discontent in the Middle West, 1900–1930* (Madison, 1951). For the influence of climate, see John D. Barnhart, "Rainfall and the Populist Party in Nebraska," 19 *American Political Science Review,* pp. 527–40 (1925). Chester M. Destler, "Western Radicalism 1865–1901: Concepts and Origins," 31 *Mississippi Valley Historical Review,* pp. 335–68 (1944), holds a view different from that presented here.

19   *Agricultural Discontent in the Middle West,* p. 547.

20   *When the West is Gone* (New York, 1930), pp. 91–92.

21   *The Pioneer Fringe,* pp. 42–43.

22   Malin, *Winter Wheat,* p. 150.

23   *The Public and Its Problems* (New York, 1927).

24   In his informed and fair description, *The Dammed Missouri Valley* (New York, 1951).

25   Notably in *Virgin Land,* but note also Webb, *The Great Plains,* p. 477, "those who read about it were not of it."

26   Vol. XXIV, pp. 15–17 (August 30, 1947).

CHAPTER V

1   Quoted by the classic historian of Missouri River navigation, Hiram Martin Chittenden, *History of Early Steamboat Navigation on the Missouri River* (New York, 1903), Vol. I, p. 116.

2   Unless otherwise documented, nineteenth-century navigation history is taken from Chittenden.

3   Harold E. Briggs, *Frontiers of the Northwest* (New York, 1940), p. 58.

4   Philip E. Chappell, "A History of the Missouri River," 9 *Transactions of the Kansas State Historical Society,* p. 291 (1905–6).

5   Samuel L. Clemens, *Life on the Mississippi* (New York, 1896), p. 107.

6   Chittenden, Vol. I, p. 417.

7   *Ibid.,* p. 421.

8   76th Congress, 1st Session, House Doc. No. 106, p. 1046 (1939).

9   10 Stat. 56 (1852).

10 Missouri River Commission, *Report,* 1885. Appendix to U.S. Chief of Engineers, *Annual Report,* 1885, p. 2991.

11 Missouri River Improvement Convention, *Proceedings* (St. Joseph, 1881).

12 Missouri River Convention, *Official Report of the Proceedings* (Kansas City, 1885), p. 4.

13 Chief of Engineers, *Annual Report,* 1881, p. 1658; 1882, pp. 226, 1732.

14 Missouri River Commission, *Report,* 1885, p. 2992.

15 Report of the Missouri River Commission, in U.S. Chief of Engineers, *Annual Report,* 1897, p. 3847. Same complaint, *ibid.,* 1899, p. 3666.

16 56th Congress, 1st Session, House Committee on Rivers and Harbors, *Hearings, Missouri River,* December 12, 1900, pp. 3–4, 15, 16.

17 U.S. Chief of Engineers, *Annual Report,* 1903, p. 1552. For condensed description of works executed under the Missouri River Commission, see Supplement to U.S. Chief of Engineers, *Annual Report,* 1902, pp. 175 ff.

18 61st Congress, 3d Session, House Doc. No. 1287 (1911).

19 Final Report of the Missouri River Commission, Supplement to U.S. Chief of Engineers, *Annual Report,* 1902, pp. 150, 177–78.

20 James J. Hill wrote to Gov. John A. Johnson of Minnesota on January 14, 1907, "To all appearances, the commerce of the country has touched a barrier which is almost insurmountable." Published in undated pamphlet of Lakes to the Gulf Deep Waterway Association, St. Louis.

21 "Mr. Pinchot also suggested to me a movement supplementary to all of these movements, one which will itself lead the way in the general movement which he represents and with which he is actively identified, for the conservation of all our natural resources. This was the appointment of the Inland Waterways Commission."—Theodore Roosevelt, opening address, *Proceedings of a Conference of Governors in the White House* (Washington, 1908), p. vi.

22 National Rivers and Harbors Congress, *Proceedings* (Baltimore, 1901).

23 Missouri River Navigation Congress, *Proceedings* (Sioux City, 1908), pp. 26–28.

24 61st Congress, 2d Session, House Committee on Rivers and Harbors, *Hearings, Missouri River,* Jan. 21, 1910, and Feb. 5, 1910, pp. 487, 493.

25 *Ibid.,* p. 494.

26 U.S. Chief of Engineers, *Annual Report,* 1912, p. 839. National Waterways Commission, *Final Report* (Washington, 1912), p. 9.

27 37 Stat. 219 (1912). Extended a few miles upstream to Quindaro Bend, 40 Stat. 259 (1917).

28 61st Congress, 3d Session, House Doc. No. 1287, p. 2 (1911).

29 *Ibid.,* p. 9.

30 60th Congress, 2d Session, House Doc. No. 1120, p. 25 (1908).

31 73d Congress, 2d Session, House Doc. No. 238, pp. 26, 723 (1935).

32 U.S. Chief of Engineers, *Annual Report,* 1923, Part I, pp. 84, 1275.

33 Major G. R. Young, District Engineer, Kansas City, to the Chief of Engineers, U.S. Army, "Report on Survey of the Missouri River, Quindaro Bend to Mouth" (with a view to securing a 9-foot channel), Feb. 10, 1930, p. 36. Typed memorandum in the files of the House Public Works Committee.

34 *Annual Report,* 1922, pp. 1277–78.

35 38 Stat. 1055 (1915).
36 64th Congress, 1st Session, House Doc. No. 463, *Missouri River from Kansas City, Missouri to the Mouth*, p. 5 (1915).
37 *Ibid.*, p. 18.
38 Memorandum cited in Note 33 above, pp. 34–36. Major Young's finding that the majority of the works "still stand" is contradicted by a remark of Major C. C. Gee, Division Engineer at Kansas City, 1924, about "almost complete destruction of the work" due to lack of funds.—6 *Mississippi Valley Magazine*, p. 14 (1924).
39 G. R. Young, Memorandum cited in Note 33 above, p. 36.
40 *Mississippi Valley Magazine*, p. 15 (1924).
41 For the impact of the Panama Canal, see the testimony in 63d Congress, 3d Session, House Doc. No. 22, *Effect Upon Commerce of the Trans-Mississippi Territory of the Through All-Water Service from Coast to Coast via the Panama Canal* (1914). The Association published, from 1923 to 1932, the *Mississippi Valley Magazine.*
42 This organization receives federal support of $3,000 a year under a continuing appropriation to the Corps of Engineers. Act of June 28, 1902.
43 Statements cited may be found in 68 *Congressional Record,* pp. 430 (1926), 1605, 1609, 1616, 1617 (1927), and the *New York Times,* December 15, 1926, p. 3.
44 70th Congress, 1st Session, House Report No. 1910, p. 54 (1928).
45 73d Congress, 2d Session, House Doc. No. 238, p. 761 (1935).
46 21 *Congressional Record,* p. 2537 (1890); 22 *Congressional Record,* pp. 3547, 3613, 3616 (1891).
47 8 *Congressional Record,* p. 1175 (1879).
48 Herbert Quick, *American Inland Waterways* (New York and London, 1909), p. 184.
49 "The Relation of Water Conservation to Flood Prevention and to Navigation in the Ohio River," Inland Waterways Commission, *Preliminary Report* (Washington, 1908), pp. 451–90.
50 Col. W. H. Bixby, "The Practicability of Storage Reservoirs to Prevent Floods and to Benefit Navigation to the Ohio and Other Rivers of the United States," in National Waterways Commission, *Final Report,* pp. 185–202. Quotations from pp. 188, 191. Mr. Leighton made a rejoinder in this report, Appendix II.
51 Hiram M. Chittenden, "Forests and Reservoirs in Their Relation to Stream Flow," 34 *Proceedings of the American Society of Civil Engineers,* p. 974 (1908). Chittenden had surveyed and reported on the Kansas River just before the 1903 flood: 58th Congress, 2d Session, House Doc. No. 82 (1903). His report disregarded flood control entirely. The negative report on flood storage he refers to is 58th Congress, 2d Session, Senate Doc. No. 160 (Jan. 23, 1904).
52 National Waterways Commission, "Preliminary Report," in its *Final Report,* pp. 24–25, 52.
53 39 Stat. 410 (1916).
54 Kansas Session Laws, 1917, Ch. 172. Printed in Kansas Water Commission, *Report* (Topeka, 1917–18), pp. 7–9.

55 Kansas Water Commission Special Report, *The Relation of the Kansas Water Commission to the Flood Problem of Kansas, 1918* (Topeka); Kansas Water Commission, *Report, 1917–18, 1919–20, 1921–22* (Topeka).

56 The results of the survey of the Missouri basin are contained in a number of individual reports on the major tributaries, consolidated with a report on the mainstem in a volume of 605 pages transmitted to Congress in 1933. It is the most recent synthesis of the findings and recommendations of the Corps of Engineers concerning the entire river system. 73d Congress, 2d Session, House Doc. No. 238 (1935).

57 73d Congress, 2d Session, House Doc. No. 238, p. 196 (1935).

58 There is a full and fascinating account of the flood in U.S. Geological Survey, Water Supply Paper 796-B (1937).

59 U.S. Chief of Enginers, *Annual Report, 1939*, p. 1295.

60 Osceola, South Grand, and Pomme de Terre on the Osage, Richland and Arlington on the Gasconade, Chillicothe on the Grand River—all in Missouri; Kanapolis, Tuttle Creek, and Milford on Kansas River tributaries. 75th Congress, 1st Session, Flood Control Committee Doc. No. 1 (1937).

CHAPTER VI

1 As much water as runs through a sluice opening 12 inches wide and 1 inch deep, with a head 6 inches deep behind it.

2 *Recopilacion de Leyes de los Reynos de las Indias* (3d ed., Madrid, 1774), Vol. IV, p. 71. The Supreme Court recently reviewed the genesis of appropriation law in *U.S. v. Gerlach Livestock Co.,* 339 U.S. 725 (1950). The standard authority on the subject is Samuel Wiel, *Water Rights in the Western States* (3d ed., 2 vols., San Francisco, 1911). But it is interesting to note that Wiel, who developed his thesis in California, strained the English judgments to hold that appropriation was common law in all but name before Story's *Commentaries* distorted it, and that riparian rights smacked of the statist traditions of the *Code Napoleon.*

3 Based on National Resources Planning Board, *State Water Law in the Development of the West* (Washington, 1943); and U.S. Bureau of the Census, *Irrigation of Agricultural Lands* (Sixteenth Census, 1940), pp. xl–xlv. These summaries are now superseded by President's Water Resources Policy Commission, *Water Resources Law* (Washington, 1950), Appendix B.

4 *Water Resources Law,* pp. 732–34.

5 Kansas State Irrigation Commissioner (George S. Knapp), *Report, 1920–1922,* p. 39 (Topeka).

6 Walter Prescott Webb treated the appropriation doctrine as one of the true adaptations of American institutions to the climate of the western Plains.

7 See the criticism of this method of administration in Kansas State Engineer, *Reports,* Vol. V (1920–22), pp. 40–41. The state engineer of Montana was equally critical of the lack of state administrative supervision of water rights in an interview during 1947. For another statement of the criticism see Montana Agricultural Experiment Station, Special Report No. 8, *Water Resources*

of Montana and Their Use (Bozeman and Helena, 1941 [mimeographed]), Part I.

8   Nebraska State Water Engineer, *Reports,* Vol. XII (1917–18), pp. 9, 15; Vol. XIII (1919–20), p. 8; Vol. XVI (1925–26), p. 283; Vol. XVII (1927–28), p. 152. For a similar problem in South Dakota, see State Land Use Planning Committee of South Dakota in cooperation with the U.S. Bureau of Agricultural Economics, *Water-Land Resources and Problems in South Dakota* (Pierre, 1941 [mimeographed]), p. 145.

9   A. C. Tilley, Nebraska State Engineer, in his *Water Reports,* Vol. XXIII (1939–40), p. xx.

10   Missouri Basin Survey Commission, *Missouri: Land and Water* (Washington, 1953), p. 195.

11   Julius M. Friedrich, "The Settlement of Disputes between States Concerning Rights to the Waters of Interstate Streams," 32 *Iowa Law Review,* pp. 265–66 (1947).

12   325 U.S. 665 (1945).

13   81st Congress, 1st Session, House Committee on Appropriations, *Hearing, Interior Department Appropriation Bill for 1950,* Part II, pp. 408, 666–71 (1949), gives Nebraska's case. Construction was blocked by riders to the Interior Department appropriation acts for 1954 and previous years.

14   345 U.S. 981 (1953). Congress had also to approve the arrangements.—68 Stat. 486 (1954).

15   Congress approved the South Platte compact in 1926.—44 Stat. 195 (1926).

16   57 Stat. 86 (1943).

17   58 Stat. 94 (1944).

18   65 Stat. 663 (1951).

19   57 Stat. 90 (1943). For the Senate debate stating this issue, and the text of the original compact, see 87 *Congressional Record,* pp. 9616–23 (1941). The veto message is at 88 *Congressional Record,* pp. 3285–86 (1942).

20   Commission on Organization of the Executive Branch of the Government, *Task Force Report on Water Resources and Power,* p. 1693 (1955, Vol. III).

21   14 Stat. 252 (1866). The policy was retained in the implementing act of 1870—16 Stat. 217.

22   Thomas Donaldson, *The Public Domain* (Washington, 1884), p. 1109. 19 Stat. 377 (1877).

23   U.S. Public Land Commission, *Report,* 1903.

24   25 Stat. 527 (1888).

25   Commissioner of the General Land Office, *Report,* 1891, p. 51.

26   51st Congress, 1st Session, Senate Special Committee on Irrigation and Reclamation of Arid Lands, *Report 928,* Pt. IV, Vol. III, pp. 5–6 (1890).

27   U.S. Geological Survey, *Tenth Annual Report,* 1888–1890, Pt. II, *Irrigation,* p. 7.

28   Benjamin H. Hibbard, *A History of the Public Land Policies* (New York, 1924), p. 430.

29   Everett W. Sterling, "The Powell Irrigation Survey, 1888–93," 27 *Mississippi Valley Historical Review,* pp. 421–34 (1940).

30 Act of August 30, 1890. 26 Stat. 391 (1890).

31 28 Stat. 422 (1894).

32 Hibbard, *Public Land Policies,* p. 436.

33 57th Congress, 1st Session, Senate Doc. No. 446 (1902).

34 32 Stat. 388 (1902). Since the act of 1902 looked for financing to the proceeds of public land sales, the definition excluded Texas, but Texas was added to the jurisdiction of the reclamation laws in 1906. 33 Stat. 814 (1905); 34 Stat. 259 (1906).

35 *Twin Falls Canal Co. (Ltd.)* v. *Foote et al.,* 192 Fed. 583 (1911).

36 U.S. Department of Justice, "Brief for the United States, Intervenor," in *Nebraska* v. *Wyoming,* U.S. Supreme Court, October Term, 1944, pp. 15, 18.

37 Bureau of Reclamation, *Land Ownership Survey on Federal Reclamation Projects* (Washington, 1946), p. 62.

38 Quoted by Richard J. Hinton, *Irrigation in the United States* (a report prepared under the direction of the Commissioner of Agriculture; Washington, 1887), p. 198.

39 For an explanation of this motive, see 80th Congress, 1st Session, House Committee on Public Lands, *Hearings on a Bill to Amend the Reclamation Project Act of 1939,* 1947, pp. 5–6.

40 Hibbard, *Public Land Policies,* p. 442.

41 For testimony by a contemporary, see the presidential address to the 19th National Irrigation Congress, *Proceedings* (Chicago, 1911).

42 80th Congress, 1st Session, House Committee on Irrigation and Reclamation, *Hearings,* February 4, 5, and 7, 1947, p. 134.

43 U.S. Bureau of the Census, *Irrigation of Agricultural Lands* (Sixteenth Census, 1940), p. xxvii. Statement of Harry W. Bashore, 79th Congress, 1st Session, Senate Committee on Irrigation and Reclamation, *To Establish a Missouri Valley Authority,* p. 368 (1945).

44 U.S. Bureau of Reclamation, *How Reclamation Pays* (1947), p. viii.

45 Repealed 36 Stat. 835 (1910).

46 Project History in the files of the Bureau of Reclamation, Washington, *Lower Yellowstone Project* (Fact Finders Report), Sec. B.1.

47 Project History, *Buford-Trenton Project* ([old], 1909–10), p. 2.

48 *Ibid.,* p. 10.

49 44 Stat. 653 (1926).

50 *A 1925 Review of the Department of the Interior,* p. 21.

51 50 Stat. 595 (1937).

52 71st Congress, 3d Session, House Doc. No. 674 (1931); *Casper-Alcova Irrigation Project, Wyoming* (1931), p. 85.

53 *Engineering News Record,* November 29, 1934, pp. 696, 699. See also the issue of September 14, 1933, p. 329.

54 A. P. Davis, Assistant Engineer, and J. H. Quinton, Consulting Engineer, to F. H. Newell, April 29, 1904. Project History, *Belle Fourche* (1904).

55 78th Congress, 2d Session, Senate Doc. 191, p. 76 (1944).

56 Project History, *Huntley Project* (Special Advisers, 1924), Sec. B-5.

57 U.S. Bureau of Reclamation, *The Huntley Project, Montana* (August 15, 1908).

58 Richard T. Ely and G. S. Wehrwein, "The Relation of the Engineer to Land Economics," *Professional Engineer,* October, 1925, p. 8.

59 "It is not surprising," says the *Annual Report* of the Secretary of the Interior, 1947, p. 11, "that often the first, the second, or the third group of settlers failed."

60 Department of the Interior, file copy of Fact Finders Report, Sec. F(h). Conclusions of higher than normal turnover are also recorded in project histories of the North Platte, Huntley, and Lower Yellowstone projects.

61 Lyman W. Wallin, *Land Transfers on the Belle Fourche and Lower Yellowstone Irrigation Projects from Settlement to 1945* (U.S. Bureau of Agricultural Economics in cooperation with the U.S. Bureau of Reclamation; Washington, 1946 [mimeographed]).

62 65 *Congressional Record,* p. 6786 (1924); 68th Congress, 1st Session, Senate Doc. No. 92, pp. 37 ff (1924).

63 Hubert Work, Secretary, *A 1925 Review of the Department of the Interior,* p. 24.

64 President's Water Resources Policy Commission, *Ten Rivers in America's Future* (1950), p. 190.

65 Project History, *Lower Yellowstone* (Fact Finders' Report), Sec. G-6.

66 Commissioner Bashore, 79th Congress, 1st Session, Senate Committee on Irrigation and Reclamation, *Hearings on S. 555,* pp. 366, 369 (1945).

67 President's Great Plains Committee, *The Future of the Great Plains* (1936), p. 33.

68 53 Stat. 1187, Sec. 9 (1939). In 1946 costs allocated to the preservation and propagation of fish and wildlife were also made nonreimbursable. 60 Stat. 1080 (1946).

69 Testimony of Robert W. Sawyer, 80th Congress, 1st Session, House Committee on Public Lands, *Hearings, Irrigation and Reclamation,* February 4, 5, 7, 1947, pp. 85–86.

70 53 Stat. 719 (1939).

71 54 Stat. 1119 (1940).

72 For an excellent account of the new horizon of irrigation land development opened by the Wheeler-Case approach, see Ivan D. Wood, "Experience in Converting Land to Irrigation Use," in Northern Great Plains Agricultural Advisory Council, *The Use of Water Resources for Agriculture in the Northern Great Plains* (Custer, South Dakota, 1945 [mimeographed]), pp. 75–93.

CHAPTER VII

1 See the comment on this constitutionally aberrant practice in Arthur A. Maass, "Congress and Water Resources," 44 *American Political Science Review,* pp. 579–80 (1950). The Pick plan is printed as 78th Congress, 2d Session, House Doc. No. 475 (1944).

2 73d Congress, 2d Session, House Doc. No. 238, p. 104 (1935).

3 Missouri Basin Inter-Agency Committee, *Report on Adequacy of Flows in the Missouri River* (Omaha, 1951), p. 71.

4 78th Congress, 2d Session, House Committee on Rivers and Harbors, *Hearings on H.R. 3961,* p. 15 (1944).

5 78th Congress, 2d Session, House Committee on Flood Control, *Hearings on H.R. 4485,* pp. 971, 979 (1944).

6 78th Congress, 2d Session, Senate Committee on Commerce, *Hearings on H.R. 4485,* pp. 610–11 (1944).

7 General E. Reybold, letter to Representative Barrett, 90 *Congressional Record,* p. 2917 (Feb. 28, 1944).

8 *Hearings on H.R. 3961,* p. 55.

9 78th Congress, 2d Session, House Doc. No. 475, pp. 3, 7 (1944).

10 78th Congress, 2d Session, Senate Doc. No. 191 (1944).

11 *Ibid.,* p. 123.

12 78th Congress, 2d Session, Senate Doc. No. 247 (1944).

13 78th Congress, 2d Session, Senate Committee on Irrigation and Reclamation, *Hearings on S. 1915,* p. 50 (1944).

14 79th Congress, 1st Session, Senate Committee on Irrigation and Reclamation, *Hearings on S. 555,* p. 431 (1945). Italics added.

15 58 Stat. 891 (1944).

16 90 *Congressional Record,* p. 8056 (1944).

17 Committee minutes of August 5–6, 1944 (mimeographed).

18 78th Congress, 2d Session, Senate Committee on Commerce, *Hearings on H.R. 4485,* p. 585 (1944).

19 78th Congress, 2d Session, House Committee on Flood Control, *Hearings on H.R. 4485,* p. 1046 (1944).

20 "Golden River; What's to Be Done About the Missouri?" 190 *Harper's Magazine,* p. 517 (May, 1945).

21 *Stenographic Transcript of Water Conservation Conference* (Chicago, 1944), p. 106.

22 79th Congress, 1st Session, Senate Committee on Irrigation and Reclamation, *Hearings on S. 555,* p. 7 (1945).

23 White House Press Release, December 23, 1944.

24 90 *Congressional Record,* p. 8627 (1944).

25 79th Congress, 1st Session, Senate Report Nos. 246, 639 (1945).

26 *The Valley "Authority" Issue* (undated, obtained from Mississippi Valley Association, St. Louis).

27 59 Stat. 19 (1945).

28 Mimeographed text, "Talk to be Presented by Brigadier General R. C. Crawford, U.S. Army Division Engineer, Missouri River Division before Annual Convention of the Upper Mississippi Valley Association, St. Louis, Missouri, November 28, 1944." Obtained from the Office of the Division Engineer.

29 George R. Call of Sioux City, 78th Congress, 2d Session, House Committee on Flood Control, *Hearings on H.R. 4485,* pp. 1036–37 (1944).

30 Missouri Basin Inter-Agency Committee, *Report on Adequacy of Flows in the Missouri River,* p. 65.

31 According to the Commissioner of Reclamation in 1945: ". . . we could not justify Garrison Reservoir for flood control. . . . We could not go along with building the Garrison as a navigation reservoir until we had assurance

. . . it would not adversely affect irrigation in the upper reaches of the river." 79th Congress, 1st Session, Senate Committee on Irrigation and Reclamation, *Hearings on S. 555*, p. 431 (1945).

CHAPTER VIII

1 82d Congress, 1st Session, Senate Committee on Appropriations, *Hearings, Supplemental Civil Functions, Department of the Army Appropriations, 1952*, p. 5 (August 8, 1951).

2 U.S. Chief of Engineers, *Annual Report*, 1954, Vol. II, p. 828.

3 82d Congress, 1st Session, House Committee on Appropriations, *Hearings, Civil Functions, Department of the Army Appropriations for 1952*, Part I, p. 133 (1951).

4 Figures taken from the annual reports of the Chief of Engineers, and from 84th Congress, 1st Session, House Committee on Appropriations, *Hearings, Public Works Appropriations for 1956*, Part I, pp. 110, 115, 120 (1955).

5 U.S. Missouri Basin Survey Commission, *Missouri: Land and Water* (1953), p. 123.

6 82d Congress, 2d Session, House Committee on Appropriations, *Hearings before the Subcommittee, Missouri River Channel Stabilization and Navigation Project*, p. 5 (1952); and *Report*, July 2, 1952, p. 3.

7 Commission on Organization of the Executive Branch of the Government, *Task Force Report on Water Resources and Power* (1955), p. 1339.

8 Department of the Army, Chief of Engineers, *Missouri River Basin: A Report to the President's Water Resources Policy Commission* (1950), Table I.

9 *Missouri River Channel Stabilization and Navigation Project*, p. 35. "The whole thing is completely unreliable," concluded the subcommittee of the House Committee on Appropriations: *Report*, July 2, 1952, p. 4.

10 *Missouri: Land and Water*, p. 122. Commissioner H. T. Person dissented at this particular point. He felt that the indirect value of the food production from 9,094 acres per year to the future national food supply should be given some weight.

11 84th Congress, 1st Session, Senate Committee on Appropriations, *Hearings, Public Works Appropriations, 1956*, pp. 755, 2148–49 (1955).

12 *Ibid.*, p. 757.

13 *Ibid.*, p. 755.

14 Missouri Basin Inter-Agency Committee, *Minutes*, May 18, 1950, p. C-8.

15 Estimates from *Missouri: Land and Water*, pp. 114–15.

16 Missouri Basin Inter-Agency Committee, *Minutes*, May 18, 1950, p. 4.

17 84th Congress, 1st Session, House Committee on Appropriations, *Hearings, Public Works Appropriations, 1956*, Part I, p. 112 (1955).

18 73rd Congress, 2d Session, House Doc. No. 238, p. 218 (1935).

19 Missouri Basin Inter-Agency Committee, *Minutes*, May 18, 1950, p. E-3.

20 This account of the origin of the flood is based on U.S. Weather Bureau, *Kansas-Missouri Floods of June–July 1951* (Technical Paper No. 17, 1952).

21 The authority for information on flood flows is U.S. Geological Survey, *Kansas-Missouri Floods of July 1951* (Water Supply Paper 1139, 1952).

22 82d Congress, 1st Session, Senate Committee on Appropriations, *Civil Functions, Department of the Army Appropriations 1952,* p. 448 (1951).

23 Missouri Basin Inter-Agency Committee, *Minutes,* February 9, 1951, pp. 6, 7.

24 82d Congress, 1st Session, Senate Committee on Appropriations, *Hearings, Civil Functions, Department of the Army Appropriations, 1952,* pp. 428–29 (1951).

25 *Ibid.,* pp. 453, 444, 446, 440, 449.

26 Public Works Administration, *Report of the Mississippi Valley Committee* (1934), p. 167.

27 78th Congress, 1st Session, House Doc. No. 342 (1943).

28 "In the Missouri Basin Project we are building dams at places where past experience shows us floods have occurred and the size of the installations is based to some extent on the greatest flood of record. It is conceivable, however, that tributary streams that have never before flooded might discharge record flows below the protecting dams and flood damage still occur. . . ."— Missouri River Division Engineer Brig. Gen. S. D. Sturgis, Jr., Missouri Basin Inter-Agency Committee, *Minutes,* May 18, 1950, p. 3.

29 House Doc. No. 342, p. 53.

30 82d Congress, 1st Session, House Committee on Appropriations, *Hearings, Civil Functions, Department of the Army Appropriations for 1952,* Part I, p. 446 (1951).

31 St. Louis *Post-Dispatch,* July 17, 1951.

32 Missouri Basin Inter-Agency Committee, *Minutes,* May 18, 1950, p. C-4.

33 82nd Congress, 1st Session, House Committee on Appropriations, *Hearings, Civil Functions, Department of the Army Appropriations for 1952,* Part I, p. 448 (1951).

34 Relman Morin, dispatch from Kansas City, July 22, 1951.

35 83d Congress, 1st and 2d Sessions, House Committee on Public Works, *Hearings, Flood Control Omnibus Bill,* Vol. III, p. 307 (1954).

36 *Missouri: Land and Water,* pp. 131–32.

37 Abel Wolman, Louis R. Howson, and N. T. Veatch, *Report on Flood Protection, Kansas River Basin* (Topeka, May, 1953). The study was made for the Kansas Development Commission.

38 84th Congress, 1st Session, House Committee on Appropriations, *Hearings, Public Works Appropriations, 1956,* Part I, p. 99 (1955). Italics added.

39 U.S. Geological Survey, *Floods of April 1952 in Missouri River Basin* (Water Supply Paper 1260-B, 1955); U.S. Weather Bureau, *Floods of 1952, Upper Mississippi-Missouri-Red River of the North* (Technical Paper No. 23, 1954).

40 President's Water Resources Policy Commission, *Ten Rivers in America's Future* (1950), p. 241; Commission on Organization of the Executive Branch of the Government, *Task Force Report on Water Resources and Power* (1955), Vol. II, p. 812; *Missouri: Land and Water,* p. 191.

41 Commission on Organization of the Executive Branch of the Government, *Task Force Report on Natural Resources* (1949), p. 28; President's Water

Resources Policy Commission, *Ten Rivers in America's Future,* p. 245, and *A Water Policy for the American People* (1950), p. 85; *Missouri: Land and Water,* p. 235; *Task Force Report on Water Resources and Power* (1955), Vol. I, p. 74; Commission on Intergovernmental Relations, *A Report to the President for Transmittal to the Congress* (1955), p. 243.

42 Department of the Interior, Missouri Basin Field Committee, *Progress: Missouri River Basin* (Billings, Mont., June, 1955), pp. 5–19.

43 According to the Commissioner of Reclamation, 79th Congress, 1st Session, Senate Committee on Irrigation and Reclamation, *Hearings on S. 555,* p. 368 (1945).

44 81st Congress, 1st Session, House Doc. No. 373, *Missouri River Basin Agricultural Program,* p. 58 (1949).

45 Interior Department Appropriation Act of August 9, 1937, as modified by 52 Stat. 764.

46 Bureau of Reclamation, *The Colorado–Big Thompson Project and the Drouth of 1954* (1954, processed), p. 7.

47 84th Congress, 1st Session, House Appropriations Committee, *Hearings, Central Section, Public Works Appropriations for 1956,* Part I, p. 66 (1955).

48 Wyoming State Engineer, *Thirty-Second Biennial Report 1953–1954* (Cheyenne, 1954), p. 17.

49 82d Congress, 1st Session, Senate Committee on Appropriations, *Hearings, Interior Department Appropriations Bill for 1952,* p. 1267 (1951).

50 *Task Force Report on Water Resources and Power* (1955), Vol. II, pp. 700–709.

51 67 Stat. 566 (1953); 84th Congress, 1st Session, Senate Committee on Appropriations, *Hearings, Public Works Appropriations, 1956,* p. 161 (1955).

52 *Toward Stability in the Great Plains Economy* (Nebraska Agricultural Experiment Station Bulletin 399; 1950), p. 50.

53 51st Congress, 1st Session, Senate Special Committee on Irrigation and Reclamation of Arid Lands, *Report 928,* Pt. IV, Vol. III, pp. 5–6 (1890).

54 *Agricultural Research in South Dakota, Sixty-Third Annual Station Report* (South Dakota State College Agricultural Experiment Station; Brookings, 1950), pp. 92–94.

55 Interior Missouri Basin Field Committee, *Missouri River Basin Progress* (Billings, Mont., November, 1952), p. 7.

56 *Economics of Grain Farming in Renville County* (North Dakota Agricultural Experiment Station Bulletin 367; 1954). See also I. W. Schaffner, *Present Farm Economy in Three Proposed Irrigation Areas of North Dakota* (Agricultural Economics Report No. 3, Agricultural Experiment Station; Fargo, 1951 [mimeographed]).

57 84th Congress, 1st Session, House Committee on Appropriations, *Hearings, Central Section, Public Works Appropriations for 1956,* Part I, p. 248 (1955).

58 Commission on Executive Branch, *Water Resources and Power,* Vol. II, p. 716.

59 84th Congress, 1st Session, Senate Appropriations Committee, *Hearings, Public Works Appropriations, 1956, Bureau of Reclamation,* pp. 187–88 (1955).

60 Report from the State Engineer, *Progress: Missouri River Basin* (Interior Missouri Basin Field Committee, Billings, Mont., June, 1955), p. 161.

61 *Ibid.*, p. 13.

62 *U.S. Census of Agriculture: 1950*, Vol. III, p. 35.

63 61 Stat. 699 (1947). The whole story emerges in the appropriation hearings. The Director of the Budget had proposed a list of dams, better investigated, and promising greater repayment. But they were not the projects promising the most immediate relief from the sort of floods just experienced. Congressman Case of South Dakota got from a Bureau of Reclamation spokesman the statement that "had the Bureau made the selection, I am fairly certain that some other projects would have been on the list." Then the House Committee inserted in the appropriation four dams from the Budget Bureau's deferred list. Of the four, three have so far failed to provide irrigation.— 80th Congress, 1st Session, House Committee on Appropriations, *Second Supplemental Appropriation Bill for 1948*, pp. 108–52, 159–61, especially pp. 142–46 (1947).

CHAPTER IX

1 In a public hearing at Topeka, 82d Congress, 1st Session, House Committee on Agriculture, *Hearings, Soil Conservation and Flood Control*, Part I, p. 381 (1952).

2 57 Stat. 567, Sec. 5 (1943), Proclamation No. 2714, December 31, 1946.

3 80th Congress, 1st Session, House Committee on Public Lands, *Hearings before a Subcommittee, Irrigation and Reclamation* (February 4, 5, 7, 1947).

4 84th Congress, 1st Session, House Committee on Appropriations, *Hearings, Central Section, Public Works Appropriations for 1956*, Part I, p. 307 (1955).

5 84th Congress, 1st Session, Senate Committee on Appropriations, *Hearings, Public Works Appropriations, 1956, Bureau of Reclamation . . .* , pp. 242–43 (1955).

6 The above quotation and those in the following two paragraphs are taken from the hearings just cited, pp. 133, 134, 136, 139, 141, 143, 146, 162.

7 80th Congress, 1st Session, House Committee on Public Lands, Hearings before the Subcommittee on Irrigation and Reclamation, *To Amend the Reclamation Project Act of 1939*, pp. 85–86 (1947).

8 Studies of the North Platte, Milk River, Huntley, Belle Fourche, and Lower Yellowstone projects are summarized in Nebraska Agricultural Experiment Station Bulletin 399, *Toward Stability in the Great Plains Economy* (Lincoln, 1950), pp. 45–50.

9 *Irrigation Farmers Reach Out Into the Dry Land* (Montana Agricultural Experiment Station Bulletin 464; Bozeman, 1949), p. 33.

10 U.S. Department of Agriculture, Bureau of Agricultural Economics, *Integration of Irrigated and Dry-Land Farming in the North Platte Valley in 1946* (1947).

11 *Ibid.*, p. 35.

12 82d Congress, 2d Session, House Committee on Appropriations, *Hearings*

before a Subcommittee, Department of Agriculture Appropriations for 1953,
p. 429 (1952).

13 *Ibid.,* p. 1145.

14 *Ibid.,* p. 156.

15 Facts on which this section was based are from T. S. Thorfinnson and
A. W. Epp, *Systems of Farming for the Tri-County Irrigation Area in
Nebraska* (Agricultural Experiment Station Bulletin 393; Lincoln, 1949).

16 Missouri Basin Inter-Agency Committee, *Minutes,* January 24, 1952.

17 Since it supplements a pre-existing system, the Bureau's Colorado–Big
Thompson project is exempted by statute from the 160-acre law. Though
in the basin, it is unconnected in law with the Sloan plan!

18 Lincoln *Journal,* October 20, 1950.

19 *Ibid.*

20 82nd Congress, 2nd Session, House Committee on Public Works, *The Flood
Control Program of the Department of Agriculture, Report* (Committee
Print No. 22; 1952), p. 30.

21 82nd Congress, 2nd Session, House Doc. No. 530, pp. 43–78 (1952).

22 *Missouri: Land and Water* (1953), pp. 132–36.

23 83rd Congress, 2nd Session, Senate Committee on Agriculture and Forestry,
Hearings, Cooperative Soil Conservation and Flood Prevention Projects, p.
106 (1954).

24 *The Flood Control Program of the Department of Agriculture,* p. 35.

25 81st Congress, 1st Session, House Doc. No. 373, *Missouri River Basin Agricultural Program* (1949).

26 82d Congress, 1st Session, House Committee on Agriculture, *Hearings, Soil
Conservation and Flood Control,* Part I, p. 475 (1952).

27 House Doc. No. 373, p. 2.

28 *Ibid.,* p. 7. Italics added.

29 82nd Congress, 2nd Session, House Committee on Appropriations, *Department of Agriculture Appropriations for 1953,* Part I, p. 578 (1952).

30 Message of July 31, 1953. 83d Congress, 1st Session, House Doc. No. 221
(1953).

31 67 Stat. 214 (1953).

32 68 Stat. 666 (1954).

33 83d Congress, 2d Session, Senate Committee on Agriculture and Forestry,
Hearings, Cooperative Soil Conservation and Flood Prevention Projects, pp.
90 ff. (1954).

34 *Missouri: Land and Water,* p. 136.

CHAPTER X

1 Some of the evidence, and the reasons for public ignorance as far as the
basin's press is concerned, appear in Richard Baumhoff, *The Dammed
Missouri Valley* (New York, 1951), Chap. VIII.

2 84th Congress, 1st Session, House Committee on Appropriations, *Hearings,
Central Section, Public Works Appropriations for 1956,* Part I, pp. 44–45
(1955).

3 Federal Inter-Agency River Basin Committee, Resolution of March 29, 1945. The Committee was rechartered by President Eisenhower's Inter-Agency Committee on Water Resources in 1954.

4 *Missouri: Land and Water* (1953), p. 86.

5 *New York Times,* May 1, 1949.

6 U.S. Commission on Organization of the Executive Branch of the Government, *Concluding Report* (1949), pp. 28–29.

7 Arthur Maass wrote the comprehensive critique: *Muddy Waters* (Cambridge, 1952).

8 Commission on Organization of the Executive Branch of the Government, *Task Force Report on Water Resources and Power,* Vol. I, pp. 37–39 (1955). The Commission proposed reorganization among the federal departments only by the creation of a co-ordinating Board in the Executive Office of the President.

9 U.S. Commission on Organization of the Executive Branch of the Government, *Task Force Report on Natural Resources* (1949), p. 97.

10 Executive Order 10318.

11 *Fighting Liberal* (New York, 1945), p. 245.

12 Council of State Governments, *Revised Draft, Missouri River Basin Compact* (January, 1953), pp. 1–2.

13 *Missouri: Land and Water,* p. 10. The dissenting members, who approved the compact device, were Dean H. T. Person of the Wyoming college of engineering, Senator Milton R. Young of North Dakota, and Representative Clifford R. Hope of Kansas (*ibid.,* pp. 12–14).

14 Frederick L. Zimmermann and Mitchell Wendell, "Representation of the Region in Missouri Basin Organization," 48 *American Political Science Review,* pp. 160–61 (1954); and Wallace R. Vawter, "Interstate Compacts—The Federal Interest," in *Task Force Report on Water Resources and Power* (1955), Vol. III, pp. 1719–22.

15 Zimmermann and Wendell, "Representation of the Region," p. 161.

16 St. Louis *Post-Dispatch,* September 8, 1955, p. 9A.

17 *Task Force Report on Natural Resources* (1949), p. 24.

18 *Ten Rivers in America's Future* (1950), pp. 161–281.

19 *Ibid.,* p. 3.

20 Message of April 10, 1933.

21 *TVA—Democracy on the March* (Pocket Books ed., 1945), pp. 166–67.

22 *Regional Factors in National Planning and Development* (Washington, 1935), the report of a National Resources Committee study led by John M. Gaus, contains the clearest thinking, from the widest survey of facts, on this point.

23 The criticism Professor Charles McKinley brought against the minority of the Hoover Commission that found "a multiple-purpose resource development program" tied together by nature and the march of technology is especially pertinent in this part of the country.—"The Valley Authority and Its Alternatives," 44 *American Political Science Review,* p. 618 (1950).

24 84th Congress, 1st Session, House Committee on Appropriations, *Hearings, Central Section, Public Works Appropriations for 1956,* p. 23 (1955). More

of the cost will be allocated to power in later estimates, but the power revenues will still be paying back more irrigation than power costs.

25 *Missouri: Land and Water*, p. 22, summarizing Part V.

26 Within the larger basin community, there is a real need to foster consciousness of the interrelated problems of particular subbasins, such as the Osage, the Little Sioux, the Big Horn, the South Platte, or the Milk. Miniatures of the Inter-Agency Committee might find a new opportunity for intensive education at this level. In smaller, single-state subbasins, watershed associations might win allegiance, more comprehensive in purpose than any have yet proved to be in fact.

27 *Missouri: Land and Water*, pp. 264–67.

28 *Ibid.*, pp. 12–14.

29 84th Congress, S. 2728 (1955).

30 A reorganization proposal may displace the Bureau, the Corps, and possibly the Soil Conservation Service programs in the basin, as would M.V.A. It may seek to change their programs by confronting them with the politically effective demands of the basin populace, as is proposed here. Or it may seek to "co-ordinate" them by superimposing an additional agency. The interstate compact commission would bring state and Presidential appointees together, but only to review existing agencies' formulated plans. The federal commission of the Missouri Basin Survey Commission, a full-time body, would stand apart from the Corps, Bureau, and Soil Conservation Service. The existing agencies, uncommitted to modify their nationwide programs for the basin, would retain the upper hand in a test of Congressional strength—for their clienteles are national.

31 In 1955 the House subcommittee dealing with public works appropriations divided itself into panels according to sections of the country, not agencies. The questions that resulted when Missouri basin requests of both the Corps and the Bureau were reviewed by the same panel were unusually penetrating. Budget requests for the Department of Agriculture's watershed works continued, however, to receive separate hearings.

32 Senator Hennings incorporated in his bill the proposal of the Survey Commission which would keep these two types of budget review distinct by having the basin budget request submitted at three alternative levels of spending. National considerations could then vary the total without rearranging the priorities within the basin.

INDEX